# THE DIRECTING

## OF

# ARCHAEOLOGICAL EXCAVATIONS

A

D

G

F

A
B

C
E

FRONTISPIECE. The layout of a small excavation
(Arbury Road, Cambridge, 1969). Note, A, processing
tent; B, Site Hut; C, Toilet; D, Car Park; E, Site guard's
caravan; F, Regular trench grid over a prehistoric enclosure; G, Single trenches sampling Romano-British
ditches and road.

# THE DIRECTING OF ARCHAEOLOGICAL EXCAVATIONS

JOHN ALEXANDER

WITH PLATES, DRAWINGS AND MAPS

London: John Baker Ltd
New York: Humanities Press Inc

© 1970
JOHN ALEXANDER
First published in Great Britain in 1970 by
JOHN BAKER PUBLISHERS LTD
5 Royal Opera Arcade
Pall Mall, London SW1
ISBN 0 212 99843 9

First published in the U.S.A. in 1970 by
HUMANITIES PRESS INC
303 Park Avenue South
New York, N.Y. 10010
(USA) SBN 391 00094 2

Printed in Great Britain at
THE CURWEN PRESS PLAISTOW LONDON E13

# Contents

# List of Illustrations

# List of Plates

It should be noted that some of these are chosen to illustrate photographic problems during the recording of a site and would not normally be published.

# Preface

Directors of excavations all over the world often find themselves faced with problems outside their training and experience. This situation is becoming commoner as the general body of archaeological knowledge becomes greater, as professional training becomes narrower and as excavating techniques improve.

Since the purpose of excavation is now accepted to be a complete record of all the human activity at a site, directors must be prepared to deal with a very wide variety of periods and types of evidence, each of which will have its own problems. A quite different set of problems awaits directors at the end of the excavation, for the days are long past when they could hope to examine and report personally on all their finds. The final success of excavations lies, equally with their skill in digging, in the directors' relationships with other specialists, and in their ability to produce a final synthesis of all the kinds of evidence.

The younger director has, as well as the problems listed above, the lonely problems of practical decision-making for which few educational establishments prepare their graduates. No matter how many excavations have been attended as a helper and assistant, or how wide his or her reading, the young director may well find his first excavations very difficult if he has not given much previous thought to planning and organisation.

It is hoped that this book will help directors to prepare themselves to solve some of these problems. It will not attempt to do this by presuming to offer regional or period models or advice, but by discussing the general principles involved, and by indicating reports useful for technical details irrespective of period. In this edition reports written in English have, as far as possible, been selected.

It will be assumed here that directors have already served the kind of apprenticeship discussed in Chapter I and that they are therefore fully conversant with the primary techniques of locating, digging, recording and publishing. A number of excellent handbooks, which are indicated in the reading lists following each chapter, have already been written to supplement that apprenticeship.

# CHAPTER I

# The Education of a Field Director,
# his Assistants and his Helpers

'The qualities to be considered are first the honesty, shown mostly
in the eyes and by a frank and open bearing, next the sense and
ability, and lastly the sturdiness and freedom from nervous
weakness and hysterical tendency to quarrel.'

Sir Flinders Petrie
*Methods and Aims in Archaeology*, 1904, p. 21

If archaeology is defined as one method used in the recovery, study and
reconstruction of the past of man,[1] then the field director is the executive
who locates, excavates and publishes the detailed evidence which
makes generalised study and reconstruction possible. It is therefore
obvious that improving excavation techniques and recognising new
kinds of evidence are the chief ways in which more authentic models of
societies will be constructed. The conscientious director must therefore
not only know and practise all the current techniques of his craft but
must always be on the look-out for new ones. To do this he must bring
to his work a much wider knowledge than his predecessors. The pioneer
days have gone for good when to find any kind of evidence was a
triumph.

It is agreed by all who have written on the subject that field archaeology is a craft.[2] To become master-craftsmen all directors must have
worked on a number of sites in an apprenticeship which will have lasted
a number of years. There is no substitute for this, and the skills cannot be
learnt from textbooks or sand models although these may quicken the
understanding.

The problems of deliberate training must therefore always be considered in the light of this requirement. For a director as for a sub-
ordinate, a wider knowledge than that found in trenches is essential
today and the qualities and qualifications necessary for a successful
excavation may now be considered.

## THE QUALITIES AND QUALIFICATIONS
## OF A FIELD DIRECTOR

The directors of excavations should be, whatever their other qualifications, experienced field archaeologists. Theoretical knowledge of any
kind, even archaeological, or field experience in another discipline is no
substitute for having worked on a number of sites under a variety of
directors in capacities ranging from a troweller to a site supervisor.
This process should have taken a number of years, since the most
important part of the work will be concerned with soil change, feature

recognition and the handling of men and machines; it can only be learnt by serving an apprenticeship on sites. To benefit from this an intending director must bring to it a mind stocked with a wide variety of information and skills in the fields of ethnographical, archaeological, environmental and chronological studies. Whilst these may be acquired as part of a university education specialising in archaeology,[3] many of them can also come from part-time study and regular local field-work.

Apart from these various kinds of knowledge which will be discussed below, a successful field director will normally need other qualities. The practical qualities will be those of one who likes working out of doors. He must be physically fit and able to enjoy mud and rain as well as fine weather. He must also have the ability to control men and women and to deal with officials and machines, for the endless minor problems of management must be handled efficiently and without diverting his attention from the archaeological problems.

Other qualities will be needed when the excavation is over. Since the director himself will be responsible for the interpretation and publication of his material he must, quite apart from the skills discussed below, have the time to work through the material, the knowledge to deal with specialist workers in other fields, and the literary and organising ability to collate their work with his own and to assemble the total evidence in a form suitable for the printers and block-makers.

This is no mean array of qualifications, and no one should lightly take it upon himself to organise an excavation (Fig. 1). It must always be borne in mind that any part of a site excavated can never be studied again, and that any area excavated improperly or unpublished is destroyed. The director alone must accept responsibility for the digging and publishing.

GENERAL THEORETICAL KNOWLEDGE

A trained field director might be expected to possess the kinds of knowledge discussed below, but this is not to say that the director of every excavation must necessarily be a professional archaeologist. This will never be possible, and when sites are being destroyed so rapidly throughout the world, to insist on it would stop much valuable work. It would also mean the exclusion of many part-time archaeologists whose specialised skills and interests contribute much to the advance of the subject.[4] Whether part-time or full-time workers, however, directors will do well to have the following kinds of knowledge of the cultural (human artifactual or social) evidence and non-cultural (derived from the natural sciences) evidence.

The cultural may be considered under the following headings:
(i) *Ethnography*
A knowledge of the scientific study of living communities is an essential

part of the background of a director. This is not to recommend the casual and specious parallels drawn in the past,[5] but the need to know something of special and chronological patterns of settlement, economic organisation and the variety of military and religious customs which occur. This knowledge will be as important for the prehistoric period as for the more recent periods. It can best be acquired by following a course of study, but might also be obtained by the judicious reading of anthropological field reports and studies of material equipment.[6] If these are read with the problem of excavation in mind the kinds of structures, artifacts, food and industrial debris likely to survive will form an invaluable background of knowledge; this is particularly true for hunter-gatherer and simple agricultural communities. It will also have the advantage of restraining excavators from the wilder kinds of interpretation.

(ii) *Archaeology*

This word may be used in this context to mean the body of already excavated evidence and its interpretation. Study has inevitably fragmented it into a number of separate disciplines, of which only prehistoric archaeology, by its very definition lacking literary evidence, is a simple study of the remains found in or on the ground. The others, for example European mediaeval archaeology, are in varying degrees integrated with literary evidence. The basic theoretical knowledge necessary in any one discipline will therefore vary, and here lies the problem of the field archaeologist. His skills should embrace all these disciplines for in his excavations he must expect to encounter remains of several periods which he must treat with equal care. He must therefore have a general knowledge of the material of all the periods he is likely to encounter. This is not as formidable as it perhaps sounds, especially for anyone working in a single province or country. It does mean that the general nature of the material remains of hunter-gatherer, subsistence agricultural (stone-, bronze-, and iron-using), and more elaborate societies developed from them should be known, and something should have been studied of the detailed nature of the evidence for each of them in the region.

If this is desirable as part of the academic background of all directors, then the increasingly detailed information required from sites must mean that each director should have specialised knowledge of one or more periods and kinds of sites (see Chapters V–XI) and should concentrate on their excavation. The detailed study of a period, as already mentioned, will depend upon the kinds of evidence available, and only in the prehistoric period will it be limited to a study of excavation reports and the material from them. For all other periods it must be a truly historical study in which a student is well grounded in the languages and literary evidence involved. In Britain, for example, this is necessary for Roman-British, Saxon, mediaeval and post-mediaeval archaeology.

Both full- and part-time students should also spend much time with museum collections; specialised collections being especially sought out. Here, preferably with experienced workers, they should handle and study the material objects from their chosen periods, for it is through such handling that experience comes.

Also important is the study of the specialised excavation reports of the chosen period. The best excavated and most informative sites over a wide area (e.g. from the whole Empire for Romano-British studies or the whole world for Palaeolithic studies), as well as those found in the chosen region or country, should be worked through in detail, and if possible the objects from them and the actual sites should be visited.

The non-cultural evidence may be considered under the following headings:

(i) *Environmental Studies*

The recovery of evidence of the interaction of man and environment is now established as an essential part of field archaeology, and a director must be equipped to see that it is done.[7] Since a whole variety of natural sciences are concerned, he cannot hope to be competent in all of them, although a specialist knowledge of one is a great asset; but he must know the ways in which they can help and what they require as evidence (see Chapter V).

In addition to this general knowledge he should have more detailed acquaintance with some aspects of the work. In geology and pedology he should be able to distinguish the main categories of rocks and soils and know the appearance of them as laid down or formed.[8] He should have studied particularly, the evidence for water and wind erosion and transport and should be able to recognise different kinds of sediments, especially in pits and ditches. He should know enough to decide when and where it will be necessary to call in, or take samples to, a specialist geologist or pedologist.

Knowledge of botanical, molluscan and entomological remains will be less necessary in the field, since identifications will come from a later study of samples in laboratory conditions. A director should, however, know the kinds of information he might hope to have from them.

A knowledge of animal, bird and fish anatomy is also desirable. Whilst the detailed study will come after the excavation, a director should be able to recognise the main classes of bones, especially their epiphyses, and so be able to suggest methods of excavation.[9]

(ii) *Chronological Studies*

A variety of relative and absolute dating methods are now available, and as many as possible should be used to check the dating on any site.[10] Few will normally be carried out in the field, but a director should be familiar with them, be able to see those which might be applied to a particular site, and be able to take suitable samples (e.g. for radioactive isotope measurement), or call in specialists (e.g. for palaeomagnetic field reconstruction). These will, of course, be especially important for prehistoric sites.

## GENERAL FIELD KNOWLEDGE

Mention has already been made of the apprenticeship which any director should serve. During it, partly by working on excavations and partly by study, he should certainly have had actual experience of, and insight into, all the kinds of work he will expect his assistants and helpers to carry out. He must also have acquired the skills of man and money management, for if organisation and planning before or during excavation are faulty much time and effort is wasted. (This is discussed in Chapter II.)

His necessary archaeological experience can be discussed under the following headings:

(i) *Planning* (Fig. 2)

The most difficult part of a director's craft is the choice of sites and trenches. Solution of the *strategic* problems of locating and choosing sites can be helped by a knowledge of the techniques available (see Chapter II), but only experience in using them can decide on their particular application (e.g. when an electrical resistivity survey may be of use). A critical study of excavation reports in seminal conditions may help to sharpen this experience.[11] Field exercises, in which individuals are asked to explain on an actual site how they would propose to survey or excavate it, are also useful.

The *tactical* problems of siting trenches, the next most important part of a director's work, can also be solved as much by the critical study of previous excavation reports (e.g. of the choice of trench sites, sections, etc.), as by working as an assistant on excavations. This facet can be developed in training by an experienced excavator producing his field notes and drawings, sections and plans and discussing them in the classroom. Films and slides can also be brought into this teaching.[12]

In addition, minor field situations (e.g. the interior of a trench) can be re-created in laboratory conditions and the methods of excavation discussed.[13] Instruction and enjoyment can come from 'situation games' in which students play the parts of director, land-owner, ministry official, etc. in pre-arranged situations.

The daily planning of work on an excavation is also something which can be improved by training. A director must be familiar with the day-to-day developments in each trench and have looked through the material from them. Only then can he arrange for the frequent alterations of excavation pattern and the redistribution of resources which will be necessary. These planning problems must always be in the director's mind, for they should underlie all his thinking.

(ii) *Excavation*

Manuals of excavation techniques[14] and discussion can help here, but it is only by having been a helper (page 11) and then a site supervisor (page 12) that the necessary experience can be acquired (Fig. 1). Having actually worked with pick, shovel, trowel and machine, a director should be able to gauge the equipment, workers and time needed to complete particular pieces of work in different conditions (page 57.) He should also know from this experience where spoil-heaps, railways, barrow and basket walks should be sited and when and where machines should be used.

(iii) *Recording*

Once again only experience, preferably as a specialist assistant (page 38), will enable a director to be sure that the day-by-day recording will be satisfactory and such that the report can be written from it. Classroom study of various recording systems which have been found to work in the field can be helpful to a director evolving his own form of recording.[15] The planning of written records will be easier than preparing for photography, surveying and section-drawing. Although instruction manuals exist[16] they are no substitute for practice, and indeed are actually dangerous when not supported by experience. This can be obtained in seminal conditions either on training excavations or practice sites.[17]

The generalised field knowledge discussed in (i), (ii) and (iii) will be necessary anywhere, but the special problems of excavating in temperate and tropical lands will require further consideration (page 45).

WRITING AND PUBLISHING THE REPORT (Fig. 8)

As already mentioned, publication is implicit in all excavation and is the unique responsibility of the director. It will require a quite different series of skills from those necessary during the excavation (see Chapter IV). In no case should a director lose control of the whole pattern of the evidence. During his training a director should have helped prepare, from the field-drawings, the plans and sections necessary for a report; should have helped sort and study the cultural finds from an excavation, should have been shown the negotiations for studying, the discussions around and the collation with other material of specialists' reports, of the samples on non-cultural evidence from a site. He should have been encouraged to be on the look-out for new ways of treating and publishing material and should have studied the best-published reports of his contemporaries with this in mind. Whilst some of the methods of study can be learnt from manuals,[18] much, including the permissible degrees of delegation of work, can only be learnt by experience.

## THE TRAINING OF ASSISTANTS

The role of assistants (surveyors, photographers, environmentalists, etc.), if indeed they are not all living within the skin of the director, is described at length in Chapter III. Much of their training must be by apprenticeship in the field, but some aspects of it can be taught in practical demonstrations, lectures and seminars.

University departments of archaeology and extra-mural studies often, in Britain, provide training of this kind.

*Surveyors and Architects.* These, whether hired professionals, young professional archaeologists in training or part-time archaeologists with professional knowledge, can benefit from some preliminary instruction.

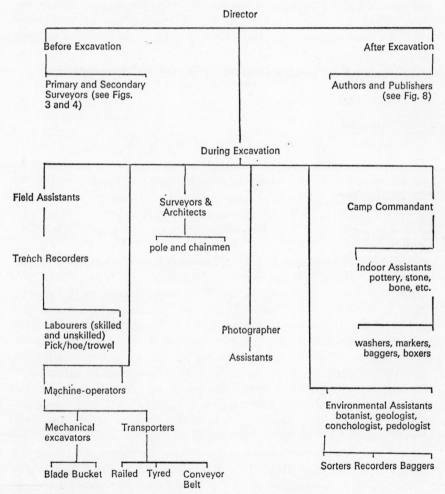

Fig. 1 Personnel of the excavation team (by function).

B

Experienced surveyors and architects should learn which techniques, particularly in photogrammetry, are best suited to archaeological work and to the site on which they are working.[20] Newcomers in training can learn to handle the equipment and practise specific tasks.[19]

*Photographers* may also be young professional archaeologists in training, amateur photographers, often with great practical experience, or hired professionals. If beginners, then classroom and practical experiments under different conditions should be carried out, but much of this should be in soil-colour and texture photography rather than indoor work.[21] Professionals and experienced amateur photographers will benefit from discussion and reading on the preparation of sites for photography and the kind of detail required.

*Indoor Assistants*, although they will be experienced in the archaeological material, may lack knowledge of recording and processing methods. This can be taught in lectures, demonstrations, and simulated field conditions.

The other *Assistants (archaeological and environmental)* (Fig. 1) will acquire most of their knowledge from their general training and from working on sites.

## THE TRAINING OF HELPERS

The training of helpers to work with trowel and brush, pick and shovel, or hoe, depends on the circumstances in any particular country or excavation. In principle the more general archaeology they know, the better the excavation, but on a research excavation a director will have no time and little inclination to offer general instruction. If he has the choice he will naturally choose workers who have already taken part in other excavations. If there are novices they will normally be put to work with those who are more experienced.

Longer-term training may come through the increasing interest in field-work among young people in many countries. In Britain, for example, with archaeology beginning to be taught in schools[22] and colleges of education,[23] this interest may increase, and opportunities to learn trowelling and other field techniques as part of courses of instruction are offered by many university extra-mural departments.[24] These are supported by evening courses in all parts of the country. Through advertisement and through the Council of British Archaeology, many of these skilled amateurs are available in their holidays to help in excavations.

Long-term excavation projects or bodies employing workers all through the year may train their own men, but whilst the practical training may be good, this lacks the theoretical knowledge which is becoming increasingly important in all stages of the work.

## SUGGESTED READING

DURING THE TRAINING OF THE DIRECTOR (starred works are particularly recommended)

*A Guide to Field Methods in Archaeology*★★, (especially for prehistoric problems), Heizer, R. and Graham, J. 1967. Good bibliography.
*Practical Archaeology*★★, (especially for historical problems), Webster, G. 1966.
*Notes and Queries on Anthropology*★, BAAS 1962.
*Procedural Manual for Arch. Field Research Projects*, Dittert, A. and Wendorf, F., Mus. of New Mexico Papers in Anthrop. XII 1963.
*Models in Prehistory*, Groube, L. *APAO* II.1 1967.
*The Classification of Artifacts in Archaeology*, Rouse, J. *AmAnth* 25 1960. 313.
*Science in Archaeology*, Brothwell, D. and Higgs, E. (ed) 1970.
*The Preparation of Archaeological Reports*, Grinsell, L., Rahtz, P. and Warhurst, A. 1965.
*Essays on Archaeological Method*, Griffin, J. (ed) 1957 (especially for the use of machines).
*Archaeologische Feldmethode*, Schwartz, G. 1967.
DURING THE TRAINING OF HIS ASSISTANTS
*Practical Archaeology*★★, Webster, G. 1966.
*Stratification for the Archaeologist*, Pyddoke, E. 1961.
*Field Archaeology*, Atkinson, R. 1953.
*The Archaeologist at Work*, Heizer, R. (ed) 1959.
*Digging up Bones*, Brothwell, D. 1965.
*Surveying for Archaeologists*, Fryer, D. 1960.
*Photography for Archaeologists*, Cookson, M. 1954.
*Plants and Archaeology*, Dimbleby, G. 1967.
*Soils for the Archaeologist*, Cornwall, I. 1958.
*The Inorganic Raw Materials of Antiquity*, Rosenfeld, A. 1965.
DURING THE TRAINING OF HIS HELPERS
*Field Archaeology*★★, Ordnance Survey 1963.
*Habitat, Economy and Society*★, Forde, C. 1964.
*Archaeology from the Earth*★, Wheeler, R. 1954.
*Beginning in Archaeology*, Kenyon, K. 1961.
*Field Guide to Archaeology*, Wood, E. 1963.
*The World of Ancient Man*, Cornwall, I. 1964.
*Archaeological Techniques for Amateurs*, Hammond, P. 1963.
SUGGESTED READING FOR TEACHERS OF FIELD ARCHAEOLOGY
The Teaching of Archaeological Anthropology, Mandelbaum, D. in *The Teaching of Anthropology*, Taylor, W. (ed) 1963.
*The Business of Management*, Falk, R. 1963.

## NOTES

1. Heizer, R. and Graham, J. 1967. 4.
2. e.g. Atkinson, R. 1953; Kenyon, K. 1952; Wheeler, R. 1954; Heizer, R. and Graham, J. 1967; Webster, G. 1966; Schwartz, G. 1967.
3. Kenyon, K. 1952. 167; Heizer, R. and Graham, J. 1967 appendix 2.
4. In many parts of the world excellent fieldworkers who concentrate on some specialised or local field earn their living in other disciplines. This is a desirable state of affairs.
5. See Sollas, W. 1924. 562.
6. As an introduction BAAS 1962 and Forde, C. 1964. For an example of a more detailed study: Stafaniszym, B. 1964.

7. Dimbleby, G. 1967.
8. Rosenfeld, A. 1965; Cornwall, I. 1958.
9. Cornwall, I. 1956; Brothwell, D. and Higgs, E. (ed) 1964.
10. Heizer, R. and Graham, J. 1967. 162 with good bibliography.
11. It has been found particularly useful to hold seminars at which all have previously read a particular report, and then, with or without the excavator, discuss its strategy and success.
12. Mandelbaum, D. in Taylor, W. (ed) 1963, especially 254ff.
13. For constructed problems see *Arc* III 1950. 175.
14. Atkinson, R. 1953 and Webster, G. 1966 are especially useful here.
15. It can be accepted that no one scheme will ever suit everybody. Each director will work out a modified system to suit himself but the principles can be learnt beforehand.
16. e.g. Cookson, M. 1954 and Fryer, D. 1960.
17. Little has been said or written about training excavations. Research excavations are not necessarily the best places for training since there is usually little time or energy for instruction.
18. Grinsell, L. et al. 1965.
19. Even in towns this can be done in parks and gardens.
20. Cookson, M. 1954.
21. Cookson, M. 1954 to be compared with Matthews, S. 1968 for the difference in approach.
22. See Syllabus for a General Certificate in Education (Advanced Level) in Archaeology, Cambridge University Local Examinations Syndicate. 1968.
23. See Syllabus for a First Degree in Education (History, special subject). University of London 1968.
24. These are carried on in all parts of England. Programmes can be obtained through University Extra-Mural-Departments and regional secretaries of the Workers Educational Association.

# CHAPTER II

# Assessing the Problems
# and Planning the Excavation

Conditions in which effective management can function: 'These are: first the objectives must be clearly stated; secondly responsibility must be defined and accepted; thirdly communication must be two-way or even three-way; fourthly the chief executives in any enterprise, of whatever size, must always control and progress the operation.'

R. Falk
*The Business of Management*, 1963, 67

The initial discovery of a site may be *casual*, part of some general *salvage* or *rescue* survey, or due to a '*problem-oriented*' research survey. The organisation of either of the latter kind of survey, developments of W. J. Arkell's and O. G. S. Crawford's archaeology-without-digging, requires a series of skills and techniques separate from those connected with excavation. These are discussed at length elsewhere and will be omitted here.[1]

In this chapter it will be assumed that a site has already been located.

## THE DECISION TO EXCAVATE

Whilst reasons for digging are as varied as excavators, few are strictly legitimate. In many parts of the world the rate of destruction is so great that the rescuing of information from sites about to be destroyed should rank above all other reasons. Where resources are not limited or where specialist teams exist, research programmes will naturally include sites unthreatened by destruction, but for local archaeological groups the principle that a site unthreatened by destruction should be left alone should be observed.

## ASSESSING THE PROBLEMS

No excavation should be started without all the problems, archaeological, legal, financial and logistical, having been studied and a detailed plan made (Fig. 2). The archaeological problems should naturally take first place, but unless all the factors are considered the excavation may fail through any one of them.

To begin with, all existing information about the site should be collected and studied. This can be a formidable business but will save much wasted effort, enable much better planning (especially of costing) and may explain many of the finds made during excavation. It may require a variety of skills and considerable tact in the investigator, and

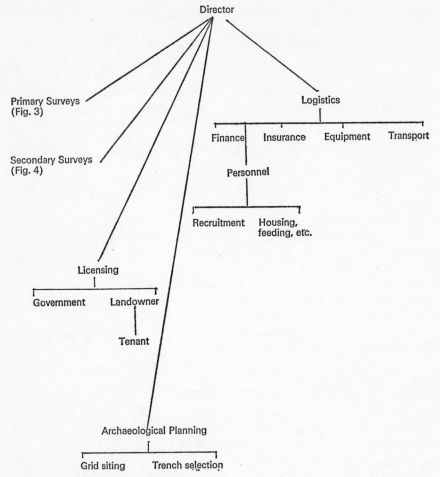

Fig. 2 Planning an excavation.

should preferably be done by the director himself. Both aural and literary evidence should be looked for and may be found in a very wide range of places (Fig. 3).

INFORMATION FROM LOCAL PEOPLE
The recent history of a site can only be discovered through conversation with people who have long known the area.[2]

In the *country*, farmers should be visited and encouraged to talk. If the present occupiers are new, their predecessors, whose knowledge may be greater, are often living in retirement and can be visited.

In cultivated areas a farmer-owner who ploughs or hoes his own land or the labourer who does it for him are likely to be most useful. They see the land under all weathers and plant, weed and harvest under all conditions. Much of the following information may be acquired in the course of conversation: the field names of the area of the site; the presence of concentrations of stones, bricks, charcoal, pottery and bones noted at any time during cultivation; patches of unexpected texture or colour (possible hearths, pits or ditches); areas of especially marshy or dry ground (possible pits or mounds) and whether any unusual objects were found and kept. It is worthwhile carrying and showing the kinds of objects which would be of special interest.[3]

Country people can also be asked whether, during the growth of crops, any variation in crop-growth was noticed, whether some parts of the field produced a very good or very poor crop, or supported special concentrations of weeds. They will also know if any pits or trenches have been dug in the field recently and perhaps remember the soil sequence in the pits and the depth of bedrock. If the field was ever

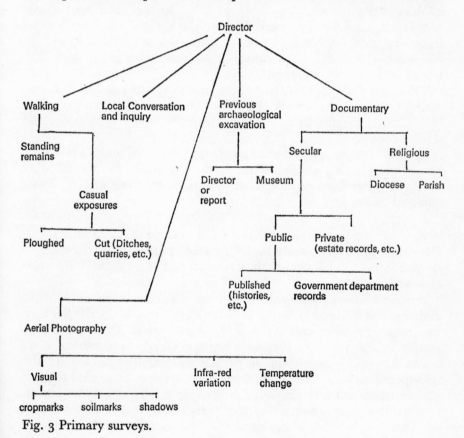

Fig. 3 Primary surveys.

drained they may know where the drains lie; whether any levelling has taken place (depressions filled, banks, trees, etc. removed) or loads of stones and rubbish brought to make up tracks or field entrances.

General questions also should be asked. Most families and villages will have someone especially interested in local affairs and these should be sought out. Local collectors are usually well known and, if tactfully approached, can be most helpful.[4] Local officials also, if they have lived long in the area, can be useful. The following information may be obtained from them: where finds of pottery, bones, etc. have been made and whether they have survived in private hands, gone to museums or have been lost; whether pits and trenches dug anywhere locally for drains or foundations have shown any unusual stratigraphy, and whether there are any legends or folk tales connected with the area.[5]

On specific points (i.e. the stratigraphy of a particular disturbance) it may well be necessary to search out the local builder or the foreman of the water, gas, electricity or road-mending gang which made it.

In a *town* the recent history of a site can best be discovered from long-established owners or tenants. In addition to the questions already mentioned, they should be asked where the gas and other services lie in gardens and neighbouring roads; where the inspection covers are, and whether any old earth closets or other buildings have been destroyed within living memory.

They may know if there have been any cracks or subsidence in the houses (which might have been due to their siting over ditches or pits), and whether digging in cellars has shown the stratigraphy under the floors or walls.

In towns stratigraphy is sometimes better preserved under roads than houses and gardens, and it is often worthwhile asking district surveyors or their gang foremen about the stratigraphy beneath the roads adjacent to the site.

INFORMATION FROM MUSEUMS, ARCHIVES AND LIBRARIES

Here the objects previously found may be studied, and references to the site in books and manuscripts consulted. The objects fall into two classes:

(i) *Casual Finds* may come from agricultural or industrial disturbance and are most likely to be found in district museums. If the site lies near the boundary of several districts, all museums in them should be inspected. The museum accessions registers should be consulted if no site indices exist. A conscientious curator will usually have marked the find-spots on a large-scale map. Particular care may be needed to trace objects which fell into the hands of private collectors and were then donated to a museum or some other person as part of a large and un-catalogued collection. If any such collection was known to have been made locally it must be traced, perhaps even overseas.[6] In all countries objects may have reached university or national museums in the period before district collectors were established.

Another source of information lies in the reports of field officers from national antiquities, cartographical and geological surveys. These are especially valuable in sparsely inhabited areas,[7] but even in Britain they preserve shrewd comments and observations not found elsewhere. If site indices are maintained by these surveys the search is easy, but in other cases the actual reports may have to be consulted.[8]

(ii) *Previous Excavation.* If this has taken place the information should be available in a published report, but if done long ago this may well be incomplete. From it or from the excavator's notes, if they have been preserved, the following information should be obtained: the exact location of trenches dug; some representative sections; the place of deposition of finds; the nature of bedrock; the depth of soil cover and the general stratigraphy.

Correspondence or conversation with the previous director, or failing him some member of the excavating team, is nearly always valuable for advice on local labour and supply conditions, legal or administrative problems likely to arise, and any local information that was obtained but not published.

If no report and no member of the excavation team is available, eye-witness accounts either from living people or as originally published in local newspapers or archaeological conference notes[9] may be helpful. These can often be consulted in district or county archives. Considerable correspondence may be necessary to trace any plans or records of finds which may still exist, but it is well worth while to take pains over this.

Written information may be considered under the following headings:

(i) *Historical Information.* Early descriptions of sites or of finds no longer available can sometimes be found in the publications of histori-cally-minded travellers, administrators, priests and school-teachers.[10] A search should therefore be made, if the site has long been known, of district histories. It is not really sufficient to look at some general summary;[11] the originals should be consulted, a district library being usually the most convenient place for this. At the same time the district or national archives may be consulted for possible manuscript local histories.[12]

Early plans of the site may also exist in district archives from surveys carried out for big private or public landowners, or for ecclesiastical bodies when establishing missions or assessing dues. If the existence of estate plans other than those in public archives is suspected, it may be necessary to consult the landlord himself. If he has a great estate or if it is owned by a university college or a religious society, this is best done through their lawyers. Title deeds to property often show or describe boundaries, and boundaries often follow the lines of even prehistoric banks and ditches, so that surface features can be sometimes proved to have existed many centuries ago.[13]

If the site is a historical one (since the introduction of written records in the region) a search of the government records, especially of the tax and legal departments, may be helpful. This is difficult and specialised work if of a period earlier than the eighteenth century, and help will have to be sought from palaeographers and historians.[14] The manuscript will normally be held in the national archive or record offices.

(ii) *Geological Information*. Before digging begins, every effort should be made to find out the nature of the soil and rocks likely to be encountered, for much time and energy can be saved by this knowledge. It may be possible to tell at what season of the year soil variation would show up most clearly,[15] when this kind of soil could be most easily excavated, and what kind of preliminary surveys will be successful.

Some of this information can come from regional publications or officers of national geological surveys, but, as has already been mentioned, it should be supplemented by local enquiry and by studying local exposures in sides of streams, ditches or pits.

(iii) *Ethnographic Evidence*. Depending upon the site being excavated, a study of local ethnographic evidence may be necessary. For example, when prehistoric sites are being investigated in areas where hunter-gatherer or simple agricultural groups still exist, a study of their material equipment and social organisation must certainly be made before excavating.[16] It would be well worth while to visit, and even sink test-trenches into, abandoned sites to observe how house-debris weathers or how postholes can be recognised. Where these groups no longer exist the evidence of earlier travellers and ethnographers should be studied.

## PRELIMINARY SURVEYS

The literary and aural sources just considered rarely by themselves provide sufficient knowledge of a site for an excavation to be planned. They can be supplemented in the following ways, the particular methods selected depending upon the site (Fig. 4).

### VISITING THE SITE

A site selected for excavation should be visited and walked over at different times of the year and in different weather conditions before excavation begins.[17] It should, if possible, be visited after ploughing and after rain, for any concentrations of ploughed-out stones, bricks or charcoal, coins, pottery, stone tools or bones will then have been washed clean and will be easy to see. Concentrations can best be located

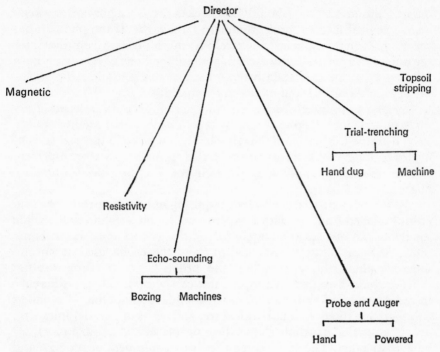

Director

Magnetic

Topsoil
stripping

Trial-trenching

Hand dug        Machine

Resistivity

Echo-sounding

Bozing    Machines

Probe and Auger

Hand        Powered

Fig. 4 Secondary surveys.

by a line of people a few feet apart walking slowly and followed by a
recorder with a large-scale plan. Any finds can then be plotted and
bagged at once. On an extensive site this kind of preparation can locate
densities of settlement (often of different periods), stone-tool and
pottery-making areas. On very large sites slow-moving motor cars have
proved useful.[18] Sites that are never ploughed should be visited when
the vegetation is low and the shadows long, to see if any surface features
remain or if there is any differential plant growth over buried features.
Sites regularly under snow for some period should be visited when snow
is melting, since this may help to show up slight surface variations.[19]

The spoil from the burrows of rabbits and other animals, exposures
in stream banks and cattle treads round ponds, or animal runs on
slopes should be watched for exposures.

AERIAL SURVEYS
If an aerial photograph of the site shows features, an enlargement of the
site area must be obtained and a plan prepared from it.[20] If the photograph was taken vertically this will not be too difficult for measurements
can be taken directly from the photograph and scaled against a large

map of the area; they should be checked by triangulation between archaeological features and prominent landmarks. If the photographs are oblique, measurements can rarely be taken directly from them, for the angles can be very distorted. Elaborate methods of rectifying have been evolved but are expensive and require considerable skill; professional help should be sought (Plate III and Fig. 34).

Any plans produced from aerial photographs should be checked on the ground before digging begins by one or other of the methods about to be described. Much futile digging has taken place in the past searching for features visible from the air. Buried features known or suspected, can be tested in the following ways: if one does not succeed another might.

(i) *Probe Surveys* are the simplest, requiring only a stout round or oval cross-sectioned iron bar with a tapered point and a T-handle.[21] A line should be set out approximately at right-angles to a suspected bank, ditch, wall, or across a suspected pit, and the probe used at 50 cm. intervals along the line. When the probe penetrates any stratum different in texture from the topsoil this can be both felt as a difference in resistance and heard as a different sound. A single line of probings can therefore discover a buried feature, and series of parallel lines 1 m. apart can define its whole shape. Two people should be able to survey an acre in a day. The method requires little equipment or practice and works well in shallow soils above hard bedrocks. It will not be of use when the depth of the top-soil is greater than the length of the probe (about 1·5 m. is the limit which most people can use); if the bedrock is of similar texture to the top-soil (e.g. sand), or if the top-soil is stony and the probe cannot be forced down.

(ii) *Auger Surveys* are in common use among pedologists and geologists and can be used archaeologically,[22] the 'corkscrew' as opposed to the 'trap' kind being more useful and less damaging. Hand augers are used like a probe but should bring up a sample every 3 cm. The details of each sequence should be recorded in the trench notebook. Especial care must be taken to clean the auger after each sample and to avoid scraping the sides of the borehole on the way up or down. One metre is the normal working limit but longer or jointed augers have been made to specification and used successfully. The advantage of this method is that colour is now added to texture as a criterion, and that samples can be studied in more detail. Several strata are often visible above bedrock, and their relative thicknesses can be recorded. Its disadvantages are that it cannot be used effectively in stony soils and should be used sparingly since it can cause destruction. It also takes much longer to carry out, for two people working together should be able to survey half an acre in a day. Augers are especially useful on complicated sites with a number of strata.

*Power-Driven Augers and Drills* are used in geological and oil surveys and are elaborate and relatively difficult to obtain,[23] but considerable archaeological experimenting has been done with them. The drills are jointed and can penetrate to great depths. Their use is greatest on especially difficult sites, for being power-driven, they have the advantage of being unaffected by stones or any hard material. They are particularly useful in penetrating to deeply buried strata (i.e. below flood debris or accumulation in towns) and have been used to locate rock-cut chamber tombs. Their disadvantages are that they are the most destructive form of testing, are relatively unwieldy, and special arrangements have to be made to buy or hire them. Samples should be taken at every 10 cm. of depth and each sequence recorded.

(iii) *Magnetic Surveys* rely upon the effect that local variations in magnetism (caused mainly by differences in soil composition and disturbances in bedrock) have upon hydrogen protons.[24] Only experiment can show the effectiveness of a proton-magnetometer or similar instrument on a particular site, and no exclusive reliance should be placed upon them. In favourable conditions they can distinguish kilns and hearths with greater precision than most other techniques; they have proved less useful so far in locating pits and ditches. In practice their use involves setting up a line of electrodes a few inches into the ground at 30, 60 or 90 cms. intervals. Anomalies between the electrodes can then be plotted. A team of three people can work over several acres in a day. The disadvantage of the instruments is that they will record the presence of even small pieces of iron in the same way as they record features, and are disturbed by wire fences and rocks with a high iron content. The instruments are expensive to buy, but special arrangements can sometimes be made to hire or borrow them. The interpretation of the plots is difficult and needs considerable experience.

(iv) *Geo-electrical Resistivity Surveys* are based on the variations in electrical resistance mainly due to varying humidities in soils and rocks.[25]

Lines of electrodes are set up as described for the magnetic survey. The resistance between each pair of electrodes is then measured by a meggor, plotted on a plan and anomalies looked for. They are best used where the top-soil is thin and the bedrock distinctive (i.e. chalk), and large features (ditches, roads, etc.) can be traced quickly over long distances.

Their advantages are that: a team of three people can cover several acres in a day; there is no destruction of evidence; and the equipment is easy to obtain in all countries since it is based on that used by all telegraph-linesmen. Its disadvantages are that: in many soil and weather conditions, especially very wet or very dry ones, the electrical resistance will be almost uniform throughout the strata; and very deep topsoil or a bedrock indistinguishable in resistance from topsoil (e.g. sand) will often give poor results.

(v) *Echo Sounding Surveys*. A variety of methods rely on reflection of sound waves by buried deposits. The simplest merely requires a heavy weight which is bounced on the ground.[26] In suitable conditions it will produce a different sound over solid rocks from that over soft earth-filled features like ditches. It is known to have worked well in areas with thin top-soils and hard bedrocks and in dry conditions. More elaborate methods involving radar devices have been experimented with satisfactorily but are not yet generally available.[27]

(vi) *Machine or hand-dug Test Trenches*. On extensive sites where time is limited the use of mechanical excavators or, failing this, human labour to assess the problem can be invaluable. Always accompanied by an archaeologist, machines especially can quickly cut trenches or clear areas through plough-soil, sterile over-burden or superimposed banks and mounds and test the underlying stratigraphies.

*Sites under water*, both those which have been flooded or harbour works, may be encountered. Work on them will depend on the help of trained divers with archaeological interest and experience.


# LEGAL PROBLEMS

No excavation should be started in any country without a knowledge of the law of the land on the licensing of excavations by state and landlord, the accident liability of employers, insurance, the ownership of finds and the disposal of antiquities. If these matters are neglected much trouble and expense can result.

Three kinds of permission may be necessary before a site can be dug; those of the government, the landlord and the tenant.

*The Government*. In most countries the excavation of antiquities of any kind is strictly controlled and there are severe penalties for unlawful digging.[28] The details of how and from whom licences to dig may be obtained are usually set out in an *Antiquities Statute*,[29] and negotiations for a licence must be begun long before the excavation is due to begin. Copies of the statute can usually be obtained through the National Antiquities Service or from the Government Stationery Office. In Britain a series of Ancient Monuments Acts gives the duty of protecting and maintaining specified monuments of public interest to the Minister of Public Buildings and Works. He exercises this power with the help of the Ancient Monuments Board and the reports of its Chief Inspector. The Minister also compiles a list of sites protected by the acts. It is an offence to interfere with a monument so specified without the Chief Inspector's permission. Few other countries have so little control over their antiquities. Any licence so obtained should make the following points quite clear:

(i) The area in which excavation is permitted.

(ii) The final destination and perhaps division of the finds and their location during the period in which they are being studied.

(iii) Date, priority and method of publishing results.

Care should be taken to see that the local authorities and landowners have copies of the licence.

*The Landowner.* Permission to excavate must be sought also from the landowner, whether a private person or a public body. It should be given in writing, and if it is at all complicated or ambiguous should be referred to a lawyer. This written permission should settle the following points before digging begins:

(i) Compensation for loss or destruction of crop (the amount of compensation and nature of the crop should be clearly stated).

(ii) Fencing during excavation (against animals, etc.).

(iii) Access (the routes helpers and visitors are allowed to take).

(iv) Reinstatement of the land (backfilling, topsoil replacement).

(v) Ultimate disposal of finds.

*The Tenant.* Permission to dig must also be sought from any tenant of the land. Details of compensation, access and reinstatement should be settled primarily with him; but the interests of the landlord should not be overlooked.

OWNERSHIP OF THE OBJECTS FOUND

This may vary greatly in different countries between the state, the landowner and the finder, and it is necessary to know the law in the particular country in which excavation is taking place. In Britain a distinction is made between objects of gold and silver and all other materials. An object of gold or silver must be reported as soon as found to the local Coroner who will then hold an inquest to decide if they are treasure trove.[30] He will hear evidence identifying and dating the objects and describing how they were found. He will then decide whether they were deliberately hidden (found hidden in the earth or in any other secret place), whether there was any intention of recovering them later, or whether they were simply lost or abandoned (e.g. in or after a battle).

If they were deliberately hidden with a view to recovery and the owner cannot be traced, they are treasure trove and so belong to the Crown by virtue of the royal prerogative. This means that they can be added to national or local collections of antiquities if their custodians desire and claim them. The full antiquarian market value of them will be paid to the finder if there has been prompt disclosure. Compensation is reduced for non-disclosure which is of course a crime. If not claimed by the national or local collections they may be disposed of by the finder.

If they were merely lost they are not considered treasure trove and they will be returned to the landowner or finder.[31] National and local collections should have the opportunity to buy them at their market value.

Any objects other than treasure trove belong to the landowner and should be returned to him unless arrangements are made for them to be donated or loaned to a museum. His permission is also necessary before pavements or other pieces of building are removed. It is a great advantage to have this latter point settled in advance of excavation.

*Human remains.* These, in England, should also be reported to the coroner, preferably through the police, if there is any suspicion of a violent, unnatural or sudden death. Technically the date is, from the coroner's point of view, immaterial but if the excavator can show that they are not recent burials the reporting usually remains a formality.

Some additional negotiations with local religious representatives may be necessary in all countries. In England, for example, if burials later than *c.* A.D. 700 are uncovered they are assumed to be Christian and should be reburied in consecrated ground. Village priests have in fact been known to claim even prehistoric men as parishioners.[32] If a Christian cemetery is inadvertently, or needs to be deliberately, disturbed, special ecclesiastical permission (a Faculty or Licence) will be necessary. In England this should be discussed with the parish priest, the archdeacon, and the diocesan registrar.[33] In other countries, any disturbance of human remains should be discussed with local religious authorities and villagers.

## INSURANCE PROBLEMS

Directors of excavations, committees of excavating societies and even workers themselves (for damage may result from the acts of fellow workers), should be insured against accidents taking place on sites. If paid workers, either full-time or part-time, are employed it will also be necessary in England as in many other countries to pay national insurance contributions.

*Accident Insurance.* Open trenches, even when fenced, are always dangerous; especially for children or animals which may get through, fall in and be injured, and there is always a possibility of compensation being claimed and awarded in court. Trench walls also may collapse or loose earth and stones may fall on workers, and in some cases those in charge of the excavation might be held responsible. Against this, general insurance may be taken out. Many insurance companies undertake this kind of cover, and usually an agent will, on request, visit the site and suggest a premium based upon the depth and size of trenches, the number of people present, the security of the fencing and the length of time involved. This, in England at least, is not usually very expensive. Adequate first aid equipment and the addresses of the nearest doctor and hospital should be available on the site.

Any insurance cover obtained should include injury to members of the public at large as well as actual workers in the excavation.

## NEGLIGENCE

Directors should also be familiar with the law of negligence of the country in which they are working. In England this creates an obligation to take reasonable precautions to prevent injury to workers, visitors and other persons likely to be affected by the conditions of the excavation. A prudent director will see that injury will not be caused by any negligence on his part.

*National Insurance.* In countries where there are national contributory insurance schemes for employed persons[34] it is the responsibility of the director to know their details and to pay his share. In some countries, including Great Britain, he is required to deduct the employee's share, buy insurance stamps and affix them to the card provided. It is also necessary for him to know local regulations concerning the payment of insurance contributions on honorariums.

## TAX PROBLEMS

Some countries, including Britain, require the employer to deduct income tax from his employees' wages. Others, also including Britain, levy an employment tax on some employers. A director must know his statutory liabilities in these matters, and have discussed them with the appropriate officials.[35]

## PUBLIC RELATIONS

These are worth separate consideration because they are often neglected and can make a great deal of difference to the success of an excavation. Friendly relationships with local archaeologists, landowners and officials, the local community and its leaders, and the national and provincial press, television and radio, are always desirable and often essential.

## LOCAL ARCHAEOLOGISTS AND ANTIQUARIES

If local workers have not already been asked for help or advice, politeness should ensure that they are told of the excavation and invited to visit it. The curator of the district museum and the officials and members of the local archaeological society are the most obviously interested parties, but local antiquaries and collectors should also be considered. In England this should include telling the county and district societies and museums.

c

LOCAL AUTHORITIES

It has already been suggested that when an excavating licence has been granted by a central government agency, copies of it should be sent by the excavator to district officials so that the legal basis of the excavation is established. If this can be coupled with a formal request from the central authorities that all possible help be given to the excavator, so much the better. Over much of the world the help of a district official in arranging labour, negotiating with landlords and tenants, providing guards, buying food, renting houses, etc. is invaluable, and much care should be taken in consulting him and explaining the needs and aims of the work. This is almost equally true of all local leaders. Depending on local circumstances, the support of a tribal chief, great landlord or religious leader may be necessary, and a courtesy visit to explain the purposes of the excavation should be made.

In Great Britain, for example, information that excavation is to take place, possibly with invitations to visit the site, can be sent to or better still discussed with, urban or rural local government officials, the Clerk to the Council, the Architect and the Surveyor being those nearest to the problems of the excavation. Whilst not to be approached lightly, these officials can often make useful suggestions (for the hire of equipment or stores for example) and they may also have much knowledge of commercial or other casual digging in the area.

If the excavation exposes considerable structural remains, it may be felt that local school children should have the opportunity to visit it before backfilling takes place. This should be arranged, in Britain, through the Chief Education Officer of the local authority.

It is also as well to inform the police that the excavation is taking place. If there is any likelihood of illicit digging, robbery, hooliganism or even too much local curiosity, it may be possible to arrange for patrolmen to visit the site at regular intervals or even to have men detailed for full-time guard-duty.


THE COMMUNITY

Contact with local community leaders, especially those interested in local history, is also desirable. As has already been mentioned, conversation with villagers will soon show who among them are interested in antiquities. A village priest, schoolmaster or leading farmer may well be able to help with both archaeological and logistical advice.

Depending on the time available and the duration of the excavation (how many seasons are contemplated), a public report to the local community is desirable after each phase of the excavation. In England this is often suggested and arranged by local societies (e.g. village clubs, Workers' Educational Association branches, Women's Institutes). It is polite as well as politic for an excavator to satisfy local interest.

THE LANDLORD

There is no need to stress the advantages of friendly relations with the landlord. Much help and advice can come from a landlord who understands, because it has been adequately explained to him, what is being done and what is needed. Regular contact will also be necessary to ensure that his feelings and complaints are attended to, for a hostile landlord can soon bring an excavation to an end.

THE PRESS

No set relationship between an excavator and journalists can be laid down, but the following general propositions may be borne in mind:

(i)   The existence of a body of informed opinion in a country is the best guarantee of increasing knowledge of the subject.

(ii)  In most countries archaeological progress depends on government support. This will only continue whilst there is knowledge and interest among officials and public at large.

(iii) Inaccurate published comment is far worse than none at all.

(iv)  Publicity before the excavation begins, especially if it includes a detailed discussion of possible findings, is undesirable. To arouse anticipations which may not be fulfilled, especially if connected with commercial fund-raising, is as immoral as the issuing of false prospectuses. It may bring the excavation and even research in general into disrepute.

Unless arrangements to show visitors around can be made and precautions to secure the site against too much curiosity are good, releases to the press are best made when excavations are over. Only then can a reliable summary be written and all dangers of illicit digging, hooliganism and the interruption of work by visitors be avoided. This of course conflicts with the natural desires of journalists, and if reporters come during the excavation some form of compromise will have to be made. The following points should be settled before an interview.

(i)   Who the interviewer represents (newspaper, press-agency, freelance journalist).

(ii)  That any report to be published will, in its final form, either be shown, or read over the telephone, to the director before publication.

(iii) No photographs are to be taken without permission. (A liking for 'lively' pictures may lead to quite the wrong impression of an excavation being published.)

(iv)  That no interview with other members of the excavation will take place without permission. (These may be more 'colourful' but less accurate than the director's account.)

(v)   That a copy of the published article and photographs be sent, for reference, to the director.

If a short statement with photograph has been prepared beforehand this can save much time at the interview. This should include a general account of the excavation, and, if necessary, the location of the site can be left sufficiently vague to make vandalism and visitors unlikely.

After the excavation has finished some publication of the results to satisfy local interest or for fund-raising may be desirable. This can often be obtained by preparing a short statement of results, i.e. 1,500 words, for local news-editors, national news agencies or the archaeological correspondents of daily and week-end national newspapers. Requests for feature articles (longer, usually illustrated articles of more general interest) are best considered separately on their merits.

Requests by journalists to join the excavation and then write feature articles of their own should be treated with reserve. If permission is granted, the articles should be read before publication. Members of the excavation team should be discouraged from private publication.

### RADIO AND TELEVISION

Requests for interviews or for information to be broadcast or televised should be treated in much the same way as press requests. Usually the requests will come from local reporters or agencies and the interviews will be tape-recorded. Whilst it is rarely possible to edit the final version, care should be taken, by spelling out proper names for example, to see that it is accurate. Only rarely will a live broadcast be made.

Interviews of this kind, like the others, are best given near the end of the excavation so that excessive publicity before or during excavation is avoided.

### THE PUBLIC AT LARGE

If there is great local interest and if the site can be protected and guides provided, a director may be considered to have a civic duty to publicise the excavation and allow visits, with the landlord's permission, by the general public. These should be organised at regular intervals under knowledgeable guides, follow a set pattern and should not interfere with the work.

### THE EXCAVATION TEAM

Those working on the excavation, whether paid or unpaid, also have a right to be told how the work is progressing and how their particular problem relates to the general pattern. They can best be told in regular (perhaps weekly) tours of the trenches, conducted by the director. If possible all taking part should be invited to the public lecture after the excavation at which the results are presented. Those who were particularly helpful should be sent offprints of the final published report.

# FINANCIAL PROBLEMS

All excavations need money even when labour is freely given by volunteers and equipment is borrowed. Provision must be made not only for expendable items (see equipment lists on page 42) but also for insurance, publication and perhaps mechanical aids. Apart from state and university-sponsored excavations, no two expeditions ever seem to be financed in the same way, and the ingenuity of committees and individuals in raising money is impressive. Here only the general principles of fund-raising and administration will be considered.

If money is being raised from a number of private and public sources a formally constituted committee with a treasurer accustomed to keeping accounts is necessary. A separate bank account should be opened and all invoices and receipts kept. Payments to workers should be registered and made against signatures or thumbprints. Day-by-day purchases from a petty cash allowance should also be supported by receipts. As much as possible should be paid for by cheque, since this makes for easy accounting.

Who should be approached for financial help and how this should be done, will vary with the country, the site and the excavator, but in all cases a full appreciation of the archaeological problem, the amount of work, the labour force and time required to solve it, and the probable cost, including publication, should all be set out and circulated. This statement can only be done if costing has been carried out in the way suggested below.

## COSTING THE EXCAVATION

Many excavations are partial failures because they neglect to match beforehand their resources to the problems of the site. This can be avoided if, after the collection of all the available evidence in the ways already described, the area, depth and complexity of strata to be removed are expressed in terms of cubic metres of soil and man-hours of work. These figures must then be considered in the light of the time available and weather to be expected. From this the amount and kind of labour, money and equipment needed, and the feasibility of excavation, can be assessed. Unless this is done and the resources of the expedition are shown to be, or can then be made to be, more than insufficient, incomplete evidence and a spoiled site are likely to be the result.

The *Area to be Excavated* will have to be decided on archaeological grounds, and although the amount may be altered (usually increased) during excavation this will indicate the minimum area of work in square metres. The approximate depth of accumulation above bedrock should be known from the surveys so that this figure can be turned into cubic metres. How long a cubic metre of a particular kind of soil will take to excavate will depend on its consistency and its archaeological complexity. Commercial costing in Britain for simple hand-labouring varies with the nature of the soil (wet clay, dry sand, etc.) round ·5 cubic metres per man-hour. Archaeological costing even for sterile deposits should never be less than this. If trowelled carefully, the same volume would take at least 6 man-hours. For example: a trench 2 m. wide through a bank or ditch 10 m. wide × 3 m. high might take 4 workers with picks and shovels a week. An occupation level 10 cm. thick over a 3 m. × 3 m. trench might take 4 trowellers 2–3 days. Calculations of this kind can never be accurate, but even rough estimates are worth making. Although attention to the siting of spoil dumps, barrow or basket runs, or the use of conveyor belts or railways helps, this cannot do a great deal to speed the work. Since trenches must always be completed to bedrock, the number of trenches which can be finished with any fixed amount of resources can be roughly estimated beforehand.

## PERSONNEL (Fig. 1)

Once the size of the archaeological problem is known, the kind and amount of help needed can be deduced. The qualifications of the director himself have already been discussed (Chapter I) but depending on the size and complexity of the excavation, seven kinds of *Specialist Assistants* may be necessary.

(i) *A Surveyor and/or Architect.* Some member of the excavation team must be competent to produce accurate measured plans (see page 57). In most excavations this is a fairly straightforward process and can be carried out by a surveyor, but if standing buildings or a succession of buildings are expected, an architect[36] should be included in the team. A director who lacks a trained surveyor or architect may well find too much of his time being given to the preparation of plans.

(ii) Unlike the architect, an ordinary professional *Photographer* is not necessary or even desirable on an excavation unless he is experienced in outdoor work and possesses considerable archaeological knowledge. One must, however, have good photographers and cameras on every excavation (see page 58) and, as in surveying, a director doing his own photography may well find it takes too much of his time.

(iii) An *Indoor Archaeological Assistant* who can deal with the material when it has left the trenches will also be necessary on many sites. He or she ought to be a good organiser and if possible should have some general knowledge of the local material of the periods expected on the site. He will be in charge of the processing services, especially the washing, marking, recording and bagging (see page 61) (Fig. 5).

(iv) The increasing importance of non-cultural evidence requires that an *Environmental Assistant* be included in the team. As pointed out in

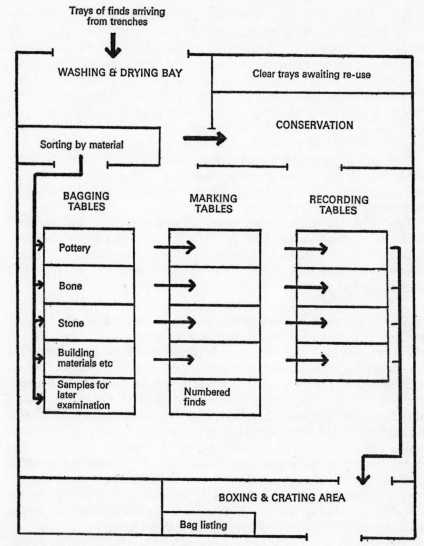

Fig. 5 Ideal layout for a site tent or hut.

Chapter V, soil, plant, animal, snail and insect remains can be located and properly sampled only if the search for them is a regular routine. Visits from outside scientists, whilst valuable, are no substitute for this.

(v) A large-scale excavation may require a number of *Outdoor Assistant Archaeologists* competent to take charge of particular sites and groups of trenches. They will normally be full-time professionals and have many of the skills mentioned above.

(vi) *Trench Recorders* (page 57) will also be needed, and whilst they need not be full-time professional archaeologists, they should be competent to record the hour-by-hour excavation of strata and oversee the work of less experienced workers in their trenches.

(vii) Problems of conserving finds in the field occur on most excavations, and when these are likely to be a major problem (e.g. in desiccated or water-logged sites), a *Conservator* may be needed. It is the responsibility of the director to see that the objects found reach the museum or laboratory in the same state as they left the ground, and no attempt at long-term preservation should normally be made in the field. Even if no trained conservator is available, it may be necessary to have special assistance in the delicate and time-consuming business of packing objects safely.

(viii) If it is necessary to arrange for the shelter, food and transport of many of those taking part in the excavation a *Camp Commandant* may be necessary (page 53). Unless one is appointed, this part of the organisation may well distract the director from his more important archaeological problems.

The recruitment of these assistants will be either from the ranks of the young professional archaeologists who are learning their craft, or the increasing number, especially in Britain, of experienced amateur archaeologists who include professional surveyors, architects and photographers. Whilst in the past such people have been recruited by personal recommendation, directors can now recruit through the publications of the Council of British Archaeology, especially the Calendar of Excavations,[37] the local archaeological societies and federations,[38] appropriate university departments and even the agony columns of the national press. Now that an increasing number of universities are teaching archaeology, both intra- and extra-murally, the appropriate departments might be approached directly by directors with requests to circulate or display notices. University departments which organise training excavations could be especially helpful here.[39]

An excavation succeeds or fails as much by the quality of its *General Labour Force* as by its director and his assistants. Although ideally all present should have some knowledge of archaeology and be capable of all kinds of work, in practice individuals will have widely differing experience, knowledge, abilities and predilections, and a director, having assessed his needs, should try and recruit to suit them. General workers should be recruited well before excavation begins and will come, in Britain especially, from a variety of sources.

The recruitment of adult volunteers (see page 18) is increasingly important for the finer work. Students can be reached through university faculties, student unions, magazines and newspapers.[40] If possible candidates should be interviewed, but if accepted by letter, dates of arrival and departure, what pay or expenses they may expect and details of lodging, feeding and transport should be settled in writing (see appendix). No one should be accepted for less than seven days, and fourteen days should normally be the minimum; even an experienced worker takes several days to become accustomed to soil changes on a new site. School children of thirteen years onwards also can be allowed to participate although the numbers should be limited in most cases to a small proportion of those taking part.

The number of workers accepted should be closely related to the number of trenches being opened. Not more than four people can work efficiently in a 3 m. square trench, and if unskilled trowellers, especially students, are accepted their number should be limited to that which can be closely supervised.

Men or women employed as full-time unskilled earth movers will normally be recruited through labour contractors or directly through a labour exchange. The number required should be worked out most carefully, and if large gangs are employed charge-hands (in charge of small groups) and foremen (controlling larger ones) will be very important and must be chosen carefully. Labour contractors will have the advantage, to the director, of paying and being responsible for their men and providing transport. Bad workers and foremen can be sent back and new ones demanded. The disadvantage is that their charges will naturally be much higher than those paid to direct recruits. Direct recruiting is cheapest, but unless labour is plentiful or the director is a good judge of men, much time may be wasted by the employment of poor workmen, and more in dealing with their personal problems, injuries, transport, etc.[41]

In parts of the world where labour is cheap the temptation to open larger areas than can be properly supervised must be resisted. Very few excavation teams today can justify the use of the hundreds of men used in the earlier part of the century.

Much of the work previously done by unskilled human labour is now better done by *Excavating Machines*. These can often be hired by the day or season for small excavations, but excavating societies and expeditions working on a large scale over many seasons might well consider buying a multi-purpose machine (page 52). Hired machines will be delivered to the site and come complete with a driver on whose skill much depends. To be used economically, they must do at least the equivalent work to that done by the men who could be hired for the same money. (In England today this is from 4–6 men for the cost of the smallest machines.) If hired they must be ordered well in advance of requirements for a precise day and time, and should have a closely planned programme, since it is most uneconomical to have them standing idle.

## EQUIPMENT

The director, having made his general appreciation of the site and of the number of workers to be employed, can then estimate his equipment requirements. Any expedition or society in the field for many seasons should buy most of its equipment, for hiring is an added expense and often unsatisfactory. Storing may be difficult, but if a site is to be returned to over some years a store can usually be hired or built locally.

The amount of equipment needed will, of course, vary greatly at different sites, but all or some of the objects in the following lists may be necessary. Unless the excavation is far from any supplies, the minimum should be taken, for ingenuity and local resources can be made to supply many gaps.

A. *Marking Out and Survey Equipment*[42]

(i) Posts (4 cm. square, 70 cm. long); nails (5 cm., 25 cm.); hammer, mallet, black and/or white paint and brush, skewers, string (builders' twine).

(ii) Theodolite (or planetable and alidade, dumpy level and staff). 30 m. chains or tapes. Ranging poles (in metres). Compass. Spirit levels (preferably a small hanging and a large carpenter's). Optical squares and artillery squares are useful but not essential. Squared paper in cms.

B. *Digging Tools*[43]

To be planned on a scale of one for each worker.

Fine digging: pointing trowel (4 in. welded), hand shovel, stiff-bristled hand-brush, kneeling-mat, bucket (lightweight), hand-pick or entrenching tool.

Coarse digging: Picks (weight to vary), or hoes (only where this is the traditional tool), shovels (8 in.). Forks may be useful in some soils.

C. *Equipment for General Use*

This will be estimated on a site basis and quantity will depend on the size of the site, amount of soil and the distance to the spoil-heaps.

(i) Site-clearing Tools. Only a few of these will normally be needed for sites covered with vegetation: sickles, scythes, bill-hooks, axes, secateurs, shears, grub-axes, rakes, for example—those covered by modern collapsed buildings: wedges, sledge-hammers, crowbars, pneumatic drills, rollers, ropes.

(ii) Earth-moving Equipment.
Wheelbarrows: One between two trenches containing four trowellers or hoe-men, or two pick-and-shovellers. Planks or metal tracks may be needed for the barrow-runs.
Baskets: Four boys or women to one hoe-man where barrows are not available. A good supply of baskets will be needed since they wear out quickly.

Conveyor belts: Of most use in deep trenches or where spoil-heaps have to be high, they can also be used on horizontal surfaces. Driven by electricity, petrol or diesel oil, they are expensive both to buy and to hire and on most excavations will only be used to solve special soil-moving problems.

Windlasses and buckets: These may be a useful and cheap alternative to belts in small or deep trenches.

Dumpers: These machines are especially useful in moving spoil from trench sides when barrow or basket walks are long and difficult. They will not be standard equipment on most excavations, but might well be hired at regular intervals if available locally.

Railways: For use where much spoil is to be moved and where it can be moved on the level or down a slope. They can often be hired relatively inexpensively and in special circumstances save much work.

D. *Specialised Equipment*

To be estimated on a site basis. Sieves (50 mm., 1 cm. or 2 cm. mesh) (it may be possible to make these as required), or screens.[44] Spades and turf-cutters. Yardbrooms and besoms.

(i) For backfilling: rammers and compressors may be necessary.

(ii) For deep trenches: revetting material, wooden planks and struts, saws, nails, hammers, or iron shuttering and struts, hacksaws, spanners and angle-pieces.[45]

(iii) For wet trenches: sludge or stirrup pumps and hoses. (The former petrol or electrically driven.) Rubber boots, buckets and ropes, tarpaulins.

(iv) Trench Covers. In wet or stormy season transparent covers over the trenches or screens on the windward side may be desirable. These should be built beforehand of light timber and plastic or iron sheeting.[46]

E. *Recording Equipment*

(i) For each trench the following should be allowed:
nails (10 cm.) estimate at 1 lb. per trench; labels (25 cm.) unstrung luggage, or tape machine[47] (estimate labels at 50 per trench). Notebooks (looseleaf, waterproof) with plain, lined and squared paper,[48] indelible pens (felt-tip, ball-point or steel nib and Indian ink), pencils and rubber. Steel tape (3 m. or 1 m.), wooden rule, spirit level, plumb-bob.

(ii) For the excavation as a whole the following will be necessary. Amounts will depend on the number of trenches being dug.
For section drawing: half and quarter imperial drawing-boards (or hardboard squares), squared papers (cm.), 10 m. and 2 m. tapes, skewers, string, plumb-bob and spirit level. For photo-

graphy: colour and monochrome film, tripod (with fitted spirit level), 1 m. and 5 cm. scales. Identification tags. Darkroom equipment (if an isolated expedition).

*F. Processing Equipment*

(i) For washing: washing bowls (one to every worker being used here), nail-brushes (one each), buckets or tanks if water has to be brought to the working area. Drying screens (if much material). These should be made up of light timber and wire netting (50 mm. mesh).

(ii) For bagging: Paper or cloth bags for pottery (in 1, 4 or 7 lb sizes). Plastic bags for stones or bones. These should be bought wholesale (by the thousand). Estimate at least 20 bags per trench; if there is much and varied material, 100 bags per trench may well be necessary.

Felt-tipped pens for writing on bags with different colours for different materials (if tape machine is not being used).

(iii) For marking: Mapping pens and Indian ink. The nibs wear out quickly, so order by dozens.

(iv) For recording: Loose-leaf notebooks or card indexes and punches.

(v) For conservation: Cotton-wool, bandages, plastic sheeting, preservatives.[49]

(vi) For packing: Collapsible cardboard cartons (size depending on weight of material and how they will be transported). Wooden crates (e.g. tea-chests) as necessary. Wood-shavings, waste paper etc. Nails, hammers, binding wire.

*G. Medical Equipment*

This will depend upon the isolation of the site and the local hazards, but should include a first aid box and a first aid manual.

*H. Huts, Tents, Caravans and Rooms*

One or more central shelters will be needed to sort and process the finds and to store the equipment. If *buildings* can be built, borrowed or rented they are to be preferred, since the shelter is complete and light and water may well be available. Sectional *wooden huts* which can also be made secure are the next most desirable, but require large vans or lorries to transport them. It is therefore difficult to set them up far from a motorable road. *Caravans* have all the advantages of huts but are expensive; their furnishings will usually have to be altered. *Tents* have the advantage of being easy to transport and erect, but cannot be locked and can blow down.

For all kinds of working areas long tables (wooden trestles, or metal and hardboard), and chairs will be necessary.

# THE SPECIAL PROBLEMS OF TROPICAL LANDS

Here a director will have to be prepared for additional difficulties.

*Climate.* This will often affect the length and times of the digging-season much more than in temperate lands. Work has usually to be restricted to the drier and cooler seasons, but is then often frustrated by hardness and dryness which makes soil change difficult to distinguish. Experiments in wet-season work[50] have shown that it is often best to excavate in dry spells within the rainy season or immediately after it. More experiments with excavations under cover might be made.

Climate may also affect health, and arrangements for medical care will be more important than in temperate zones. A higher sick-rate among staff is to be expected and planning should make allowance for it.

*Location of Sites.* This will be particularly difficult in tropical forests, and discovery will usually await clearance by man, bush fires or floods. Aerial photography will be of little use unless differential growth reveals settlements or old clearings.[51] Large-scale surveys will be needed in advance of any other fieldwork.[52]

In the grasslands aerial photography may be more useful and both shadows and crop marks may be helpful if a flying programme is carefully planned. After fires and at the beginning of the rainy season might be especially suitable times.

Deserts, whether hot or cold, are particularly valuable since organic remains may survive in a desiccated or frozen form. Aerial photography, especially when the shadows are long, is most rewarding[53] and much close survey can be done from slowly moving cars or animals.

*Excavation.* Here the main problem will be labour, for although unskilled workers will often be available, there may be a complete absence of skilled trowellers and recorders. The great temptation is to employ more unskilled labour than the director and his assistants can efficiently control, and to excavate too much. A related problem will be the control of men since this will require knowledge of the local language, working customs, payment methods etc.

Preservation in the field may also require greater forethought and the provision of a variety of materials, since no archaeological laboratory may be within reach.

*Processing the Material.* If sites are far from the director's home or working base; if transport is difficult; or if the removal of finds is forbidden, special arrangements to register, photograph and/or draw the objects during or immediately after the excavation will have to be made.[54] Planning should include a draftsman in the excavation team and special arrangements for the local examination of non-cultural samples. If the material is to be removed or even stored for some time, termite-proof bags and especially strong crates may be necessary.

## SUGGESTED READING

PRELIMINARY SURVEYS

*Field Archaeology*★★, Atkinson, R. 1953. Part I sec. i and p. 42.

*A Guide to Field Methods in Archaeology*★, Heizer, R. and Graham, J. 1967. Chaps 3 a, e and g, Chap 5 a and b.

*Field Archaeology*, Ordnance Survey 1963. 8.

*The Uses of Air Photography*, St. Joseph, K. (ed) 1967.

A Technique of Surface Collection, Alcock, L. *Antiq* XXV 1951. 75.

*Alla Scoperata della Civilta sepolte*, Lerici, C. 1960.

A new type of locating device, Colania. *Antiq* XLII 1968. 109.

Studies on the Chemical Analysis of Archaeological Sites, Cook, S. and Heizer, R. *UCPA*. 2 1961.

PLANNING AND ORGANISING

*Field Archaeology*★, Atkinson, R. 1953.

*Practical Archaeology*, Webster, G. 1966.

GOOD EXAMPLES OF PLANNING

*Stanwick*, Wheeler, R. 1954 (earthworks). *Colchester*, Hull, M. 1958 (town). *Degannwy*, Alcock, L. *ArchJ* CXXIV 1967. 190 (stone work).

## NOTES

1. See Heizer, R. and Graham, J. 1967. 14 and Mandelbaum, D. in Taylor, W. 1963, for good introductions to field surveys of all kinds. Fay, G. 1965 gives equipment lists.
2. This must be done without asking leading questions. Conversation is much more likely to produce results than correspondence. See Webster, G. 1966. 20.
3. Particularly pottery, slag and building material.
4. In all countries private collectors can be secretive but their confidence may sometimes be won if it is made clear that there is no question of interfering with their collections.
5. For folklore connected with burial mounds in England see Grinsell, L. 1953. 70.
6. This may be particularly important for workers in regions where missionaries and administrators from Europe have long been interested in antiquities. See Webster, G. 1966. 8.
7. The field reports of the Antiquities Service in the Republic of Sudan, for example, or of the earlier Ordnance Surveys in Great Britain.
8. In Britain the card-indexes of the Ordnance Survey (Archaeological Division) or of the National Monuments Record (now held by the Royal Commission on Historical Monuments) or the records of the British Museum are good examples of information brought together over a long period.
9. Emmison, F. 1966. In Britain, for example, in journals like *The Gentleman's Magazine*, or in the early volumes of local antiquarian societies, objects brought to meetings were reported in some detail. Newspapers are available centrally at the British Museum (Colindale).
10. The reports, for example of Muhammed ibn Abdullah ibn Battuta from North Africa and Asia in the fourteenth century. Gibb, H. 1929 (ed).
11. Such as the Victoria County Histories in Britain.
12. Emmison, F. 1966. In England these have sometimes survived in the papers of local workers, and have been deposited in national collections (e.g. the Society of Antiquaries of London).
13. West, J. 1962. Landowners should be written to personally.
14. Beresford, M. 1963.
15. For example see *HSNJ* II. 4 1964. 465f. for a discussion on digging in a tropical rainy season.

16. Australia has excellent examples of this, e.g. *PPS* XXX 1964. 400f.

17. In this, local directors have a great advantage over those who can come to a site for short campaigns only. The latter should recruit local help.

18. In the surveys preceding flooding of the deserts near Wadi Halfa (Sudan) 1966. In the large new field systems of Britain this may also be of use in the future.

19. St. Joseph, K. (ed) 1967. Griffin, J. (ed) 1957.

20. Trorey, L. 1950 and Atkinson, R. 1953. 26–9. In Britain some commercial firms (e.g. Aerofilms and Aero Pictorials Ltd.) and government departments (e.g. Ministry of Overseas Development, Director of Overseas Surveys) as well as university departments (e.g. Director of Aerial Photography, Cambridge) have these.

21. Atkinson, R. 1953. 29–30.

22. Atkinson, R. 1953. 30.

23. Lerici, C. 1959, also *Ex* 5.3 1962. 5.

24. Aitken, M. 1961. As an example Rainsborough: *PPS* XXXIII 1967. 296.

25. Atkinson, R. 1953. 31–9, with full description. For other forms and comment see *Ex* 7.2 1967. 4f: *AmAnth* 28 1962. 199f, and *PPS* XXVI 1960. 64.

26. Atkinson, R. 1953. 31.

27. For example Infra-red Imaging. *EMI Electronics Ltd.* Leaflet I.I.E. 1/1.

28. The Sudan Antiquities Statute is a good example of the more comprehensive type. See also the U.S.A. National Historical Preservation Act 1966.

29. Britain: *CBA* 1964. For U.S.A.: Heizer, R. and Graham, J. 1967. 206; France: *BSPF* 1929. 24.

30. *AntJ* X 1930. 228f. and *Antiq* XLII 1968. 307 with bibliography.

31. In England usually to the landowner, but a recent decision awarded an object to the finder.

32. Jessup, R. 1930.

33. The expense of drawing up the petition for a faculty and of the faculty itself is borne by the petitioners.

34. Local regulations may distinguish between building and civil engineering and agricultural labouring. A director must know to which group he is considered to belong. For English practice see Atkinson, R. 1953. 82–3.

35. In Britain with the local officials of the Ministry of Social Security. Exemptions for archaeological projects can sometimes be obtained.

36. For an architect's view see Weaver, M., The Misuse of Architects by Archaeologists. *LRS* (duplicated), London 1967.

37. Published monthly from March to August from 4 St. Andrew's Place, London, N.W.1.

38. Their field research sections often include a large number of active local workers.

39. The University Extra-mural Departments have been particularly active in this field in England in the last ten years, and a considerable number of experienced assistants have been trained.

40. Here again the training excavations and evening courses organised by universities and local societies have resulted in a large number of volunteers now being available.

41. Woolley, C. 1942, gives some hair-raising examples of this.

42. Atkinson, R. 1953. 127–38. Fay, G. 1965.

43. See Atkinson, R. 1953. 44–5 for a discussion of tool types.

44. Heizer, R. and Graham, J. 1967. 42 discuss screens and give further references.

45. The Manual of Civil Engineering (ICE), London 1966.

46. In areas of sudden heavy showers these will be essential.

47. The portable, dial and trigger kind, have been found to be successful.

48. Quarto looseleaf covers for each trench have been found very useful.

49. Heizer, R. and Graham, J. 1967. 192–30 give a list of useful materials.
50. For example *HSNJ* II, 4 1964. 470.
51. St. Joseph, K. (ed) 1967.
52. Davies, O. 1967 shows what is possible in Africa.
53. The survey of the Middle Nile in Khartoum Museum is a good example of this.
54. This problem has been with tropical expeditions for many years. Punch card systems may help; see Soudsky, B. 1967 and Clarke, D. 1968 for European, and MacPherron, A. 1967 and Binford, S. 1968 for American, references.

# CHAPTER III
# Organisation during the Excavation

'Rule 4. Brawling, fighting and the carrying of weapons by workmen are strictly prohibited in the excavation.'
'Rule 5. Loafing villagers are not permitted to come as spectators into the excavation.'

W. Bade
*A Manual of Excavation in the Near East*, 1934

During excavation, as well as his general archaeological problems of controlling and understanding the excavation of the trenches (Chapters V–XI), the director will have a variety of organisational problems, of which the handling of workers and machines and the recording, processing and packing of their finds will be the more difficult and important. These groups of problems may be considered separately (Fig. 1).

## THE CONTROL AND USE OF LABOUR AND MACHINES

The intelligent use of labour, using each worker's skill, temperament and strength appropriately, can only be done if the director comes to know each personally. This will be partly through the initial interview, but more through his regular peregrination of the trenches when he will see the evidence of their work.

The allotting of work will usually be the first task of each day, and the director or the site supervisor should have decided in advance what is to be done. On the previous evening the work in each trench should have been reviewed, and its importance in relation to the general progress of the work and the kind of labour best suited to its problems considered. This review will show if changes are needed. If, for example, an occupation layer with many finds and features which needed careful trowelling has given place to an archaeologically sterile layer, a change in the speed of work, and possibly of the people carrying it out, may be necessary. Workers should be individually instructed daily and, if possible, kept at work in the same trenches. The director will also decide whether trowels, handpicks or large picks and shovels will be used, the depth of spit to be worked and whether sieving or screening will be necessary.

A daily routine should be established from the beginning of the excavation. Times for food and drink breaks as well as starting and finishing work should have been decided in advance and be kept to fairly closely. Movement about the site except when necessary should be discouraged, and sitting on baulks forbidden.

During the day the director or, if there are many sites, the site supervisors, should visit all trenches several times as a routine and

D

should be available at any time to advise a worker who is in doubt. Only by such close touch can the siting of temporary baulks, the change in depths or speed of digging spits, the decisions to sieve or photograph be taken. In these visits the director should, however, avoid interrupting the flow of work by too many changes of instruction. Trench supervisors/ recorders should see that spits or features are dug as directed.

The relationships between a director and his labour will vary greatly depending on his temperament, but he must be able to handle archae-ologically unskilled labourers who are used to being assessed on the amount of soil moved as well as volunteers interested mainly in archaeological discovery. In this problem he is perhaps closer to sixteenth-century sea captains than he suspects.[1] Masters of handling professional earth-moving labourers[2] can describe but not explain their methods, and only experience will tell what to do. The labourers will expect to be fully employed, to work with tools to which they are accustomed, to work regular and locally acceptable hours and to be paid regularly. Their work should be planned ahead and, unless some instruction is given in archaeological interpretation, must be closely watched. Much will depend on the quality of chargehands and foremen, and special care should be taken over their promotion and training.

All excavations will need some work (e.g. the removal of archae-ologically sterile layers) with picks, hoes and shovels rather than with trowels, and whilst those who wield them should ideally be archae-ologically experienced, if unskilled labourers are employed then it is better to use them here than on the more significant strata. Workers of this kind can also be used for thick layers in which stray finds and features may be found (e.g. tips in large banks). The way in which they are accustomed to work makes them quite unsuitable for complicated tasks, although if the same workers are employed for many weeks or seasons they can become expert at the recognition of soil changes, finds and features.

Since labourers are paid by the hour in many countries, and are thereby expensive to employ, a director must see that they are con-tinuously employed, for much of the excavation funds will be invested in them. In some cases machines are now an alternative to this kind of labour (page 52). In Britain at least, this is fortunate, for it is becom-ing more and more difficult to recruit experienced labourers.

Since much excavation will be done slowly with small tools, the relatively small amounts of earth to be removed are within the physical capabilities of healthy people of all ages and both sexes. Previous field experience and a general knowledge of archaeological evidence are therefore of greater importance than brute strength. In England in particular, but in growing numbers elsewhere, many adults spend their holidays working voluntarily on excavations and their winter evenings studying archaeology. It is through them more than anything else that the great improvements in excavating standards can be attained. It is now usual to make some contribution towards their expenses, and this is money well spent.

Where no skilled adult volunteer assistance exists, the fine work may have to be done by unskilled students or by adult (preferably female) labourers.[3] These kinds of worker will need training which will have to be given on the excavation.[4] Supervision will also have to be closer, and probably more archaeological assistants will have to be employed. Volunteers, selected for their archaeological experience, knowledge or enthusiasm, will desire a more detailed understanding of their work than labourers and discussion in the trenches should be supplemented by regular (perhaps weekly) tours of the excavation. The volunteers will best be controlled by a director in his role as 'archaeologist-in-charge' rather than as the 'employer' he appears to the paid labourers.

Registers should be kept for all present at the excavation and should be entered up daily, so that weekly worksheets can be made out. Men should be paid at some agreed time and day each week and worksheets given out with the money.

## SPECIAL EXCAVATION PROBLEMS
## CAUSED BY GEOLOGY

Quite apart from the nature of the archaeological problems, the geology of the site will affect the way in which problems have to be tackled.

Working in *clays* for example, can be almost impossible in very wet or dry conditions. If very wet, tool-blades can only be kept unclogged by regularly dipping in water, and objects can only be found by fingering or by hosing against screens. Layer boundaries can often be seen only in section. Sumps and baling or pumps will be necessary. The only advantage of digging when wet is that any colour changes become clearer. In dry weather clay is very hard, cracks easily and is colourless. Wetting it rarely helps, for the surface will merely crack and peel, but soaking the trench floors overnight can help. Sections will have to be drawn piecemeal while they are still damp. Important areas and strata should only be worked when conditions are between the extremes of humidity and trowelling is possible.

Working in *sands* presents quite different problems—those of burrowing and collapse. Work with trowel and spade can go on in all conditions, even during rain, and soil colours show up excellently when wet. In dry weather regular sprinkling of trench floors, but not sides, is helpful. Brushing usually obscures distinctions. Animal runs of all kinds are likely and must be traced, so that their contents, which may include material brought down to line nests, can be discounted. Baulks should be wider than in other soils and rocks and traffic should be kept away from the edges. Since sections will soon dry and collapse easily they should be drawn as quickly as possible, perhaps in stages. If trenches are more than 1·5 m. deep they should be revetted, and in wide trenches support-buttresses should be left against the baulks.

Working in *gravels* will much resemble working in sand, but with the problems exaggerated. Features and strata will become more difficult as the gravel becomes more pebbly, and sections will be harder to interpret and will collapse more easily. The original sides of pits, ditches etc. will probably have collapsed soon after they were exposed, and true feature-profiles will be hard to obtain.

Working in *hard rocks* (chalk, sandstone etc.) will be relatively easy, since drainage will often be good and features dug into the bedrock will preserve their original profiles. Difficulties will be great if the rock surface has been badly weathered or eroded.

## THE HANDLING OF MACHINES

As already mentioned, machines are expensive, and if they are engaged their programmes should have been worked out in advance and should then be closely followed. The areas which they are to work should be marked by posts and their operators given precise depths to dig to and places to dump soil. An experienced archaeologist should be watching each whilst it is working to check soil changes and to look for features and finds. They must never stand idle and should be sent back at once when their programme is complete. The work-sheets of drivers should be marked up and signed before they leave the excavation. Travelling time to and from the excavation will be charged and should be assessed before booking the machine.

The kind of work they can be given will vary, but they cannot, except in an exploratory way, be used on any layers with archaeological material. Two kinds of machines can be distinguished although many machines combine several functions.

*Blade Machines.* These, with a wide horizontal blade, may be wheeled or tracked and will merely push off or back strips of soil. They are particularly economical for clearing plough soil or other disturbed layers from a wide area in preparation for an extensive area excavation. They will cut near-vertical sides along the long axes, and these can often be aligned to the site survey-grid. They leave slopes and spoil dumps on the short axes. A good operator will leave a clean level floor to his cutting, and a bad one ridges and hollows. They should be stopped at least 6 cm. above the level required and should be kept from needlessly running over the cutting since this hardens and compresses it. They are equally efficient at backfilling, are much cheaper than handwork, and can consolidate the filling as they work. If they are available locally all spoil dumps should be sited with an eye to their use (e.g. where the machine can manoeuvre behind them and push straight to the trenches). The tracked machines work faster but are more expensive, require a transporter to bring them to the site, and crush and harden the soil. The wheeled machines are cheaper, more versatile, can be driven along roads and over fairly rough country and, if relatively small areas are to be cleared, are the more efficient.

*Bucket Machines.* These can scoop either backwards or forwards with a 60 cm.–2 m. or more wide bucket, can be dragline or hydraulically operated and are wheeled or tracked. They are most uneconomical in clearing an area, but in the hands of a skilled operator will cut trenches very accurately. They are therefore particularly useful for trial trenching and removing sterile layers within trenches. Dragline machines tend to dig less cleanly than hydraulically operated ones, but often have longer jibs and so can dig deeper and dump spoil farther than the others. Hydraulic ones work more precisely, have a depth limit of *c.* 4 m. and are often more manoeuvrable.

## DOMESTIC PROBLEMS

It may be necessary to arrange for the shelter, feeding and transport of those taking part in the excavation. If so the director will be well advised to employ an efficient camp commandant assisted by caterers and drivers, for the day-to-day problems will absorb much time. He will also be well advised to keep the number of workers recruited to the minimum and to work out the arrangements in detail in advance. Where possible hired equipment should be avoided, but any hired or borrowed objects should be insured.

### SHELTER

If householders live nearby and are willing to offer board and lodgings, these are perhaps the most satisfactory arrangement, since feeding and washing problems are solved at the same time. In villages and towns this may mean the director searching out suitable lodgings many months in advance of excavation by advertisement or house-to-house visiting. In Great Britain local authorities or societies,[5] may help in this. A list of addresses, once compiled, can be sent to accepted workers who will then make their own arrangements.

If lodgings are scarce it may be possible to borrow or hire a school, college or village hall[6] and then to provide beds, bedding, and food. These buildings will probably have the advantage of lighting, heating and sanitation, but will mean employing full-time staff to look after them. If nothing of this kind is available a tented camp may be the only answer.[7] In good weather this will be the most pleasant but will bring in extra problems of lighting, water and sanitation. A compromise can offer central tents or huts for washing and eating and leave it to individuals to bring their own tents and bedding. This has the disadvantage—to all except the young—of requiring them to carry their own tentage and bedding. In wet or stormy weather living in tents can also reduce the efficiency of the excavation.

FOOD AND DRINK

In a hostel or camp far from shops this will have to be provided, for it is too much to expect helpers to shop and cook for themselves in the little time left over from excavation.

Costs will have to be worked out and money put aside, for one or more full-time caterers will have to be employed. In Britain, Colleges of Domestic Science have often been most helpful in recruiting them.[8] Arrangements will have to be made for bulk buying and cooking, and utensils, cutlery and crockery hired. Dining huts or tents, with furniture, will also have to be provided.

If the excavation camp is near a town or village it may be possible to recruit workers who will look after themselves if transport and time for shopping are provided. A dining hut/tent will still be needed. This last arrangement simplifies the director's problems and is much to be preferred. It is not usual to provide food for paid daily-workers.

Drinking-water should be available all through the working day, especially in hot climates, and morning and afternoon tea or coffee is welcome under all conditions. Bottled-gas heaters or stoves and kettles, a vehicle or animal for carrying water and large churns or containers will be needed. If there is no water nearby, relatively large amounts will have to be transported for water will also be needed for washing finds, and, if there is a camp, for workers, and for cooking.

Lavatories will have to be provided on all excavations. They can often be hired, but screens and chemical closets should be bought if the expedition is in the field for several seasons. Disinfectants must be supplied in all cases. Washing facilities (tents or huts with basins and stands) will also have to be provided if workers are camping.

TRANSPORT

On all excavations two or more cars, preferably with their own drivers, are essential. It is most useful to have a lorry or van which can take quantities of equipment or many workers. If the terrain is difficult four-wheel-drive trucks may be necessary, but in many countries more economical ones will suffice, especially if a trailer can be used with them.

Unless helpers are camping nearby, only regular collection and delivery of them will enable regular working hours to be kept. If labourers are hired through a contractor he should be made responsible for bringing them to the site. A 'bus service' may be necessary for workers scattered in lodgings.

Before, during and after the excavation there will be much movement of equipment for which a lorry or van is essential. There are also many small chores and visits during the excavation for which a car is needed, and workers should be encouraged to bring their own. Petrol should be paid for if they use their cars on excavation business.

## THE RECORDING OF INFORMATION DURING EXCAVATION

Systems of recording vary greatly,[9] and if all is set down daily in such a way that not only the director but, if he should die, others can understand and use it, then the system matters little. The following system has proved successful on a number of excavations and is offered as an illustration of general principles.

From *each trench* being worked, a daily detailed account of the layers dug will be necessary, and a separate notebook for each trench on a complicated site, or for each two or three closely contiguous trenches on others, is desirable. If an expedition or society is to remain in the field for several seasons, water-proof loose-leaved file-covers with lined, plain and squared paper should be provided, for the covers can

---

Site A                          Trench D                          Page 6

Layer: 5                                          Comment
12.VI.69 Surface level and featureless when exposed.
   2 cm removed. Stony in NW corner, damp in SE.
   Brown sandy loam. No finds; few stones.
   Dug by C. C. F. and K.L.

13.VI.69 Second 2 cm removed. Continued stony in
   NW. More stones in general. Sherds and bones in      Stones not found in SE Pit?
   centre (see plan 4).
   Dug by C.C.F. and F.C.

14.VI.69 Third 2 cm. removed. Continued stony in
   NW (sample kept). Few stones, many sherds, bones
   (one articulated leg bagged separately).
   Charcoal concentration in SE (see plan 4).           Deeper level of Pit?

15.VI.69 Layer ended after 1 cm. Laid stones in NW      Part of hut floor? Check
   corner (on plan 4). Many sherds lying horizontally.  trenches C and E.
   Charcoal, round stones.
   Coin (SF 18).                                        Pottery all mediaeval.
   Dug by C.C.F. and F.C.

Sketch of west section (15.VI.69) on next page

Fig. 6 Specimen sheet from a trench notebook.

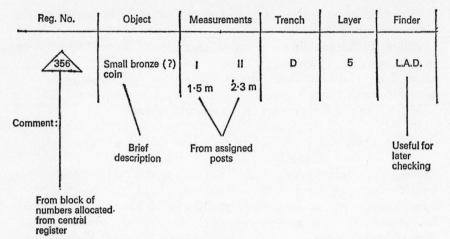

| Reg. No. | Object | Measurements | | Trench | Layer | Finder |
|---|---|---|---|---|---|---|
| 356 | Small bronze (?) coin | I    1·5 m | II    2·3 m | D | 5 | L.A.D. |

Comment:

Brief description

From assigned posts

Useful for later checking

From block of numbers allocated· from central register

Fig. 7 Specimen entry in a finds register.

be reused many times. In shorter excavations thin school exercise books will suffice. The book should remain in the trench whenever digging is going on and will be entered up day by day or hour by hour as necessary by the trench recorder (see below). It should contain on separate sheets:

(i) A brief general description of the surface of the trench before excavation began.

(ii) A list of layers each described in one or two words at the moment at which it is distinguished.

(iii) A detailed description of each layer (Fig. 6) reporting on its colour, texture, features and finds. This should include comments from the workers actually digging the level (e.g. special areas of dampness, stoniness or stickiness) and from the recorder or director (possible interpretations and similarities with other trenches).

(iv) Measured small-scale plans (say 1:50) of the trench or the surface of each layer showing features, and larger ones (say 1:25) showing features (e.g. postholes and their fillings) in greater detail. These can be done by the trench-recorder.

(v) Sketch sections of all the sides of the trench drawn freehand as soon as a succession of strata are visible. These can be added to or redrawn as more strata are found. They should have the strata numbers on the list (ii) above marked on them. If these are drawn when the sections are fresh they are most useful in the measured section drawings made later on.

(vi) Special Finds Register. This, on a separate page, will list all important objects found with their layer number, three-dimensional measurements and central register number (Fig. 7).

A system like this is to be preferred to any central system of recording in the form of a site book or day book, for, when not kept by someone working in the trench, details may be missed. The director or an assistant should regularly check the books.

The work will progress fastest and be most accurately recorded, if an experienced worker is put in charge of each trench. The duties of a *Trench Supervisor/Recorder* are to keep the trench notebooks, label all trays and sections and to watch over the less experienced workers in the trench so that they do what, and do no more than, they have been told to do by the director or his assistant. The keeping of the notebook has already been described, but the register of special finds deserves more notice. These finds are usually recorded in both the vertical and horizontal planes from a fixed datum,[10] although slopes or interruptions in levels often mean that the measurements tell very little afterwards. When finds are many, a director must decide which objects are 'special' and deserve this treatment; when scarce, all may warrant it. If many are found on a surface it is sufficient to number and enter them on a large-scale plan and then to bag them serially. In all cases the position of the object inside the layer should be recorded.

All the finds which it is decided to record in this way should be listed in the site book with a serial number, and bagged separately with all details concerning it written indelibly on the bag.

*Labelling* will involve the trays and, when any new layer is recognised, the sections. The recorder will give the layer a new number in the trench notebook and lay out new trays for the finds from it. These will contain two labels on which the site, trench and layer letters and numbers are indelibly written or stamped.[11] He should also see that fragile objects and objects associated in the ground are sent separately to the processing hut. If this is done conscientiously any mixing of finds from different levels can be avoided.

Labels with the same indelibly written code should also be pinned by nails to the junction of the new layer and the one above it, on all the sides of the trench on which it appears. This can be a great aid in keeping a continuity of recording and interpretation in the trench, especially when sections come to be drawn.

*For the Site as a whole* more general recording will have to be done by the director or his surveying, archaeological and photographic assistants.

The *duties of the Surveyor* will be to make general plans by one of the usual techniques.[12] These will include: a small-scale one (1:500), contoured and showing all the trenches in relation to non-archaeological features; a series of larger-scale plans (1:100) of groups of trenches. There should be one of the latter for each main period of the site, and on it the features of the period should be entered (Fig. 20, 22, 34).

Particular surface profiles, and other levelling will be done as required.[13]

The *duties of the Photographer* will be to take a series of record photographs and, as directed, a smaller series of more carefully considered ones for probable publication. Record photographs should be in colour, should be quickly taken and should not interfere with the flow of the work. The composition and choice of angle will normally be left to the photographer. The photographs will be of features or finds in various stages of excavation, and there will often be little opportunity to spend time in preparing the area for the photograph or to wait for the best lighting conditions. These photographs should be freely taken throughout, for they will be a great help in preparing the report. A record of the trench layer and orientation should be kept by the photographer[14] (Plates IV, V and XV).

Subjects which it will be desirable to publish as photographs will be recognised by the director during the excavation. He should, over a period of days or weeks, with the photographer, note the angles, lightings and weather conditions in which they could best be recorded. These considerations may influence the way in which the feature is excavated (e.g. which part of a ditch is sectioned). Visits to the site to take photographs before excavation begins, especially if surface features exist, will be necessary and during excavation other general views, either from the air or from a tower,[15] may be necessary if extensive features are found (Plates III, XIV). These should all be taken in monochrome as well as colour.[16] Since expense will limit the number of photographs published, only subjects which will add something to the understanding of the site, which the drawings lack, should be considered for publication. When these have been decided upon by the director, extra care and time should be taken in their photography. They should be taken with a tripod and reflex camera, so that the angle can be seen and the picture composed by the director. The lighting should be studied over a period of days and the cleaning up and defining carried out in the way so well described by Cookson.[17] This preparation can consume much time and labour—an additional reason for restricting it to important subjects. 'Faking' or changing by differential scraping, wetting or taping should always be avoided. The technological details, e.g. choices of lens, filters, scales, etc., will come only with experience although the study of manuals may help.[18] If possible the negatives should be developed and checked before work begins again and the trench is disturbed (Plates II, VII, IX, XIII, XVI and XVII).

The *Recording of Sections* will also have to be done by the director and his assistants, for this is the most subjective and difficult part of recording yet one of the most important kinds of evidence. No truly objective way of recording a section has yet been devised; drawing relies entirely on the integrity of those drawing, for it cannot be checked once the excavation is over. Photography can be used only if soil variations are sufficiently obvious to show, and then can only be used for measurement if the camera is set at right angles to, and as near as possible to, the section[19] (Plates IV and XI). Spraying with plastics and, when hard, rolling up with a surface coating of the section adhering can be useful but gives only a false appearance of objectivity.[20] On balance there is so far no substitute for a carefully measured drawing (Fig. 16b, 36, 56, 60). Ideally all the sides of all trenches, and a number of intermediate sections within the trenches, should be recorded in this way, for this makes the preparation of the report easier. In practice there is often neither the time nor experienced helpers able to do this, and selection thus becomes necessary. This selection must include:

(i) those giving complete cross-sections of the site along its main axes;

(ii) Those through the main features, not necessarily at a trench side but where the nature of the feature shows best (e.g. across the centre of a pit);

(iii) those which show the succession of strata or intersection of features particularly well. These too may not necessarily be at trench sides.[21]

The optimum moment for drawing a section should be looked for as carefully as for a photograph. Under some conditions (in heavy clay or sand) it may be necessary to draw in a series of successive zones, for drying out or collapse may make it impossible to wait until bedrock is reached and the whole trench side exposed. If possible, drawing should wait until all is exposed and all photographs taken. It can then be seen if drying out has helped or hindered the recognition of layers. If the former, then only the time of day chosen for drawing will need care (e.g. bright sunshine, if oblique to the trench makes it impossible to see the strata). If the strata only showed when damp, they may have to be re-wetted (although this is often a failure) or the whole face cut back 30 cm. or more and drawn at once.

The most important sections should be drawn by the director himself, and all others by experienced assistants and then checked by him. Two people should work on each (one drawing, one measuring) and one should be the trench recorder or someone who has worked in the trench, preferably from its opening. The actual techniques of drawing are well described elsewhere,[22] and here only a few additional points may be stressed.

(i) There should be no hurry over drawing, and individual stones, bricks, etc. should be measured in.

(ii) Both the drawer and the measurer, one near and one at a distance, should study the section with the sketch sections of the trench notebook. At intersections or the junctions of layers the measurer should trowel vigorously and, if necessary, cut back the section if there is any doubt of the line. Any questions unanswered when the section is finished will always remain unsolved.

(iii) The drawers must be perpetually alert to distinguish the significant from the casual (e.g. a junction of two siltings from a random scatter of impressive stones).

(iv) All layer numbers should be entered on the section and a scale of not less than 1:20 used.

Section drawings should always take place after the photographs have been taken, so that as much trowelling as the drawers feel necessary, can be done.

## THE ENVIRONMENTAL ASSISTANTS

As has already been mentioned, the inclusion of environmental assistants in excavation teams is becoming increasingly necessary, although much of the interpretation must be done when the excavation is over. The taking of suitable samples for study and the day-by-day investigation of soils and features (pits, ditches, postholes, etc.) can provide full employment on a large excavation for one or more special assistants. Their suggestions whilst the dig is in progress may make the final picture of the community many times more complete (Chapter V). Since environmental archaeologists are still rare, it may not be possible to find one, but this can no longer be regarded as an excuse for failing to acquire sufficient knowledge to choose and take significant samples (page 87). If this is done it is likely to be a full-time job for one assistant. Specialists will still have to be consulted and asked to visit for specific problems.

*The Field Duties* of such an Assistant will be to examine the layers in all trenches and to help decide their character. This might involve sampling for *geological determination* (to see if a layer was likely to have been deposited naturally by wind, water, ice, etc.); for *pedological* (to see if a soil existed, its nature, and whether it was likely to have developed *in situ*); for *botanical* (to test for the possible survival of plant remains) and for *entomological and conchological* (to test for the survival of insects and molluscs). If the presence of any of these remains were established in the field, then he would be responsible for taking further samples and arranging for their examination.

He would also be responsible for the processing of the non-cultural material brought in in the trays from the trenches.

## PROCESSING THE FINDS

*The Huts, Tents or Rooms.* These should be sited quite close to the trenches, the approach road and to water; the relative importance of these factors depending on the site. The number and kind of rooms will also vary, but if much processing is being carried out on the site and if there is much material, then a good deal of space will be needed. A suggested tent layout is given in Fig. 5. If a building is available (e.g. an empty house) a series of rooms, one for each stage and process, is the ideal to be aimed at.

## THE FINDS AFTER EXCAVATION

When the trays of finds leave the trenches, either because the stratum to which they belong has been completely excavated, or because they are full, they should be taken to some covered area or room for further treatment. It is very bad practice to allow them to leave the site unwashed and unsorted, for they are in their most vulnerable state, and if the tray labels are displaced they will have to be counted as unstratified and relatively valueless. The director will have arranged and equipped a hut, tent or room for their treatment, and if large quantities of material were expected, a special Indoor Assistant to take care of it. The *Duties of the Indoor Archaeological Assistant* will include the supervising of the essential processing; the washing, marking, bagging and conserving, and of such other preliminary work in sorting and registering as it is possible to do.

As the trays come in from the trenches they should be laid out near the washing area. *Washing* should go on daily and can be done, under supervision, by unskilled helpers of any age. It is an especially useful job for children and for those who would like to help but cannot dig or can spare only a few hours.[23] The area should be provided with bowls (one for each tray being washed), nail or toothbrushes and drying racks. The latter should be a series of small wire-netting frames, but corrugated iron sheets, boards or even newspapers (one for each tray-group) can be used. Any fragile objects (e.g. soft-surfaced pottery or charcoal) should be taken out and bagged separately before washing begins. Great care must be taken to see that the labels, suitably weighed down, stay with their tray contents, and no tray should ever be left, even for a meal-break, half washed. If water is plentiful, washing and rinsing bowls should be provided. All objects except the fragile ones brought in from the trenches should be washed.

As the tray contents are drying the preliminary sorting can take place, for potsherds, stone artifacts, bones, shells and building material can be grouped together on the drying-rack. At this point it is useful for the director to see the drying-rack or tray contents as part of his daily routine. This will ensure that he knows the kind of material coming from each trench and layer and therefore its approximate date and significance. If natural objects put into the trays by workers have no significance they can now be discarded. All objects washed and dried in a day should be bagged before nightfall.

*Bagging* should follow at once upon drying. The different classes of material sorted out during drying should be bagged separately, the site, trench and layer code being written upon each bag and the labels going inside it. Bags of cloth, paper or plastic (the latter not for pottery) can be used as the climate dictates, and should be available in a number of sizes (see equipment lists). The bags should then be boxed by the material they contain.

If time and labour permit, marking should go on continuously throughout the excavation so that all material leaves the site with little chance of it being misplaced. Here as in the washing, unskilled juvenile and temporary helpers can be of great use. If the amount is not too great, all human artifacts and all food-bone fragments should be marked with the site, trench and layer code. This should be done in indelible ink with thin-nibbed pens. If very large quantities of industrial debris from, for example, flint-knapping or pot-making are found there may be time to mark only tools and weapons or rims, bases and decorated sherds respectively. The director might also require all the objects from particularly important levels and groups to be marked. The marking should be done so that it does not disfigure the most interesting surface.

On many sites conditions will allow no further processing to be done, and the compiling of *bag lists* should precede the crating. A simple register of bags showing their trench and layer numbers, and the box or crate they were placed in, can be of great help when the material is being worked on later.

The final stage will be *crating* the bags ready for their removal from the site. This should be by material, bags from the same trench being crated together. The composition of the crates will depend upon the journey ahead of them. If by sea, train or air, strong wooden boxes will be necessary and they should be bound with steel tape as well as screwed down. Contents lists will be necessary if they are to go through Customs. If removed by private car direct to a house or museum, stiff cardboard boxes are adequate and quantities of collapsible ones can be bought wholesale. All boxes should have details of the site and their contents stencilled or painted on them.

*Special Finds* will arrive from the trenches individually bagged and listed. They should be kept apart from the other finds, be further separated into groups of different materials and, if time permits no more, be boxed up together. If possible, before this, they should be listed, with details of their find spots, in a single central register or card index.

Such immediate *Conservation* as is necessary should also be done in the tent or hut, either by the conservator or the Indoor-assistant. As already mentioned, it should be kept to the minimum necessary to allow the objects to reach the laboratory in the state in which they were found. The elaborate and lengthy work of cleaning and mending should not be attempted in the field. In effect this will normally mean maintaining the moisture content and sealing the objects in airtight containers.

A wide variety of *Samples* for environmental studies will also be brought into the hut or tent. If no further processing is to be done, the Assistant must check that the bags, or if necessary the jars or boxes into which they are transferred, are adequately labelled and tied and then see them packed by material.

## SECONDARY PROCESSING: THE ANALYSING OF THE MATERIAL

The writing of the excavation report will be much advanced if more than the foregoing minimum of processing can be done on the site. With large amounts of material the mere opening and sorting of boxes and bags can take much time, and many directors will not have as much help available at home as they have in the field. A large well-lit room supplied with tables and chairs will be needed.

Analysis will depend on having sufficiently experienced Indoor and Environmental Assistants; and if much specialised material is expected (e.g. foundry slags and ores or flint-knapping debris) a special effort to engage an assistant conversant with the material should be made.

The *Cultural Objects* will have already been bagged by material, and secondary processing will usually involve the laying out, perhaps by several people, of the objects of each kind of material, sorting them into types, perhaps measuring and sketching, and entering the details in a series of loose-leaf registers or card indexes.[24]

If a mechanical system of analysis is wanted it will be necessary to code the information and to have it transferred to punched cards. This will be necessary when much material is involved, when it cannot be taken from the site or when various types of evidence need to be measured and cross-analysed in a number of ways. In all cases the details required must have been worked out beforehand and standard coding frames evolved. When this has been done much featureless material can be discarded. A director should always check all material before it is rejected and see that all the artifacts from especially significant levels and groups are kept.

The materials can now be considered separately:

### STONE

All tools and weapons will naturally be kept for future study and any sorting would first put them aside. The remaining debris for each square metre of each layer should then be classified into flake and core types and individual classes counted, weighed, measured[25] and indexed. A hand or stand magnifying glass or low-power microscope will be needed for this work. Since the aim of the study will be to recreate the stages in the industrial process, examples of the various stages will be set aside for publication.

If a team is working overseas and regulations do not permit even the tools to be taken away for further study, then they should be sorted into types and registered by layer. All should be drawn life-size in three aspects (back, front and edge), photographed, and a written description (including wear, patina and type of flake scar) made. Further stages in processing are discussed in Chapter X.

POTTERY

This should also be laid out by layers and sorted on the basis of form, fabric and ornament. The various groups should then be counted, weighed and registered. It may be necessary and economical to use mechanical methods to analyse fully the distribution of each group. For example the rim diameters might be measured, grouped and compared against such other variables as form and fabric. Specially interesting groups or unusual sherds should be marked in the register, and if the Assistant is experienced a generalised dating for the group can be suggested. Mixed groups (e.g. in Britain: Mediaeval and Roman pottery found together) should also be noted. All rims, bases, handles and decorated pieces should be kept, but featureless sherds may be discarded at this point except for those from especially important strata and groups (from which all finds should be kept).

If the sherds cannot be taken away from the site or country and must be worked on further, card indexes or registers of forms and fabrics and the strata in which they were found must be built up, and good examples of each form be drawn and photographed; each fabric should be described in writing. These are further discussed in Chapter X.

BUILDING MATERIAL

All this should have been kept; if in large quantities near the trenches or in the trays if rare. Although on urban sites there may be much of it, it should be registered before being discarded. Types of materials should be distinguished so that the size and shape of the bricks, masonry, wall, floor and roof tiles and the types of cement and plaster are recorded. All faced fragments of plaster should be examined for paint. Once listed, only a few good examples of each type of material need be kept.

BONE, WOODEN, GLASS AND METAL ARTIFACTS

These and any others will have been listed as 'Special Finds', and only if local regulations refuse to allow them to be taken away for study, should they be worked on during the excavation. Objects of each material should then be sorted separately by type, and each example drawn and photographed and a written description made, preferably in a card index.

*Environmental* material may also be further studied in the field if skilled help is available and if the interpretation of the archaeological material is far enough advanced. The latter point is the more important, for once the significance of the strata on a site is known, many of the samples previously taken will be known to be valueless (e.g. from mixed, irrelevant or intrusive levels). Those from non-significant layers can be discarded and only the remainder processed. These can be considered by kinds of material.

*Bones* of various kinds will have been bagged unsorted, and these may well be further processed on the site. They should be laid out by layers, and the identifiable bones should be recorded by name, species and layer. From single-period archaeological levels all bones which may be measured and articulated groups in particular should be kept. Unidentifiable fragments, when they have been studied for methods of breaking and cutting, may be discarded.

*Soil, charcoal, slag, mollusc and other samples* should be laid out by strata in the same way and their significance assessed in terms of the archaeological material. Those from mixed levels can be discarded and the rest boxed for laboratory study.

## BEGINNING AND ENDING THE EXCAVATION

Special problems occur at the beginning and ending of the excavation.

SITING THE TRENCHES

This is very much the problem of the director, and his decisions will be based partly on the preliminary surveys (Fig. 3 and 4) and other existing information (Chapter II) and partly on the kind of site (Chapters V–XI).

Each new trench should be marked out accurately with string and nails, its workers and tools allotted, and its recorder, also with his equipment, appointed. Thought should be given to its *spoil-dump* which should be sited to leeward, near at hand, and where digging will not be likely to be necessary later. It should not be sited where spoil will roll into, or push down, the side of the trench, and should be approachable either horizontally or downhill. If the trench is to be backfilled mechanically the dump must not be on a steep hillside, and an approach track for the machine must be preserved. If space is limited the dump

E

can be built up high[26] or be removed regularly by machines (say at weekly intervals). Barrow, bucket or basket routes should also be laid down, and if many people are using the same route, a one-way traffic system laid down. Soft or muddy routes should be planked.

CLEARING UP THE SITE

At the end of the excavation there will usually be an obligation to fill in the trenches and restore the original surface. From the beginning therefore the topsoil will have been piled and the turf cut and stacked separately from the other soil. This is particularly important if the backfilling is to be done by machine.

Every effort should be made to backfill by machine, for to do it by hand is costly and time-consuming. Spoil dumps should be sited with an eye to easy mechanical backfill (e.g. where there is a clear push-back to the trench). Dumps should not normally be placed so that the machine must try to work along a steep slope.

It is often cheaper to take tenders from a number of firms for back-filling work than to do it oneself.

If the surface should return to its previous level then the soil must be compressed at intervals during the infilling to stop subsidence. This can be done by running the machine to and fro over it, by hand-compressors, or by ramming.

## SUGGESTED READING

*The Business of Management\**, Falk, R. 1963.

*Essays on Archaeological Method\**, Griffin, J. (ed) 1957. (Especially for machine-use and new survey techniques). Some new ideas on Excavation, Biddle, M. *LRS* (duplicated) 1967.

*Archaeology from the Earth*, Wheeler, R. 1954 especially Chap. 4.

*Practical Archaeology*, Webster, G. 1966.

*Procedural Manual for Archaeological Field Research Projects*, Dittert, A. and Wendorf, F. 1963.

*Stratification for the Archaeologist*, Pyddoke, E. 1961.

*Surveying for Archaeologists*, Fryer, D. 1960.

*Photography for Archaeologists*, Cookson, M. 1954.

*Archaeological Photography*, Simmons, H. 1969.

A Practical Method for Preserving Soil Profiles, Drummond, D. *AmAnt* 29. I 1963. 116.

*Manual of Civil Engineering*, ICE 1966.

*Simple Photogrammetry*, Williams, J. 1970.

## NOTES

1. Whilst not pressing an analogy with the gentlemen-adventurers and the crew of those days, the difference in attitude between volunteers (whether paid or not) who are working because of an interest in archaeology, and professional earth-movers digging for a living has perhaps some points in common.

2. Petrie, F. 1904; Woolley, C. 1942.

3. Many sixth-form schoolchildren and university students will soon learn to work intelligently and well. In countries where female labourers exist (e.g. Poland), they have been found excellent at delicate work. In men the ability for delicate work varies with temperament.

4. The techniques to be employed by individual helpers are well dealt with in many books, e.g. Wheeler, R. 1954 and Webster, G. 1966 for England, and Hammond, P. 1963 for North America. Other references were given at the end of Chapter 1.

5. In Britain, borough or district advisory services and chambers of commerce often keep lists of lodgings. Members of local archaeological societies may also help find private accommodation.

6. This will have to be arranged through the local authority.

7. Tentage is expensive to hire, and if the excavation is to continue through many seasons it should be bought.

8. Senior students of, or recent graduates in, Domestic Science, may be interested in the experience of catering for a camp.

9. Most experienced directors have evolved their own systems, but Heizer, R. and Graham, J. 1967 go too far in suggesting that general principles need not be discussed.

10. Kenyon, K. 1952.

11. Atkinson, R. 1953. Rubber-stamped labels and metal tags have been successfully used.

12. Atkinson, R. 1953. Fryer, D. 1960 for photogrammetry. For stereo-colour, *PhotJ* 101 1961. 211. Williams, J. 1970.

13. Atkinson, R. 1953.

14. Cookson, M. 1954.

15. These can be very varied. The simplest is a ladder guyed by three ropes, the most elaborate are mobile towers used for repairs. Simmons, H. 1969. For the use of balloons see Guy, P. *Antiq* VI 1932. 148.

16. As a check against a camera failing and because monochrome usually reproduces better than colour. *PhotJ* 101 1961. 211.
17. Cookson, M. 1954.
18. Matthews, S. 1968 and Simmons, H. 1969 supplement Cookson, M. on the more recent technical points.
19. McBurney, C. 1968 used this technique.
20. Since the various rock and soil changes recorded have to be interpreted. *AmArch* 29. 1 1963. 116.
21. The director must always watch for these points and leave temporary baulks to record them.
22. Kenyon, K. 1952; Webster, G. 1966. Experience has shown that draughting film with a polyester base (e.g. Ilford Supermattex), is useful in drawing sections in the rain.
23. In Europe and America there are often local people who will be pleased to help in this way. In other parts of the world it is easy to recruit full-time workers for this.
24. For an example of this kind of processing see Macpherron, A. 1967.
25. McBurney, C. 1968.
26. Atkinson, R. 1953.

CHAPTER IV

# The Writing and Publishing
# of the Report

'Publish and be Damned.' Attributed to Arthur, Duke of
Wellington (1769–1852).

It is self-evident that any site excavated but left unpublished is destroyed
and responsibility for publishing must be accepted by the director
personally and delegated only because of illness or death. Since many
months of work and considerable sums of money will be necessary to
write and publish the report (Fig. 8), time should be allocated in the
period immediately after the excavation when memory is still fresh, and
money be set aside from the first moment of planning. Several useful
accounts of the stages in the preparation and publishing have been
published in recent years[1] but deal mainly with detailed problems; here
the strategy of the post-excavation period and aspects not stressed in

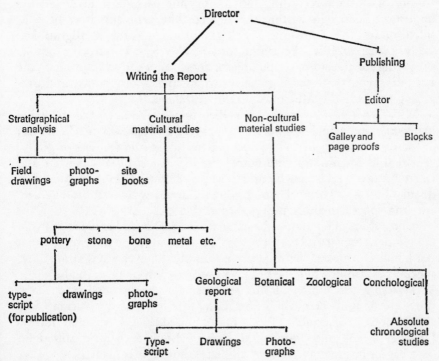

Fig. 8 Writing and publishing the report.

the literature will be considered. Readers will be referred to other sources for the discussion of particular points of detail.

The problem of writing and publishing can be considered separately, but for both it is necessary to have read and looked critically at many other reports. It will also be necessary to know the format in which the report will finally be published, but in any case the final presentation should be in typescript on quarto paper and should be double spaced with wide margins.

## INTERIM REPORTS

It has become fashionable in Britain in recent years to publish long interim reports. Whilst it is a great advantage for other workers to know the general results of excavations within a few months, interim reports should be brief, for the limited space in journals should be reserved for full reports publishing the factual evidence.[2]

## WRITING THE REPORT (Fig. 9)

This must always be the personal concern of the director, since he will not only be able to co-ordinate all the kinds of evidence but will, in the field, have been the only person to have seen the excavation as a whole. In spite of excellent recording, his memory and personal notes are always important factors in writing the report. The problems may be considered under the following headings: producing the stratigraphical study which will be the framework of the report; carrying out or arranging for the study of the objects and samples so as to produce the specialist reports; preparing the drawings and photographs; and preparing the period syntheses of all the evidence.

At the end of an excavation a director should have the following material upon which to work: the *recorded evidence* which will consist of the trench notebooks; the plans and sections; a long series of photographs and his own private notes: the *objects and samples* bagged and listed by layer and trench; and a series of special finds registered in detail (Fig. 8). To work on this material he will need storage and working space, furniture and good lighting.

*Storage space:* This should be as near as possible to his place of work, since much sorting and carrying may be necessary, and so arranged that the labelled crates of material are accessible. Shelves are desirable and special precautions may be necessary against insects or animals.[3]

*Working space:* Unless all the evidence has been coded beforehand the material must be available for many months[4] and the working area should contain a number of long tables and shelves, have good natural lighting, a sink and water. The shelves should either be slotted for drawers, or large numbers of small boxes should be collected for storage during the period of preparation (Fig. 12).

**Introduction**
General description of site.
Summary of previous knowledge.
Acknowledgments of help.
Photographs (aerial, pre-excavation general views).
Plans (national and regional location).
Destination of finds and records.
Summary of evidence from all periods.

**Description by Periods**
A correlation of stratigraphy, features and objects. Each period (chapter) to contain:
    Description of evidence (features and objects) by phase and trench. (Objects
    included by cross-reference to material chapters).
    Discussion of the implications of the evidence, comparison with other sites.
    Sections, period and phase plans, photographs.

**Description by Materials**
Specialist chapters on cultural and non-cultural objects by materials.
Each cultural material chapter to include:
    Numerical summaries of all the evidence.
    Detailed discussion of selected pieces with comparisons and relationships with
    other sites.
    Diagrams, drawings and descriptions of selected pieces.
Each chapter on non-cultural evidence to include:
    Numerical summary of all the evidence.
    Discussion of its significance.
    Diagrams and tables.

Fig. 9 Tabloid summary of a report.

*Studying the evidence:* Since the aim of the report is to present the complete history of the use of the site by men, and since at any one place in most parts of the world, men will have left traces at different times, the material will be divisible into a number of chronologically distinct groups. Some of these will, of course, contain more evidence than others, but all must be studied. The director's first task will be to isolate these groups and then to study the evidence from each of them separately.

A start should be made by studying the stratigraphical evidence, for until this is done the objects have relatively little meaning. No specialist reports should therefore be started until the stratigraphical study is well under way and the significance of many of the layers has become apparent. Unless this is done much time can be wasted (e.g. in a detailed study of material from mixed levels).

## THE STRATIGRAPHICAL STUDY

This can never be delegated, for much, in spite of elaborate records, will depend upon the director's observations during the excavation and his personal notes. The primary recognition of chronological periods will usually have taken place during excavation, for they are often clearly distinguished (e.g. by sudden changes in building methods or plans, by sealing deposits due to destruction or by nonconformities caused by erosion). The director will have traced these events through many trenches and so have given himself correlations over a wide area. Using the trench notebooks, plans and sections, the layers of each main period can be separated out (setting aside for the moment any uncertain ones) without reference to any cultural material, and tables of layers based *solely on the stratigraphy* constructed. For example on a complicated settlement site a director's preliminary notes might resemble Fig. 10.

Notes on probably contemporaneous strata in the group of neighbouring trenches (I–Q2) at Site I.

| Lowest layers and features (tentatively Period I) | Resting on or cut into bedrock and covered by a thick layer of soil. |
|---|---|
| Trench I | None certain. Possibly Ditch 32 |
| H | None certain. Possibly level 26a, 27, 28 (certain if 132 is here) |
| J | Pits T, Z, Y, R, X, K, S, P, O, W, W1 (certainly here, sealed by soil layer) |
| G | Pits 26, 26a, 30, 23a (certainly here, sealed by soil layer) |
| H1 | Pit 30 (includes levels 26, 25, 28, 27, 32) Postholes 23/4 and 25. (All sealed by soil layer) |
| H2 | Nothing certain. Pit 17a? |
| J1 | Pits 20 (includes levels 20a, 18). Postholes 16, 17. (All sealed by soil layer) |
| J2 | Nothing certain. Pit 17? |
| N2, K1, K2, L1, L2, M1, M2 | Nothing |
| N1 | Gully 21 |
| Q1 | Gully 10a–b (same as Gully N1 21) |
| Q2 | Postholes 11 and 12 |

Sheets like this should be worked out for all sites or groups of neighbouring trenches. The whole complex of features and levels which may be broadly contemporary can then be considered together.

Fig. 10 Page from a director's notebook kept during the preparation of the report. Compare with Fig. 11.

Within each period, but still based only on stratigraphy, a succession of events will often be recognisable in each trench and from the correlation of features and layers in the neighbouring trenches sub-periods may be distinguished. This can also be expressed in table form. For example the example taken above, further sub-divided

Period I. (a) Trench I ditch 32. Trench H layers 26, 27, 28. Trench G layer 26. Trench J layer 30 and pits T, Z, Y and R (possibly pit S).

(b) Trench J pits X, K, S. Trench G layer 26 (possibly 30).

(c) Trench H pits 29 and 29a. Trench J pits O, W and WI. Trench K layers 16, 17, 18 and 19.

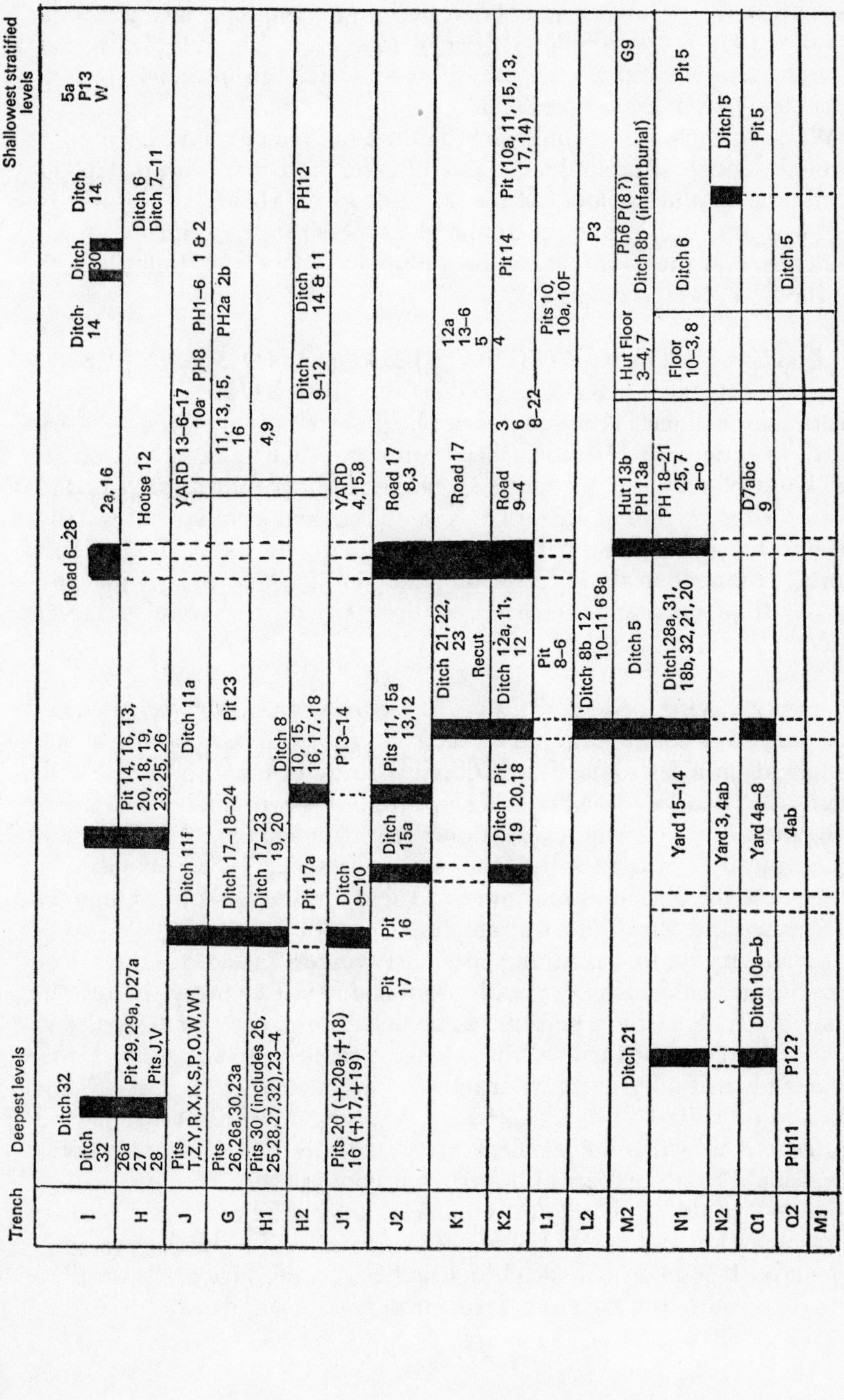

Fig. 11 Group of layers from neighbouring trenches roughly correlated during the writing of the report.

This can now be further interpreted and the groups of features and layers in each phase will give some indication of the problems to be studied. In the example given above, period I(a) might be interpreted in the director's notes as follows: 'Seems to contain a group of pits and several postholes and ditches as well as a possible ground surface. It is apparently a settlement problem.'

Work on these lines should, by the time the records have been gone through, enable a preliminary table of layers to be drawn up. Fig. 11 continues the development of the example given above.

When the tables are as complete as possible from the stratified evidence, and there will always be a number of layers 'in limbo', work on the finds can go on.

## THE STUDY OF THE OBJECTS AND SAMPLES (CULTURAL AND NON-CULTURAL)

Work on the objects and samples can begin when the preliminary work on the stratigraphical records has been done, but until reports on *all* the kinds of evidence are received, no general account of each period can be attempted. The many kinds of objects and samples will usually have to be considered separately by their materials, often by specialist workers other than the director himself. Finding, discussing with, and assimilating the results achieved by these workers is one of the most difficult parts of the work.

### LOCATING AND COLLABORATING WITH SPECIALIST WORKERS

The degree of collaboration a director requires will vary from a quick comment on a few objects to a detailed study of many of them, and, whilst the need for some kinds of help will be known in advance, others will emerge only during excavation.[5] Arrangements made beforehand are naturally the most satisfactory since the specialist can then, if he wishes, see the objects as they are excavated, decide on any preliminary processing and select his own samples.

Arrangements for recruiting specialist workers either in cultural or non-cultural subjects vary greatly from country to country. In Britain it is usually done by a personal approach by the director to someone known or recommended to him. General requests to research institutions, university departments or national archaeological bodies are less likely to be satisfactory, but in either case acceptance may often depend on the way in which the problems are stated. All requests for collaboration should be accompanied by: (i) an account of the excavation; (ii) a summary of the problem and how these may affect the final results; (iii) the nature and amount of material offered or likely to be available for study. It should be made clear whether general advice or a detailed report is required; if the latter, separate publication under the specialist's

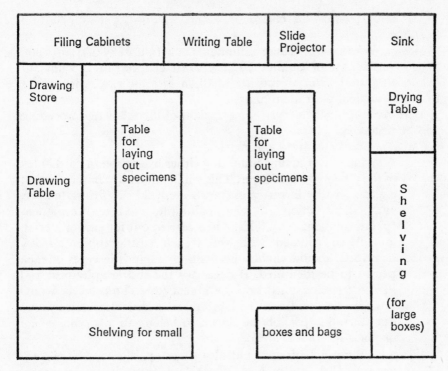

Fig. 12 A layout for a workroom.

name should be offered. If collaboration is agreed, discussion before and during the excavation should take place if so desired by either partner. If the collaboration is arranged after excavation, the material sent to the specialist worker should, unless he has specifically requested something else, be kept to the minimum and should have been processed as far as possible. In all cases it should be arranged by trench and layer (with a full explanation of the excavation labelling system) and have notes on the significance of each object and sample sent. Great effort should be made to see that it is as full, and as free from jargon, as possible. During the report-writing period, the director should keep in touch with the specialist and discuss any new questions which arise from the work and to which he would like to have answers. This should eliminate the possibility of a specialist report becoming, after much work, valueless to the general account.

The categories of material a director will study himself will naturally depend upon his interest and abilities, but where one category dominates (e.g. ceramic or stone artifacts) it is desirable that he study it himself, for the necessity to link it closely with the excavation records will make it difficult for other people to share it.

The material may be considered under cultural and non-cultural headings.

*Cultural Objects*, defined here as human artifacts, usually of stone, clay, bone or metal, are best published in separate chapters or appendices.[6] Where the numbers of objects are small, a director may, with advice from others, deal with them himself.

With *each category of material* some variant of the following procedure will be necessary:

(i) An initial cleansing and marking.

(ii) A laying out, studying and listing either by register or card index of the objects in each layer. This will be done by characteristics: e.g. pottery by forms (jugs, bowls etc.), fabric (firing, temper, etc.), construction (thrown, coil-built, etc.) and ornament (paint, incision, etc.). This, when carried out for each material, and when collated with the trench stratigraphies already described, should enable the main characteristic types of each period to be identified. If necessary the stratigraphy observed in the trenches must now be amended.[7] Those layers whose position was undetermined before or whose stratigraphy was doubtful may possibly be shown to belong to a specific group on their internal evidence.

(iii) This same collation should also show up the most significant groups of objects in each phase (e.g. those in single graves, kiln-firings or on sealed floors). It will also be possible at this point to select the best-preserved and most typical examples of each category and the most significant groups for drawing and photographing. When this has been completed for all layers and trenches, the bulk of the objects can be returned to store, labelled boxes making future recourse to them easier. Attention is now to be concentrated on the indexed information, and the selected groups and objects. The indexed information studied in conjunction with the excavation records should confirm the existence of distinct phases within a main period (e.g. difference in the pottery below, in and above a house). The total evidence of each phase might be portrayed as a scatter diagram or histogram.[8]

(iv) The selected objects, which will include examples of all the main characteristics noted, must now be related to the material from other sites both published and unpublished. If this period has been much studied, most of the comparative material will be in published excavation reports of the region. These should be worked through for detailed parallels and suggested correlations.[9] If the material has been little studied, a search through museum collections and unpublished excavation material will have to be made. Precise references and attributions should be noted for publication. Discussions with other workers in this field, the sending or taking of puzzling fragments to particular persons and the subjecting of individual specimens to special techniques[10] will become necessary.

(v) When this stage of the work is complete, the written descriptions and measured drawings of the selected objects and, if necessary, photographs of them can be arranged into a chapter or appendix ready for the printer.

(vi) Technical studies of the composition, source, and method of manufacture of the material may well be necessary.

The final method of preparing reports on different materials, all of which will differ greatly in the way in which they are studied, is best studied by reading a wide range of reports.[11]

*Non-Cultural Remains*, here defined as evidence obtained through a natural science technique, will find few directors competent to deal with them. As with the cultural material, no clearing-house or research centre exists in most countries and it has to be done either by insertion into existing research programmes, or in the spare time of research workers or by payment from the excavation funds.[12] Finding collaborators will therefore be similar to finding cultural-material specialists, and the methods of briefing and discussion will be the same (page 74). It may be very important, in these fields, for the discussion to take place before the excavation begins, so that the specialist-worker can himself see the problems and either take samples, or arrange for them to be taken. Special care should be taken to see beforehand that these workers know the information which would aid the archaeologist most.

Examples of the kinds of reports to be hoped for should be studied.[13]

Separate chapters or appendices on each group of samples or collections should be prepared when the reports are received from the specialist. If collaboration has been close they should need little modification, but if they do, this must be discussed with the specialist.

## PREPARING THE DRAWINGS AND PHOTOGRAPHS

From the stratigraphical and specialist studies already discussed the director will be able to decide which plans, sections and site photographs and which object drawings and photographs need to be published

### PLANS, SECTIONS AND SITE PHOTOGRAPHS

While any plans or sections necessary to demonstrate the succession of periods and the nature of features must be published, care should be taken to eliminate any which merely duplicate a point or which are uninformative, since the illustrations will be the most expensive part of the report. There is some difference of opinion whether they should be prepared before the body of the report is written. While it is a great advantage to have some of the more obvious ones drawn beforehand, others will only be realised to be necessary during the writing of the stratigraphical summary. Drawing methods and the use of conventions have been well discussed in recent years[14] and no further discussion is needed here, but uniformity in style is desirable and metric scales should be included.

*Plans.* From the actual plans made on the site probably only a few will be suitable for direct copying on to some transparent medium for publication. The most obvious of these will be a small-scale plan of the whole area, contoured and with all the trenches shown (page 188), and the large-scale plans of features (complete buildings or rooms, stake complexes, etc.) (page 125).

Most plans made on the site will need to be re-drawn, and in so doing the shape and scale, line thickness and conventions can be suited to the final format in which the report will be published.[15] One necessity will be a small-scale map which can often be based on an existing cartographic survey (e.g. in Britain the O.S. 25 in. or 6 in. to the mile maps), showing the site in relation to the modern landscape. Permission to use it will have to be obtained from the appropriate government department. There will also need to be, in large and complicated sites, small-scale plans of each period, or if there are successive phases within it, for each sub-period. These will usually need to be drawn from plans of various areas[16] (Fig. 22, 42, 49).

*Sections:* These should be selected to show the relationship between different periods and phases (e.g. successive buildings) and to illustrate the nature and composition of features (e.g. foundations, ditch-siltings). It should be remembered that so long as the position of the published part is shown on a plan, parts of long sections can be extracted and drawn separately; in this way, parts illustrating particular points (e.g. objects in a ditch) can be drawn on a scale which will show the detail without requiring expensive fold-out figures (Fig. 56, 62, 63).

All sections can usually be traced from the field drawings, and as long as the lettering and symbols are scaled to the final publication size, the reduction can be left to the printer. The following will be necessary:

(a) Long sections showing surface profiles in relation to the main periods excavated. These will have to be greatly reduced, and little detail can be shown on them. Fold-outs may be necessary, but should be avoided if possible since they are expensive.

(b) Short sections, preferably taken from (a) above, which illustrate important points in the text either of the relationship of periods and sub-periods or of features.

The methods of preparing the drawings and the use of symbols, or written descriptions are well discussed in recent publications and will not be discussed here.[17]

*Site Photographs.* These will be selected from those taken during the excavation and in most cases monochrome negatives will already exist. Expense usually rules out colour photographs,[18] and if necessary, monochrome negatives will have to be made from the transparencies. Blocks for photographs are usually the most expensive single printing item in the report costs, and should be introduced only when they show something that the drawings cannot. The following are likely to be necessary (Plates I, II, III, IX and XVI):

(a) Pictures or photographs of the site before excavation.

(b) Aerial photographs taken before and during excavation.

(c) Vertical and oblique views of particularly well-defined and complete features.

(d) Oblique views of standing buildings.

## DRAWINGS AND PHOTOGRAPHS OF OBJECTS

From the detailed studies of the objects and samples, both cultural and non-cultural, will come the remainder of the drawings and photographs. As already described (page 76), the best-preserved examples of all types of objects will have been put aside during their study, and it will now be necessary to draw or photograph them. As a guiding principle measured drawings are to be preferred to photographs except in the case of objects of intrinsic beauty, or where surface texture is important.

*Drawings.* These will need to be done either full size or to a scale selected with the final size of the publication in mind. Line thickness and detail will depend on this scale. Objects will usually be brought together either by material and period (e.g. all pottery together in a chronologically arranged series of plates) or by period only (pottery, metal, bone, etc. together) and must be accompanied by short written descriptions of each piece.

The actual drawing and the arrangement of plates have been well discussed in the literature[19] and will not be dealt with here.

*Diagrams.* Much of the evidence of both the cultural and non-cultural reports will have been reduced to histograms or other diagrams. The drawing of these will have to be planned with the final size of the report in mind so that the detail shows clearly.[20]

*Photographs.* Especially fine objects or groups of objects (carvings, jewels, etc.) will need studio photographs. These require great skill and are preferably undertaken by a professional photographer.[21] A metric scale will be necessary in each photograph.

## WRITING THE GENERAL ACCOUNT

When a director has drafts of his cultural and non-cultural chapters as well as his stratigraphical summaries and the finished drawings, he can begin the most interesting and significant part of his work, the collating and interpretation of the evidence, and writing the general account of each period. Here literary skill as well as factual accuracy is necessary,[22] and it may be that further discussion with some of the specialist workers, and possibly with some in new fields of study, will prove necessary at this point.

First, the relevant materials for each sub-period must be brought together. They will be: the stratigraphical summary, the relevant cultural material from each of the specialised reports (pottery, metal, glass, bone, wood, stone, cloth, leather), and environmental (soil, pollen, mollusca, etc.) evidence. The director can then start to write, beginning perhaps with the earliest phase of the earliest period.

In each phase a model of the society should be created. The *Features* found (e.g. buildings, ditches and graves) may be considered in turn with references to the objects found in them, the relevant plans, sections and photographs with figure references, and any other evidence about the features. Finally suggestions can be made at the end of each feature-account, in a separate paragraph, as to its significance (e.g. why the pit was a rubbish and not a quarry pit). Possible reconstructions might be suggested for structures. *Groups of Features* must then be considered together and their significance analysed (e.g. a group of pits, ditches, postholes and foundations might be discussed as a settlement). Once again page and figure references to points in the plans, sections and specialist reports will be necessary.

When each of the phases within a period has been treated in this way an *Account of the Whole Period* should be given. It is here that the director must show that he has studied the contemporary evidence from other sites in the region both published and unpublished. With detailed references, he must show his own finds in their full chronological and cultural setting. When this has been done for all periods, the main part of the report is complete. In retrospect the report should show for each period of human occupation:

   (i)   the use to which the site was put.
   (ii)  the annual, daily or other cycles of human cultural events.
   (iii) the material culture.
   (iv) the date of its beginning and end.

## THE FINAL FORM OF THE REPORT

In addition to the main body of the report which has been described, introductory paragraphs or chapters will be necessary. In its final form the following should be present:

*Introduction* including: (a) map reference, circumstances of discovery, descriptions of the site before excavation and of any previous finds from it; (b) acknowledgments of help or money, and where finds and records are to be found; (c) geological and soil descriptions of site.

SUMMARY OF RESULTS

*Chapters on each period* giving the stratigraphical history and correlating all the kinds of evidence.

*Appendices or chapters on the cultural finds* by materials and non-cultural finds by discipline.

## PUBLISHING THE REPORT

This is the final duty of the director, and very rarely will a duplicated report with photostat illustrations be sufficient to relieve his conscience.[23] The usual way, if the report is of considerable interest and reasonably short (10–20,000 words), is for it to be accepted by the journal of a local or national archaeological society. If longer (*c.* 60,000 words) and of more general importance it may be accepted by a publisher, a research institution or a publishing foundation for publication as a monograph.

The policies and finances of *Journals* will vary greatly so that to have a report accepted by one will require a knowledge of its aims and procedures. Journals will usually be regional (and so accept local reports of all periods) or national and therefore more specialised (selecting either for importance or for period). No approach to the editor can usually be made until the report is nearly finished.

In writing to the editor the length of the report and approximate number of illustrations should be given. If he shows interest the text should be sent and if accepted, will usually be printed at the expense of the society publishing the journal, the money coming from either government, philanthropic foundation or society funds. A recent discussion of the position in England serves to show the wide variety of conditions which exist.[24]

The particular conventions in abbreviations, footnotes, etc. of a journal should be studied (these are usually available on request from the publishing society) and the report prepared to suit them.

*Monographs* will be larger, more expensive undertakings and will need to be of great general interest. They will then perhaps command the funds of research institutes, benevolent foundations or public bodies if suitable application is made.

The author's role in the preparation of the book is usually restricted to examining the proofs and 'pulls' (impressions of the figures and plates).[25] It is a considerable advantage to understand printing techniques,[26] and as a minimum of knowledge, 'line', 'half-tone' and

F

'colour' reproduction and proof correction will have to be understood.[27] Methods of presenting footnotes and abbreviations should be discussed before the manuscript is finally submitted.

## SUGGESTED READING
*The Preparation of Archaeological Reports*\*\*, Grinsell, L. et al. 1965.
*Field Archaeology*\*, Part IV, Atkinson, R. 1953.
*The preparation of manuscripts and correction of proofs*\*, CUP 1964.
A review of Techniques for Archaeological Sampling. Ragir, S. in Heizer, R. and
 Graham, J. 1967. 181 and appendix I.
*Practical Archaeology*, Webster, G. 1966. 139–99.
*Science in Archaeology*, Brothwell, D. and Higgs, E. (ed) 1970 (for reports on non-
 cultural evidence).
Notes for Contributors, *AJA* 62. 1 1958.
Notes for the guidance of Archaeologists in regard to expert evidence (duplicated)
 *CBA* 1964.
*The Application of Quantitative methods to Archaeology*, Heizer, R. and Cook, S. (ed) 1960.
A method of chronologically ordering archaeological deposits. Robinson, W. *AmAnt*
 XVI. 4 1951.

DESCRIPTION OF MATERIALS
Four codes for the description of artifacts, Gardin, J. *AmAnth* 60 1958. 335.
*Principles of Automatic Data Treatment applied on Neolithic Pottery*\*, Soudsky, B. 1967.
The classification of Artifacts and Archaeology\*, Rouse, J. *AmAnt* XXV 1960. 313.

EXAMPLES OF GOOD DESCRIPTIONS
*Environmental*: Galatea Bay *PPS* XXIII 1967. 107.
*Stone: The Haua Fteah*, McBurney, C. 1968. Hengistbury Head and Downton. *PPS*
 XXV 1959. 236 and 276. *Windmill Hill and Avebury*, Keiler, A. 1965.
*Pottery: Beaker Pottery of Great Britain and Ireland*, Clarke, D. 1970.
*Bone and Antler: Star Carr*, Clark, J. D. G. 1954.

DRAWING AND PHOTOGRAPHING
Archaeological Draughtsmanship\*\*, Piggott, S. *Antiq* XXXIX 1965. 165.
Archaeological Draughtsmanship\*\*, Hope-Taylor, B. *Antiq* XL 1966. 107; XLI
 1967. 289
Wheeler, R. in *AnInd* III 1947. 143.
*Photography in Archaeology and Art*, Matthews, S. London 1968.
*Maps and Diagrams*, Monkhouse, F. and Wilkinson, H. 1964.

EXAMPLES OF GOOD DRAUGHTSMANSHIP
Sections and plans: Little Woodbury, *PPS* VI 1940, 30. *Maiden Castle*, Wheeler, R.
 1943; Rainsborough, *PPS* XXXIII 1967. 207. Tollard Royal, *PPS* XXXIV 1968.
 102.
Objects: *Roman Colchester*, Hull, M. 1958; *Hod Hill*, Richmond, I. 1968; *Windmill Hill
 and Avebury*, Keiler, A. 1965.
*Photographs: Maiden Castle*, Wheeler, R. 1943; *Olduvai Gorge I*, Leakey, L. 1965.

## NOTES
1. Grinsell, L. et al. 1965, is the best general account. For others, see reading list
 for this chapter.
2. e.g. in *AntJ* (*passim*). Annual summaries of results can be useful, e.g. in *JRS*
 (*passim*).
3. Rats will soon destroy bags and boxes if they can nest in privacy. Termites may
 eat both containers and objects.
4. Coding may have to be done if the excavation is far from the workroom and the
 material cannot be moved. Whilst useful for a permanent record, it is to be avoided
 as a unique way of studying material for publication.
5. For a discussion of this see *Notes for the Guidance of Archaeologists in the Use of
 Codes CBA 1964*.
6. *AmAnth* 60 1958. 335f. *AmAnt* XXV 1960. 341f.

7. It may be possible to recognise intrusive or mixed levels which were missed in the excavation. If there is any doubt about the significance of the stratum's chronological position it should be excluded from the main account.

8. Heizer, R. and Cook, F. (ed) 1960. Ragir, S. in Heizer, R. and Graham, J. (ed) 1967, chapter 15.

9. It is necessary to see the actual material as well as the report when detailed comparison is being made.

10. e.g. thin sectioning of particular sherds. See BIA 3 1963. 58f also Williams, J. 1967.

11. Semenov, S. 1967. See pages 145 and 167 for bone.
    Stone: *PPS* XXV 1959. 236f (Palaeolithic); ibid 209 (Mesolithic); *PPS* XXVI 1960 276f (Neolithic).
    Pottery: Piggott, S. 1962 and Kenyon, K. 1948.
    Wood: *PPS* XXXII 1966. 246.
    Metal: Hull, M. 1963.
    Glass: *JGS* V 1963.

12. Expensive laboratory processing (e.g. C 14 dating) may have to be arranged commercially, but in many cases it is to be hoped that the work can be done by voluntary collaboration. Any development by which workers above a technician level had to be hired would be retrogressive. Much more use might be made, for the simpler processes, of natural scientists teaching in schools.

13. Brothwell, D. and Higgs, E. (ed) 1964; with selected reports in the section bibliographies. Examples of good reports from particular disciplines.
    Botany: *JRIC*, 4 1963. 364f. Conchology: *PPS* XXXI 1965. 75f; *PPS* XXVI 1960. 299. Zoology: McBurney, C. 1968 Chapter 2. Pedology: *PPS* XIX 1953. 129f.

14. *Ant.* XXXIX 1965; Atkinson, R. 1953. 189f.

15. Monkhouse, F. and Wilkinson, H. 1964.

16. Examples of plans: *AntJ* XLIV 1964. 188; XLVII 1967. 43 and 51; XXXIX 1959. 1. *MedArch* VII 1956. Fig. 18. For discussion *AnInd* III 1947. 143.

17. Atkinson, R. 1953. 199; Webster, G. 1966. 148; *Antiq* XXXV 1965. See McBurney, C. 1968. Fig. I. 8–9 for a use of colour photographs.

18. The present state of colour reproduction suggests that it has little to add to the drawings. (Compare McBurney 1968. Pl. III.2 and IX.13.)

19. Grinsell, L. et al. 1965. 27 with a good description of drawing techniques. See also *Antiq* XXXIX 1965. Examples: Hull, M. 1963. *Star Carr*, Clark, J. 1954.

20. Monkhouse, F. and Wilkinson, R. 1964. Example: McBurney, C. 1968.

21. Matthews, S. 1968 also Cookson, M. 1954.

22. Piggott, S. 1962 is a nice example of style. For the comments of an historian on archaeologist's prose see Humphreys, S. LRS 1967 (duplicated).

23. Webster, G. 1966. Chapter V.

24. Grinsell, L. et al. 1965. 2–4.

25. In this the archaeologist is like any author.

26. Wheeler, R. 1954. 196f. *Antiq* XXVII 1953. 12.

27. CUP 1964.

## CHAPTER V
# Field Problems of Environmental Archaeology

'Palaeological reconstruction based on data from a single science
is skewed.'

J. Hester
*The Reconstruction of Human Environments*, 1964

The possibilities implicit in the study of the environment of human
groups have only slowly been realised by archaeologists.[1] Many reasons
may be advanced for this, but three may be selected as especially
important.

(i) Many different natural science disciplines are concerned with
environment and specialisation in them is such that it is only when
workers trained in them become aware of, or interested in, archaeological problems that the possibilities of their techniques become known.

(ii) Few archaeologists have any training in environmental studies
or, especially when working in historical periods, any conception of
their possibilities.[2]

(iii) A lack of interest in the ancient evidence among natural science
research institutions and departments, has led to a reluctance to
recommend students to study archaeological problems.[3]

Until recent years the relationship between archaeology and the
environmental studies, of which the most important are geology,

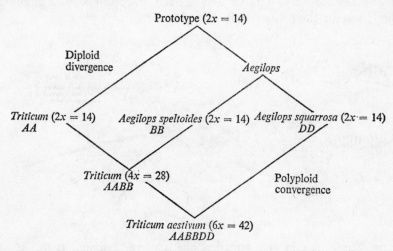

Fig. 13 The phylogeny of *T. aestivum*. The late pleistocene distribution of the
$(2x = 14)$ forms, should be an archaeological field problem.

pedology, botany, zoology and entomology, has been a relatively simple and formal one, so that Pittioni[4] could describe them as 'Auxiliary Sciences'. In that relationship they played a relatively passive role, their practitioners being consulted, being asked to visit excavations to take samples, or being sent samples after the excavation for analysis and comment. There were in most archaeologists' minds three kinds of results to be hoped for in this relationship:

(i) The establishment, in a very general way (e.g. by formation or species), of the animal, vegetable and mineral environment of the human group being studied.

(ii) In prehistoric excavations, the establishment of a relative chronological horizon based on environment.

(iii) The recovery of some details of diet and agricultural practice.

Whilst these still remain important, many new fields of study have been discovered, and there has been a growing interest among some workers in the environmental field in man's impact upon his surroundings.[5] This more positive approach among natural scientists opens up the way for much more cooperation, and several of the new developments might be mentioned by way of illustration.

Increasingly detailed study of the cytology and ecology of botanical cultivars is being undertaken[6] (Fig. 13) and with it there is greater interest in archaeological evidence of all periods. This includes interest in pest complexes (animal, insect and plant) as well as the actual survival of the cultivars themselves. Zoologists are also increasingly interested in evidence from the past, and for many periods—the immediate postglacial period is the most obvious—it is logical to think of archaeological excavations being undertaken for the collection of environmental rather than for the human-cultural evidence.

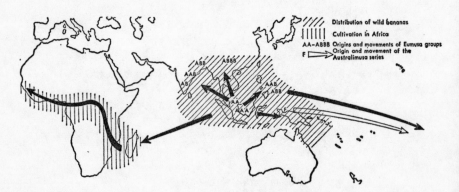

Fig. 14 The evolution and spread of the domestic banana. If the spread through Africa is correct, then archaeological field research in Central Africa should look for the eastern connection.

Among environmental students of all kinds there is increaing interest in the ecology of wild plants and animals of all periods (Fig. 14). The skills of field archaeology are uniquely necessary to the earlier period of this study and offer scope for much future collaboration.[7]

The increasing specialisations in the study of plants and animals (including lower organisms) make their techniques of study applicable to many kinds of archaeological problems; for example, the study of human nutrition from faeces, stomach contents and bone tissue;[8] of animal husbandry from bone, horn and antler tissue as well as from bone mensuration and the interpretation of features from pest infestation.[9]

## THE ROLE OF THE DIRECTOR

Whilst all archaeologists are now confronted by the necessity to consider the possibilities of environmental evidences, the field director has a positive duty to understand and ponder them, since it is obvious that they are the part of his evidence most likely to expand. In the creation of accurate models of human societies in all parts of the world, nothing else offers similar possibilities.

That environmental studies should be part of his general training has already been stated (Chapter I) and here his role as the collector of evidence is considered. The field duties fall into two groups.

(i) In planning his excavation and in recruiting his team the director must realise the potentialities of his site for environmental studies and must plan to exploit them. This may necessitate recruiting specialists in particular fields as environmental assistants.[10] It may also require him to consult other specialists before excavation, to explain and discuss the site problems with them, to invite them to visit the excavation regularly and to arrange for material to go to them afterwards.

(ii) He must see that the evidence or samples containing it are properly collected from suitable areas, are properly recorded, labelled and packed.

The problems of the main environmental disciplines may now be considered individually.

## GEOLOGY

Three groups of geological problems will need to be solved on all sites, and no director without geological training should rely on his own interpretation of the evidence.

(i) *Strata sealing archaeological remains.* It should be established whether these have been accumulated by natural agencies. If so, their nature and cause must be determined (e.g. whether wind or water-deposited, whether solifluxion or boulder clay etc.).

(ii) *Strata containing archaeological remains.* Many naturally deposited strata will contain human artifacts either dropped by their makers or removed mechanically from elsewhere. It is important to establish the nature of these strata in both cases; in the former because it may help interpret the community, in the latter because the finds must be considered as archaeologically unstratified and the artifacts may be of very different ages. In excavation, the latter material will be recorded in the normal way (see (i) above), but will be of much less significance than complexes of objects found where their users dropped them.

(iii) *Strata below archaeological remains*. The identification of these, the 'bedrock' of archaeologists, is essential on all sites, for excavation must go on until geological strata undisturbed by man are reached.[11] Identification can be difficult for although preliminary study will have shown its general nature, several small exposures of, say, a river gravel or a boulder clay, may be quite unlike each other. The surface may also be very weathered and eroded, and only the cutting of trenches deep into it, which can often be done quickly with a machine, will show its true nature. If the evidence of bedrock is to be particularly important (e.g. a river terrace or a raised beach) it should in England be related to the Ordnance Datum.

Separate problems after excavation will include the *Petrological* (perhaps including *Spectrographic* and *Thin Section*) examinations of rock fragments used by man (e.g. as querns, axes or hones). These should identify the materials and perhaps their sources. This study need not require a visit to the site by a specialist, and the samples may be put aside to be sent to a geologist.[12] Anything too precious to the report for partial destruction by thin sectioning should be labelled as such before packing.

## BOTANY

The long survival of plant remains, particularly in very wet or very dry conditions, has long been known and utilised, but the fact that they occur in smaller but still useful quantities in soils and features of all kinds and periods is less well known and often neglected. The evidence and the use to be made of it has been set out for archaeologists by Dimbleby,[13] and since the help of plant remains in interpreting the behaviour of human communities is so great, directors should strive to find them. All accounts of excavations should include reports on these remains or should indicate the reasons for failing to include them. On sites where much botanical evidence may be expected (e.g. in desiccated, waterlogged or airtight strata), a botanist should be included in the excavation team, but often it may be sufficient for a director or an assistant to be experienced in the taking of suitable samples, since the identifications will have to be done under laboratory conditions. Samples should be packed at once in polythene bags and labelled with a brief description of the layer as well as with the code. Evidence will be obtained in two ways:

(i) By *visual recognition* of plant remains during excavation. In flotation, floculation and sieving, seeds, leaves and the woody parts of plants may be recognised. Trowellers and trench recorders should be warned to expect them, especially in very wet or dry conditions in pits and ditches which may have been used for rubbish dumping or have remained open for some time, or in postholes, especially those which may have been part of stores. When fragments are found the treatment of the feature will depend on the nature of the site. On a prehistoric site where they would be of very great importance, all the feature's filling should be sieved through. On sites of all periods, large samples should be taken if it is not possible to sieve the whole. Ground surfaces should be similarly checked with special attention to kitchens, hearths, mills, presses and store-rooms and their surroundings. The most common remains are likely to be carbonised fragments near fires, all of which should be kept for further study. Large fragments of beams or of posts should be either taken up complete and wrapped in polythene sheeting or, if too large, should be cut transversely so that complete cross-sections are preserved. These should be packed in rigid boxes. Comments on their position and the soil around them as well as the excavation code should be noted on the labels.

(ii) Evidence may also come, after the excavation, from the *microscopic study* of samples. If possible preliminary work of the kind already discussed (page 77) should be carried out on the site so that only significant samples are submitted for laboratory study. On prehistoric sites, even when nothing is immediately obvious, half-kilo samples should certainly be taken and tested from all soils and floors and features. In special conditions, samples, e.g. in waterlogged pits where a series of samples should be taken from top to bottom, or in graves where samples from round the body might be taken, will be examined later for pollen grains or for plant and fungus spores.[14] Details of the layer should be included on the label as well as the excavation code.

Plant evidence may also come from other sources. A preliminary check of all pottery and burnt clay for matrix impressions may possibly be made on the site if sufficient skilled help is available. This will involve the checking of *all* fragments for the burnt-out impressions of plants and their retention for further study. Animal or human faeces, if found, should also be kept for study with plant evidence in mind.[15]

## ZOOLOGY

The importance of the study of animal, bird and fish remains has been spelt out by many people[16] and there is no excuse for failing to keep and deal with them properly. The collection of all bone fragments by strata is, today, as standard a procedure as the collection of potsherds, and like them articulating groups should be bagged together (in polythene) in the trenches. With most creatures sieving will be necessary to recover all the remains. Fragments of horn, antler, eggs, feathers, faeces and scales may be found.

Fragile bones may need strengthening before removal from the ground or immediately afterwards,[17] but most can, like pottery, be washed, sorted and bagged on the site. A considerable amount of sorting, discarding and even measurement can be done on the site if suitable help is available. Only bones from single-period sites are perhaps worthy of the most detailed age, sex and other statistical studies now being given to bones. From multi-period sites, especially from the later levels, where contamination from earlier levels is likely, only a simple enumeration of species is perhaps worthwhile. It should be made clear to the vertebrate zoologist who studies the bones after the excavation, what kind of evidence is required and which strata are worthy of detailed study.

Bird remains will usually need separating from those of animals for sending, with any eggshell fragments and guano, to a separate specialist.[18]

Fish remains will also have to be separated.[19] Scales as well as bones are possible finds. They should be looked for especially in sites near water.

## CONCHOLOGY

The study of molluscs, especially the land species, is now known to be of great importance in interpreting human behaviour as well as climate.[20] Since they are found in a wide variety of soils, especially calcareous ones where pollen grains are rare, and since species can be identified when no more than 2-mm. fragments survive,[21] care should be taken to look for them. Trowellers and trench supervisors should be made familiar with the appearance of the fragments. The evidence will come, in part, from hand collections when, during excavation, large snail fragments will usually be recognised by trowellers and placed in the trays. When these reach the site hut or tent they should be bagged separately and kept with the soil samples discussed below, for the large species may well be missing from the latter.[22] The smaller species will only be obtained in sufficient numbers from large soil samples (c. 3 kilos), and these should be taken from all snail-rich surfaces and features (e.g. ditches or open pits) where evidence would be especially useful. The samples might be given a preliminary examination on the site to make sure that they contained snail fragments. After the examination the archaeologist will need to discuss in some detail with the specialist the implications of the species found, and a statistical summary will be necessary for publication.

Sea species will normally be identified in the study of the hand collection and treated like the land ones. Where collected for food they must be counted by species and published statistically.

## ENTOMOLOGY

Fragments of insects (cuticles, wing-covers, legs, eggs, etc.) have now been shown to survive in a surprisingly wide range of climate and soil conditions.[23] Since they are excellent indicators of climate and human economy they are to be prized, and trowellers and trench supervisors must be warned to look out for them. Fragments will rarely be visible to the naked eye, but can be identified with a hand lens, and pit and posthole fillings as well as hearths and middens should be sampled for examination with this in mind. If suitably qualified help is available, a preliminary check for fragments can be made on the site, but for egg identification a laboratory examination will be necessary.

Samples should be taken for examination especially from suspected latrines, dung heaps and middens[23] and be packed in glass jars.

## PEDOLOGY

The significance of soil (the products of the decomposition of the land surface under the influence of weather and vegetation) in archaeology has been well discussed by Cornwall,[24] and directors should be familiar with his comments and suggestions. Of primary importance in an excavation is the establishment of the ground surface at different periods, and it is only when the archaeologist's interpretation is supported by a pedologist's analysis that a buried ground surface can be considered proved. A laboratory study of a soil can also tell much of the climate and vegetational conditions under which it was formed. This can be done only in the laboratory, and, if possible, a pedologist should be invited to visit the site to advise on the taking of samples. In his absence adequate samples can be taken by a well-briefed archaeologist; they should be a series of 4 gm samples taken vertically and continuously through the supposed soil, bagged in polythene, and their position indicated on a measured section. A similar section should be taken through the present top soil.

Some simple tests (e.g. acidity and phosphate content) may also be carried out on the site.

The archaeologist must discuss the findings with the pedologist so that he is sure that the questions to which he requires answers are known.

## SAMPLING FOR CHRONOLOGICAL EVIDENCE

Much evidence of the dating of particular strata may come indirectly from the various disciplines already discussed, but it may be necessary to take samples for other physical or chemical studies.

### RADIOACTIVE ISOTOPES OF CARBON (C-14) AND POTASSIUM (P-40)

The significance and limitations of these dating techniques have given rise to a literature of their own.[25] Here only the director of a prehistoric site must be reminded of the possible need for submitting specimens for trial runs. The sampling techniques can be carried out by archaeologists.[26] Great care must be taken to see that the 0·25 kilo organic samples (wood, shell etc.) are well stratified, and unlikely to have been contaminated by later or earlier remains. They should be packed at once in polythene bags. In the few cases where P-40 determinations may be useful a similar technique will be necessary.

### ARCHAEOMAGNETISM

This requires areas of burnt soil or rock containing iron particles, which have remained undisturbed since they were burnt. The taking of samples from these areas requires great precision in measuring their orientation and in lifting and should be left to a specialist.[27] If it is known well in advance that evidence of this kind is likely to occur, a team-member could perhaps be trained to take them.

### THERMOLUMINESCENCE

This requires a group of fairly large potsherds in well-stratified positions which have been under 0·3 m. of soil for at least two-thirds of their burial time; pits or the final floor surfaces of collapsed buildings are therefore the preferred sources of material.[28] A typical sample of the soil within 0·3 metres of the sherd is also needed. Both sherds and samples should be bagged at once. The following extracts from the instruction to fieldworkers issued by the Oxford Research Laboratory for Archaeology and the History of Art is a model which could well be copied by other workers:

'From each archaeological context we need a group of about 6 sherds. Here, context means a span of up to 10% of the age (e.g. 500 years for 3000 B.C.).

Sherds should be as thick as possible: minimum thickness normally acceptable is ⅛ in. (3 mm.). The pieces need not be large—1 in. (25 mm.) across is adequate.

Well-baked fabric preferable. Surface decoration or glaze does not matter.

Only sherds that have been buried to a depth of a foot (0·3 metre) or more for at least two-thirds of their burial time are normally acceptable. This means that pits and ditches that have filled up fairly quickly (either by silting or by ancient man) are ideal sources, also burials. On the other hand potsherds lying under a foot of soil on the floor of a tomb (for example) are unsatisfactory unless there is good evidence that the soil got there rapidly as, for example, in the case of a primary burial that has been sealed over; sherds from the last context are excellent.

Please avoid any unnecessary exposure to bright sunlight (five minutes doesn't matter but please do not leave it in direct sunlight for any longer). Store in a brown paper bag—or something comparably opaque.

Unwashed sherds are preferred (plus any lumps of earth attached). If washing is essential please do not use detergent or other additives in the water; shade the sherds from the sun when drying them.

Avoid excessive heating of the sherds. Their temperature should not exceed the boiling point of water (100° Centigrade, 212° Fahrenheit).

Avoid exposure to ultra-violet, infra-red, X-rays, beta-rays or gamma-rays *at all costs*.

We require a handful of the soil *that is typical of that in which each group of sherd is buried*. If the sherds are lying against a wall or on a floor, we need a sample of the wall or floor material in addition to the soil.

Exposure of the soil to light and heat does *not* matter.

From any one site we prefer to have groups from several contexts but this is not essential.

Please, above all, avoid sherds whose inclusion in a group is in any way doubtful. The method gives the date at which the pot was made; consequently we do not want residual pottery from earlier periods.

Any available information about burial conditions etc. is welcome (e.g. nature of soil, state of sherd when excavated—dry or wet).

The sherds are destroyed in the course of measurement.'

## VARVE ANALYSIS

This will only be possible on a very limited number of excavations since it depends on a long series of annually deposited sediments.[29] If these exist, then a complete and continuous series of samples, drawings, photographs and possibly a plastic strip section will be necessary.[30] A sedimentologist should also visit the site.

## TREE RING ANALYSIS

This, based on a principle of annual variation similar to the varve analysis, will also require special circumstances to be of significance.[32]

All large timbers should be sectioned as a matter of routine. This should be done either by sawing out a complete cross-section or by preserving a radial segment.

## SUGGESTED READING

*Environmental Studies and Archaeology*★★, Dimbleby, G. 1963.

*The Reconstruction of Past Environments*★★ (especially sections 3 and 4 with good bibliography), Hester, J. and Schoenwetter, J. (ed) 1964.

*Ancient Environments*, La Porte, L. 1968.

*Ethno-zoology of the Upper Great Lakes Region*★ (especially Chap. 3 and Appendix F), Cleland, C. 1966.

*Ethno-Botany of Pre-Colombian Peru*★, Towle, M. 1961.

*Principles of Palaeo-ecology*, Ager, D. 1963.

*Environment and Archaeology*, Butzer, K. 1964. (Chap. I).

*The Domestication and Exploitation of Plants and Animals*, Ucko, P. and Dimbleby, G. (ed) 1969.

*The Identification of non-artifactual archaeological material*, Taylor, W. (ed) 1957.

*Notes for the Guidance of Archaeologists in regard to expert evidence*, CBA 1964.

Archaeological Field Sampling, Rootenberg, S. *AmAnt* XXX 1964. 181.

*Soils for the Archaeologist*, Cornwall, I. 1958.

*Plants and Archaeology*, Dimbleby, G. 1966.

*Molluscs in Archaeology and the Recent*, Drake, R. (ed) 1962.

*Science in Archaeology* (Section 2), Brothwell, D. and Higgs, E. (ed) 1970 edition.

*The Inorganic Raw Materials of Antiquity*, Rosenfeld, A. 1965.

*Archaeoentomology*, Speight, M. *LRS* 1970 (duplicated with good bibliography).

*Water, Weather and Prehistory*, Raikes, R. 1967 (Part I).

## NOTES

1. Recently discussed in Hester, J. and Schoenwetter, J. (ed) 1964. See also Butzer, K. 1964 Chapter 1, Dimbleby, G. 1966 and Coles, J. in Brothwell, D. and Higgs, E. (ed) 1964. 93.

2. Departments studying early human environments are still rare, and too many fieldworkers still ignore environmental evidence. Others do not know how to obtain it or make little effort to get it examined.

3. More progress has been made by American than European workers in this field. See Ager, D. 1963. Notable local successes are Towle, M. 1961 and Flannery, K. *PPS* XXXIII, 1967, *Science*, 147 1967. 1247.

4. Pittioni, R. in Haekel, J. (ed) 1961. 10.

5. For a general discussion of results see Ucko, P. and Dimbleby, G. (eds) 1969, and Hutchinson, J. (ed) 1965.

6. Riley, R. in Hutchinson, J. (ed) 1965. 103 or Symmonds, N. 1962.

7. e.g. at Rampart Cave. *AJS* 259, 1961. 102.

8. Brothwell, D. in Ucko, P. and Dimbleby, G. (ed) 1969.

9. Latrines from parasites: *Antiq* XL 1966. 293; also Alexander, J. in Ucko, P. and Dimbleby, G. (ed) 1969. 123.

10. This will mean developing much closer connection than is at present the case in England, with appropriate university technical and training college departments. Another possible area of recruitment will be among the natural scientists working in schools.

11. Archaeologists' conceptions of bedrock vary. It should really mean pre-pliocene deposits, but the possibility of palaeolithic remains is often ignored.

12. See Hayne, V. in Hester, J. and Schoenwetter, J. (ed) 1964. 66.

13. Dimbleby, G. 1966.

14. e.g. Bishop's Waltham: *PPS* XXIII, 1957. 137.

15. Pollen analysis from prehistoric human faeces: *AmAnt* XXX, 1964. 168.

16. e.g. Cleland, C. 1966 especially Chapter 3 and Appendix F.

17. Brothwell, D. 1965. 12.

18. Howard, H. 1939. 311. Dawson, E. in Brothwell, D. and Higgs, E. (ed) 1964. 279, with good bibliography.
19. Rider, M. in Brothwell, D. and Higgs, E. (ed) 1964. 294.
20. Drake, R. (ed) 1962. For an example: Goleta, *AmAnt* 26 1961. 3.
21. The stratification of molluscs in chalk soils. Evans, J. G. *LRS* 1966 (duplicated). Identifiable fragments of no more than 2-mm diameter may pass unharmed through a worm's gut. But see Cheatum, E. and Allan, D. in Drake, R. (ed) 1962 for limitations of the method.
22. See *PPS* XXVI, 1960. 301, for a comparison of the two methods.
23. *Archaeoentomology*, Speight, M., *LRS* 1970.
24. Cornwall, I. 1958. See also *Antiq* XXXI 1957. 219.
25. Well summarised by Willis, E. in Brothwell, D. and Higgs, E. (ed) 1964. Section I, Pt 6, with bibliography.
26. Libby, W. 1955. For collection technique see Polach, H. and Golson, J. 1966.
27. Cook, R. in Brothwell, D. and Higgs, E. (ed) 1964. 63.
28. Aitken, M. 1961.
29. Zeuner, F. 1952. 20.
30. For archaeological field sampling see *AmAnt* 30, 1964. 181.
31. Zeuner, F. 1952. 6. Cook, S. and Heizer, R. 1965.

# CHAPTER VI
# Problems in the Excavation of the Settlements of Hunter-gatherers and Pastoralists

'... site of a recent Bushman encampment. There were the light screens of grass and acacia branches to shelter them against the sun and dew, and all round the sand was thickly strewn with broken and empty nutshells, wilted melon skins, rabbit fur, porcupine quills, tortoise shells, and the hooves of animals. There were several fresh giraffe shinbones cleared of every scrap of meat. ... Finally there were the unscattered ashes of their fires and a torn leather satchel sewn with sinew and decorated with ostrich egg-shell beads.'

L. van der Post
*The Lost World of the Kalahari*, 1958, 189

The excavation of these settlements, which are often assumed to be the simplest of all, is complicated by the variety of ways in which they are organised; by the immense period of time during which they are known to have been made; and by the marked change in climate experienced by many parts of the world during this time. This means that no assumptions can be made of the nature of any settlement of this kind until its environment has been recovered. To do this should therefore be the first aim of the excavation. A second complication is that recent local ethnographic evidence is not a sufficient basis from which to approach this type of site, for it may well, especially in temperate zones, be quite inappropriate in the environment of the group being studied. Excavators must have prepared themselves by a wide general study of food-gathering techniques and cycles and of the material equipment of widely different groups and settlement patterns of as many hunter-gatherer communities as possible.[1] This is not to suggest that a post-excavation search for modern parallels should be undertaken, for any attempt to see close similarities between groups long separated in time or space is likely to be fruitless. The preparation should take place beforehand so that an excavator approaches a site of this kind with the widest possible appreciation of its possibilities. He will also need exceptional receptivity during the actual excavation if he is to understand the evidence of the slight remains which is all he can expect to find.

These remains might, from ethnographic analogies, suggest answers to the following questions:

*What was the nature of the settlement?* (e.g. kill site, snail, seed, root or fruit collection centre). This might be answered from the animal bones

G

or other food debris, from the weapons or tools, and other stone-artifact distributions.

*How long was it occupied and at what time of the year?* This may be answered from a study of animal and especially bird bones (for seasonal variety), pollen and plant remains, including charcoal.

*What was the size of the group?* This might possibly be answered from the plan of the whole settlement.

*What was the pattern of settlement?* Perhaps to be answered by studying the arrangement of shelters, hearths, cooking and working areas and middens.

*What was the daily routine?* Sleeping (study of shelters, beds or sleeping hollows). Cooking and eating (study of hearths and cooking areas, or middens). Relaxing (study of toys, gaming pieces, smoking equipment).

*Personal appearance?* Answered from a study of skeletons, clothes and ornaments.

*Religion?* (Discussed separately in Chapter IX.)

*What crafts were practised?* Stone working? Answered from industrial debris and artifacts. Wood-working? Answered from stone tools and surviving fragments of wood. Bone/ivory/antler/horn-working? Answered from debris, tools and artifacts. Leather-working? Answered from tools and surviving fragments. Basketry and thong-making? Answered from fragments and possible soil-impressions. Shell-working? Answered from fragments and artifacts (Chapter XI).

*Economy? Collecting* What was collected? Answered from food debris.

*Hunting* What was hunted? Answered by a study of the animal bones and a study of their proportions.

How was it hunted? Answered by a study of the artifacts, possible survival of traps, bows, etc. The kinds of animals hunted and their numbers may also help (e.g. mass slaughter or single animals).

Were the animals butchered where they fell or carried away? This might be discovered by a study of articulated bone groups or by finding only selected joints.

*Fowling?* Which birds were killed? Do they indicate a special season? A study of the bones might show migrant groups. How were they killed? Study of weapons (i.e. bird arrows).

*Fishing?* Was it river, lake, sea (inshore) or deep-sea fishing? To be established from a study of the bones, scales, teeth (species percentages important), and possibly boats. What techniques were used? Answered from a study of the objects.

Hunter-gatherer settlements are today usually temporary encampments either in the open air, or in the comparatively few areas in which these exist, in caves and beneath rock overhangs. The problems of excavating *Open-Air* and *Cave Sites* are very different and will be considered separately.

## OPEN-AIR SITES

Ethnographic studies show that in most cases hunter-gatherers make little disturbance of the areas in which they camp, even when the same area is revisited on many occasions, and have relatively few material possessions. Whilst therefore the thickness of occupation debris may well be not more than a few centimetres, it may consist of a number of

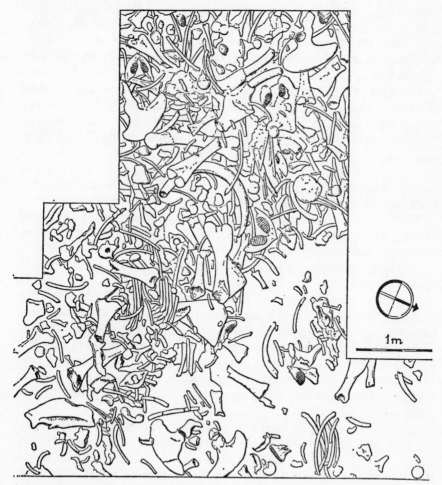

Fig. 15 Planning of the excavation of a hunter-gatherer camp-site, Dolní Věstoniće, Czechoslovakia.

consecutive settlements situated above or near each other and may cover several acres. Special circumstances may alter this pattern and produce elaborate and permanent settlements,[2] but these are very much the exception and are considered separately (Plate XVII).

Since sites are often occupied only for short periods and the debris left at them is very slight, all that normally survives will be concentrations of stone-knapping debris or bone fragments. Locating these sites is therefore very difficult. In some regions, particular geographical formations have been found to have been favoured at certain periods, and if some predilection is known then the search for sites can be intensified in those areas.[3]

Since sites are chosen for immediate and often quite ephemeral reasons (e.g. proximity to fruit-bearing trees or a kill), no logical search pattern for them can be suggested. Casual finds of sites may occur anywhere, but river or stream terraces or hill-slopes above valleys, especially those with a view of natural game funnels, may be especially searched.[4]

The most valuable types of sites will be those recognised in the sides of streams, ditches, quarries and pits of all kinds, for if found at any considerable depth, the settlement is less likely to be disturbed. The material might appear as a horizontal stratum of debris (bones, charcoal, areas of reddened stone as well as knapping debris).[5] If loose debris is found at the foot of a quarry face or stream bank, then the face itself, from which the debris may have fallen, rather than the valley or quarry floor, should be examined.

The far commoner but less rewarding method of finding sites is by locating spreads of debris by field walking after ploughing or when topsoil is removed (e.g. in advance of quarrying). Searches after rain are likely to be more fruitful, since stone will be washed clean and will show up better.

The great disadvantage of this kind of discovery is that the disturbance that made it visible has often destroyed its stratigraphy. Sites on slopes near dunes, or the edges of lakes or marshes (whether dried-up or no), have more potential interest than the others, for part may still be intact under later sand or silt accumulations.[6] Waterlogged sites are of particular importance because of the preservation of organic material, and if ancient lakes are known then the searching of their edges should be a priority.[7]

Few of the techniques used to locate other types of settlement (aerial photography, magnetometer, resistivity, probe or auger surveys) are likely to be of use here. It is possible that hollows were made in the ground and that these may show on such a survey, but it is unlikely. Augering can be used to establish the depth of the cultural accumulation.

## PLANNING THE EXCAVATION

Only through large-scale excavation can such a site be interpreted.[8]

If the area is a very large one and selective excavation is inevitable, then valley areas and the lower parts of slopes or lake-side where an overburden to the archaeological levels can be hoped for are to be preferred.

The reference grid (20 m. square) should be laid out over the whole area over which debris has been found and carried on as an interrupted grid along the main axes of the site at least 20 m. beyond the finds.

The excavation grid should vary with the size of the site but should be as large (10 m. squares) as possible. Test trenches along the main axes of the grid, down to but not through the highest cultural stratum, can establish the size of the site and allow more detailed planning. When features are located (hearths, hollows, etc.) intermediate baulks should be laid out to section them where they are best preserved.

When a well-sealed site has been discovered the first problem will be the removal of the overburden, very often of purely geological interest. This may be expensive and difficult, especially since only one dimension of the site will be known. If not too deep, the overburden should be removed by hand, since it may provide dating evidence for the levels below. If the overburden is very great, part of each layer in it should be dug by hand and the rest removed mechanically, a strict and continuous watch being kept on the machine since other occupation levels not visible in the exposed section may exist. It should be possible to align the trenches to the large grid (20 m. squares) and to preserve the section by drawing 2 m. at a time before removing them. Mechanical digging should be stopped at least a metre above a known occupation surface.

If the site has a long and complicated history, a number of settlements long separated in time may be found between or inside successive geological strata. The removal of the latter will follow normal archaeological principles (surfaces recorded, strata dug in 2 cm. levels, etc.), but the interpretation requires a quite different range of knowledge, and the excavator should either be a trained geologist, have one as an assistant, or arrange for one to visit when necessary. If this is not possible then he should at least be able to record, photograph and sample geological deposits so that they can be studied later. Human artifacts and bones of all kinds should be carefully noted and kept distinct from those found in the true settlement layers. The surface of strata and any temporary surface inside them should be studied particularly carefully, since it is here that settlements will be found.[9]

Land surfaces on which camping took place will often be recognised only by the concentration of stone-knapping debris, bone and stone artifacts, food debris (bones and shells) and fires or spreads of charcoal, ash and burnt stone (Fig. 15). The fires, and the spreads of burnt material from them, are particularly important for establishing the surface, since they may be distributed by wind or treading to some distances from the fires. The position of objects lying horizontally on the surface may also extend the recognisable surface. A stratum located in this way should be sampled to see if it represents the surface of an intact soil.

When established, the whole of the area of the occupation layer should be exposed in each trench without the removal of any archaeological material. All excavation must be by trowel, brush and knife, and only skilled helpers should be used. The surface should then be planned (a 10 cm. wire grid would be useful here) and photographed, the varying density of objects on, and any irregularities in, the surface being especially studied. From this study the next stage in the excavation should be deduced, for the hearths, sleeping-hollows, etc. described below may be identifiable. If no features and no changes in strata are recognised, the top 3 cm. of the occupation surface might be removed. The objects in it (including all fragments of bone and stone) should be collected from 10 cm. squares and be coded and bagged separately. All artifacts should be recorded three-dimensionally.

If local densities or horizontal spreads of stone etc. are found they should be uncovered without moving them and recorded in a series of plans, one for each spread. Samples taken from individual spreads might show botanical and other non-cultural remains.

If no densities are recognised in the first 3 cm., stripping by 1–3 cm. strata should go on with the same care in digging and recording until an archaeologically sterile layer is reached. The surface of this should be completely uncovered and studied for depressions and post or stake-holes which may not have been distinguished above.

Features (cooking, sleeping or working areas) should have temporary baulks set out across both axes and then be excavated on the quadrant method (page 213). Excavation should be 1 cm. strata and all soil should be sifted through a fine (50 mm.) mesh, as well as sampled for microscopic examination.

Special care will be necessary to recognise the depths and limits of the features. Perhaps only the angles at which objects are lying in them will define them.

*A cooking area* will probably be first recognised by charcoal fragments darkening an area of soil. A number of cooking areas are to be expected in any camping site and may consist of a complex of fires, middens and cooking-pits. They should be exposed, planned and photographed as a unit.

*Fires* should be easy to recognise from the concentrations of charcoal and the even longer-surviving reddening of the soil and stones nearby.[10]

Thin horizontal scraping might show the presence of *hearths*; deliberately made fireplaces usually of stones or clay. They should be
sectioned for a detailed recording of their construction and sampled for
magnetic dating and identification of the charcoals.

Methods of cooking and food-preparing may be deducible from the
tools and features found round them. Grinders, pounders, graters,
choppers and scrapers are to be expected. They should be planned *in
situ* before they are removed. Where a concentration is found, soil
samples from round about should be taken and tested for food remains.
It may be possible to detect stone or wooden spits and tripods beside
and over fires. Groups of burnt stones used in this way will easily be
detectable, but the presence of post or stake-holes round or near the
fire will only be recognisable by horizontal scraping, special care being
taken to note any angles of inclination. If groups of these can be linked
by their inclination, their position, or their filling, specific cooking
furniture may be suggested.

*Cooking Pits and Earth-Ovens.* If pits are found near the fires, their area
should be defined by trowelling and then they should be sectioned. If
they are filled with charcoal and have their sides reddened and burnt,
they may well have been used for cooking; their size may suggest what
kind of cooking. The filling should be sieved on a fine mesh for recognisable wood, bone and other carbonised remains.

*Middens.* Heaps of food debris, especially bones or shells, may be
found near the cooking area, especially if the camp was used over a
long period or revisited regularly.[11] They may be very large ($70 \times 10 \times 1$
m. high) and show radial or linear growth. In conditions favourable for
organic survival, all large patches of staining might be treated as
middens. If a midden is suspected, a quadrant grid should be laid out
over it so that on the main axis the surface profile is preserved. Tip-lines
and the way in which the pile seems to have accumulated should be
recorded, and the angles of rest of the objects should be noted. A special
watch should be kept for articulated groups of bones. In a large mound,
or pit, a special attempt should be made to recognise the chronology
of its accumulation. This may show in a study of the soil accumulation
between tips, variation in the rubbish, etc. Growth may have been in
one direction radially from the centre. If the midden was of any height,
its lee may have been used for camping, burial, etc. and it should be
watched for features of this kind. It may be possible to recognise special
types of midden from the material in them. Those with great bone
accumulation will emphasise the hunting aspect of the society and may
enable 'battue' sites to be distinguished.

Middens with a few bones may illustrate the gathering aspect of a
society. The middens are likely to be small since vegetable harvests
leave little rubbish. If a site is visited regularly piles of nuts or snail

shells (land or sea) may be found. No special problem arises in their excavation. Specialised coastal gatherers living largely upon shell-fish can leave very large middens as the result of many seasons' return to the same area. No special problems arise apart from their size in the excavation, but concentrations of specialised tools, limpet-scoops, fish-gutters, etc. should be looked for.

### WORKING AREAS

In camps there are sometimes special areas where the processing of various materials is carried on. These may appear during excavation as concentrations of stone-knapping, bone or ivory debris, or of specialised tools or sharpening spalls. Structures are unlikely, although stakeholes for leather-working might be found. The concentrations should be photographed and drawn before anything is removed since the distribution of objects may give a clue to the techniques involved. The excavation of these areas is discussed in Chapter XI. (Fig. 17.)

### TEMPORARY DWELLINGS AND SLEEPING-PLACES

In most modern hunter-gatherer communities, shelters are erected even for a stay of a few nights.[13] The simplest are likely to be straight or curved screens, erected on the windward side of the fire. Their only surviving trace might be short lines of stake-holes or stone walls. Careful trowelling of the original surface near the fires may show even the former. When sectioned, the angles at which the stakes were inserted and the fill of the holes should be recorded, since they may enable the type of windbreak to be reconstructed.[14] In specially favourable conditions the panels of woven branches or grasses might be found.

Lines of stones will be easier to recognise and excavate (page 124) and might be combined with stake-holes and screens.

More elaborate shelters might consist of a frame of stakes or posts or bones to which woven thatchings of grass and leaves were added. In excavation the pattern of stakes or posts in plan would be more elaborate, forming rectangles or ovals. The post-holes might even contain packing and be suitable for half-sectioning. The angles of inclination of the stakes or posts are extremely important and all should be sectioned and recorded. In especially favourable conditions thatching might survive as organic staining or even carbonised vegetation. Samples should be taken and may show the materials used.

Skin tents are an alternative to woven shelters and may sometimes be deduced.[15] If the trowelling of the surface of the settlement, in this case probably at some distance from the fires, shows patterns of post or stake-holes or even circular or rectangular settings of large stones, these might indicate the use of tents. Usually in modern parallels, a few large posts are used; these may be one or more central posts or lines with ridge poles. The height of the poles usually means that they are placed in post-holes or on stones rather than hammered in. Alternatively peripheral poles may be set into the ground at acute angles and lashed at the centre. Both of these patterns should be recognisable archaeologically. Pegs or weights are also used to hold guy-ropes and walls in place. Peg-holes should be recognised from the angle of inclination, which will be away from the tent. Stone, bone or even ivory weights may take the place of pegs and be found in lines round the circumference.[16] Possible additional features, such as sunken interiors and stone and earth walls are considered below.

*Earth and Stone Shelters* are still more elaborate types of shelter which may be built for cold or wet season occupation.[17] Some may utilise slopes to hollow out a small artificial cave, the front being extended by either a wooden framed shelter or an earth and stone wall on which a roof, also perhaps earth-covered, can rest. Others may merely be sited in the open. They may be first recognisable either from the lines of wall debris and post-holes or from the sunken interiors. If the walls and post-holes are recognised first then the method of excavation will be like the walls of much later houses (page 117), and the probable construction, especially reinforcement posts, original height, way in which they fell, etc., recorded. Care should be taken to search for entrances. The roof will probably lie on the floor and may survive as a stratum below the earth, stones and domestic rubbish which were piled on top. It should be carefully distinguished from the real floor (see below). A search should be made in it for fragments of rafters. Through the collapse of the roof the floor may well be intact, and in a structure of this kind it will be the most important part. In make-up (beaten earth, stone slabs, etc.) it may approach those of the more permanent houses described previously, and should be excavated in the same way. Hearths, beds, store areas, drains and even shrines may occur.[18] Objects lying on the floor should be drawn and photographed *in situ* before being moved.

Many shelters of this kind are sunk some distance into the ground and will be recognisable in plan as a discolouration in the soil. They may consist of a shallow pit, the soil from which is piled round the edges to make a low wall which supports the roof, and can be very large (20 × 5 m. by 1 m. deep) and irregular. Any large pit found should be treated as a potential shelter. When it has been defined and planned it should be excavated on the extended quadrant with temporary baulks along its main axes (page 213), and these should extend well beyond the visible edges of the pit, for there may have been walls of stones, sods, etc. These may be simple soil heaps from the excavation of the pit or properly built walls. The roof construction may show from post or stake-holes at the edges and in the pit, but the roof debris or absence of it will show during the clearance of the pit. It may have had a wooden frame, which the excavation and study of the post-holes (page 122) will reveal. It may have had a skin roof or solid roof covered with earth, turf and domestic rubbish. In the latter case the collapsed roof may be visible in excavation and a search should be made for rafters. An absence of roof details and the presence of many stake or post-holes at the edge of or in the pit might suggest a skin roof. This might be reinforced by finding outside the lip of the pit and even outside the wall a line of stones, bones, tusks, etc. which could have weighed down the edges. It is also possible that a drainage channel was dug round the outside along the line of the eaves. This should be excavated as described. As the pit is cleared its sides and bottom should be studied. The regularity or irregularity of the sides should be noted for recesses, steps, ladders and wattle or skin linings. The junction of the floors and walls should be especially checked for stake-holes which supported linings of this kind. The floor (beaten earth, stone slabs, etc.), when it has been distinguished from the collapsed roof, should be cleared and studied for features (hearths, beds, cooking areas, shrines, etc.). Objects found on it should be drawn and photographed *in situ* before removal.

Snow shelters may be mentioned here for the sake of completeness and for the reason that in times of widespread glacial conditions they may have been more common.

*Sleeping-Hollows and Beds.* These may be expected near fires with or without shelters. On modern analogies, slight hollows (1–2 m. in diameter and 50 cm. deep) may have been made and filled with bedding (branches, reeds, grass).[19] Careful horizontal scraping may recover these hollows, which should be recognisable in plan from the difference in texture and colour of the fill. Temporary baulks should be laid out on the main axes and the hollows dug on the quadrant method. In favourable conditions the bedding may survive and the fill should be studied for laminations and organic fragments; samples should be taken for layer analysis. Alternatively a pattern of stake-holes suggesting a raised platform bed might possibly be found.

Specialised camping sites connected with hunting may also be located. In *Battue Sites* animals will have been driven in large numbers to destruction at the hands of hunters, or perhaps over a cliff or into a swamp.[20] Excavation will be similar to other large middens (see above). During excavation very large accumulations of bones may be encountered, and the kinds of bones and the degree of articulation should help to distinguish the method of slaughter.[21] The greater the degree of articulation the greater the need for care in excavation, for broken and missing bones should be noted. All articulated groups should be drawn and photographed *in situ*. Control baulks should be kept to a minimum and large areas (10 m. squares) cleared. The presence of soil accumulation between bone strata should be looked for and sampled, since this may indicate periods between visits and so the presence of a series of drives. At *Kill Sites* a group of bones belonging to one animal may be found; the result of a single kill. The animal, if a large one, might well have been butchered and partly eaten where it fell.[21] Excavated on the quadrant method, this might be recognised by finding during excavation an incomplete skeleton. Articulated groups of bones from inedible parts (i.e. feet and lower legs) might be found. Missile points might also be found among the bones, and a scatter of choppers and knives, made for the butchering and then abandoned, found round about. A fire with spits might be found nearby (Fig. 15).

## ROCK SHELTERS AND CAVES

Overhangs of rock, *rock shelters*, are much more widely found, and on modern evidence more widely used for settlement than true *caves*. Their location and excavation provides different problems from open-air sites.

Rock shelters can be sought for systematically, for the areas in which they will occur can be predicted. Sites will be confined to the faces of cliffs or rocky outcrops, but since the collapse of overhangs is frequent, many sites may have been buried.[22] Where the overhang is still visible, the ground surface immediately beneath it and a wide area of hillside in front or below should be examined for debris. It may well be that the settlement is buried, and only on the slopes below will objects eroded out of it be found. Where no evidence is found on the surface but there is other evidence of a depth of deposit, the area beneath the overhang should be tested. Test pits should stop at the first signs of occupation material and give place to a proper grid of trenches.

Collapsed shelters can only be recognised if material from them has weathered out from the edge of the slope.[23] If loose material (knapping debris, charcoal, bone fragments, etc.) is found on the slope the area above should be examined, and the slope scraped in the area of greatest concentration, for beneath the loose surface scree the true stratification may be visible (Fig. 16a). Once located, the overburden of geological deposit should be excavated and studied as already described. These sites may also be located by regularly watching quarrying.

*Caves* are common only in those comparatively few parts of the world where soluble rocks are found, although rare ones may be found in all areas. On modern analogies they are lived in only in special circumstances (e.g. intense cold, heavy rain, when in a good look-out position). Settlement in a cave is likely to be in the area reached by daylight, inside near the entrance. The darker interior is more likely to have been used at night or in cold weather. The great importance of caves is that

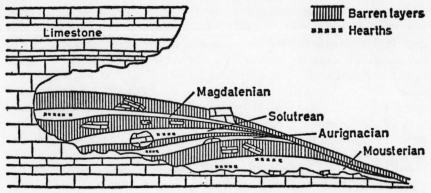

Fig. 16a Idealised diagrammatic section of a rock-shelter used by men in late pleistocene times in Europe.

remains of settlements in them are likely to be less disturbed, better preserved and better stratified than those in the open air. Ethnographic knowledge is of less than usual use in these excavations, whilst geological knowledge and general experience of excavation are of more importance. Because caves are rare, cave excavation is one of the most specialised techniques, and should only be attempted when the experience of the excavator and the resources available have been carefully matched to the site.[24]

The search for caves can be more logically ordered and their discovery is less a matter of chance than for open-air sites. It will be limited to certain geological formations (e.g. limestone), and likely regions can be systematically walked, driven through or flown over. Local information is likely to be useful and accurate. The present size of the cave is no indication of earlier size, and small caves in which there has been great accumulation may have more archaeological potential than large ones with little. Collapsed caves or caves with blocked mouths are much more difficult to find and will probably only be located fortuitously during quarrying, by local information or by trial-digging of suspected sites.

Once a cave has been located the assessment of its archaeological potential is still difficult. Roof-falls or other natural accumulations will usually have sealed all occupation levels other than the most recent, and unless the floor of the cave has been much disturbed there will be no signs of any ancient remains.[25] The spoil from any digging or from animal burrows should be carefully examined. If the cave floor is soft and not too stony (i.e. a water-deposited sand) then a probe, auger or echo-testing survey may give some idea of the depth of deposit above bedrock and an auger would even give some idea of the stratigraphy. It will not, unless charcoal is present, give any indication of human occupation. If the accumulation is stony these surveys will be impossible.

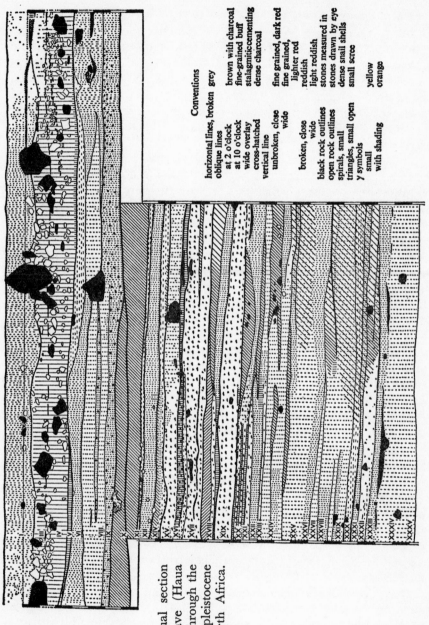

**Conventions**

| | |
|---|---|
| horizontal lines, broken grey | brown with charcoal |
| oblique lines | fine-grained buff |
| at 2 o'clock | stalagmitic cementing |
| at 10 o'clock | dense charcoal |
| wide overlay | |
| cross-hatched | fine grained, dark red |
| vertical line | fine grained, |
| unbroken, close | lighter red |
| wide | reddish |
| | light reddish |
| broken, close | stones measured in |
| wide | stones drawn by eye |
| black rock outlines | dense snail shells |
| open rock outlines | small scree |
| spirals, small | |
| triangles, small open | yellow |
| y symbols | orange |
| small | |
| with shading | |

Fig. 16b Actual section through a cave (Haua Fteah) used through the later and post-pleistocene period in North Africa. (Scale in feet.)

The area outside the mouth of the cave, or at the foot of the slope below it, should also be searched, for bones, stones and pottery may have been thrown or have been eroded out. If found, it may be possible to track this material back to its source. This is likely to be the platform in the open air immediately in front of a cave (the talus). This is often made up of materials linked with those in the cave (see Fig. 16), and if the slopes of the talus are studied and possibly scraped so that their stratigraphy shows clearly, then layers of settlement debris may be visible.[26]

If the situation of a cave is especially attractive, if for example it commands a game-funnel or a water-hole, and if no surface indications of settlement are found, then test pits are the only method of making sure that none exist. If it is decided to try test pits, they should be marked out near the entrance and on the talus within the framework of a grid. At the start, small ones (1 m. square) with a maximum depth of 60 cm. should be dug, and if occupation debris, especially ash or charcoal, is found then the test pit should at once be abandoned in favour of a proper grid of trenches. If nothing is found in the top 60 cm. the test pits should be enlarged to 20 m. squares before going any deeper. It should be kept constantly in mind that test pits are dangerous, they are too small for features to be recognised and can do much destruction to stratigraphy. Under no circumstances should a scatter of small deep test pits be dug over the cave. All test pits including sterile ones must be recorded in detail on the plan.[27]

## THE EXCAVATION OF CAVES AND ROCK SHELTERS

The layout of the grid in these excavations is particularly important, for space is restricted and the problems of spoil-disposal and safety are greater than usual. The grid, preferably not less than 2 m. square, must include, therefore, the talus as well as the interior and be so arranged that several sections are obtained on both axes of the site. Baulks should be kept wide at first since there may be a considerable depth of deposits, and barrow-runs or basket-carrying tracks will be needed to the exterior. Sufficient space must also be left outside for screening-frames and sieving.

If the cave is an ancient one and has experienced many climate changes, the human occupations will be interleaved between geological strata caused by widely differing events.[28] The removal and interpretation of these purely geological strata may well be the greater part of the work. Whilst the techniques of excavation will differ little from the archaeological (surfaces of strata to be exposed and recorded, layers to be removed in spits, etc.), the interpretation will require a specialist knowledge.[29]

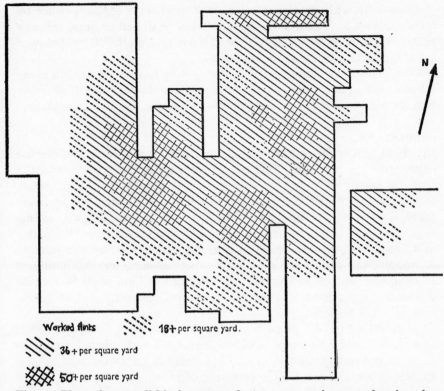

Worked flints     18+ per square yard.

36 + per square yard

50+ per square yard

Fig. 17 Plan of a mesolithic hunter-gatherer open settlement, showing the distribution of worked flint. Star Carr, Yorks. In the key each square of shading is in the proportion 1 : 115.

The occupation layers, as already mentioned, will be recognisable from the scatter of bones, stones, etc. on a near horizontal surface, and many of the objects should be lying horizontally. The stratum may be found on or inside a geological deposit and may vary in thickness from a few centimetres to several metres. If thick, it will probably consist of many thin superimposed settlement layers. Although the surface of the layer may be nearly flat, the base may be very uneven and fill interstices in the rock below. Its composition may be very mixed and patches of sand, ash and charcoal will be found. The latter, since ash and charcoal and burnt stones may be scattered far from the fire, are particularly useful as indicators of surfaces. The study and excavation of the settlement will be the same as for open sites and should be uncovered and dealt with in the same way.

The objects and features will also be similar to those found in the open-air sites (page 102), although in any constructions, stone may well be used more than wood.

Caves with wide entrances might well have these reduced either by a wall or a fence. The walls would probably be dry-stone ones, and any tumbled line of boulders should be treated as a wall.[30] Fences should show themselves by stake or post-holes.

Within the cave similar walls or fences may have been used to make partitions, and any group of stones on surfaces should be studied *in situ* both in plan and by temporary cross-baulks at intervals across them.

SPECIAL PROBLEMS

Bad light will make outside sorting and sieving necessary for internal cave settlement deposits. This should be a continual process, and the place of origin of each basket or bucketful should be known. Sieve-meshes will vary with the nature of the material, as will their arrangement. Dry loose deposit (sands and gravels) can be thrown against sloping screens or sieving frames on the leeward side of the site. Muds and silts, if wet, need to be hosed through against the sieves or panned in troughs. Conglomerates may need either breaking up with hammers or dissolving out in acid baths. All work of this kind must be carried out under supervision and special systems of recording will be necessary.[31]

Thought should be given beforehand to the need for special tools (e.g. crowbars for layers of boulders, hammers and chisels for conglomerates and stalagmites). Artificial light may be necessary, and so may timber or metal struts for the revetting of trenches. A light railway or conveyor belt may be necessary for spoil-removal. Safety may also require the provision of mining-helmets.

Although the sterile strata may be thick and the work hard, it is still difficult to use unskilled labour on this kind of site, for it is particularly important to expose the surface of any occupation levels, and these may be thin and difficult to locate.

The *Settlements of Pastoralists* will often be similar to those of hunter-gatherers since cloth or skin tents will often be used. For the kinds of evidence to be expected see pages 145 and 163.

## SUGGESTED READING

*Man the Hunter*★★, Devore, I. and Lee, R. (ed) 1968 (especially Clark, D. on Implications for Archaeologists).
*Habitat, Economy and Society*★, Forde, C. 1964. (Part I and IV. 18).
*Notes and Queries on Anthropology*★ BAAS 1962. 236–46.
*Guide to Field Methods in Archaeology*, Heizer, R. and Graham, J. 1967. 63 with good bibliography.
The presentation of a Cave Survey, Rennie, R. *SS* I. 2/3 1965.
Cave Sediments in Archaeology, Schmid, E. in Brothwell, D. and Higgs, E. (ed) 1964.
Archaeology and Shell Middens, Ambrose, W. *APAO* II/3 1967.
*Field Archaeology*, OS 1963. 20–25.
Observations on the Butchery Techniques of some aboriginal peoples, White, F., *AmAnth* 17. 1953 and 19. 1954.
Dolní Věstoniće, Klima, B. 1963.
The First Ground plan of an Upper Palaeolithic loess settlement, Klima, B. in Braidwood, R. and Willey, G. (ed) 1962.
*Star Carr*, Clark, J. G. D. 1954.
*The Haua Fteah*, McBurney, C. 1968.
*Das Altsteinzeitliche Rentierjägerlager Meiendorf*, Rust, A. 1937.

## NOTES

1. Forde, C. 1964 Pt. 1, p. 11–131, and Clark, J. D. in Devore, I. and Lee, R. (ed) 1968.
2. British Columbia provides some of the best ethnographic evidence of this. Forde, C. 1964. 69. Lipenski Vir (Jugoslavia) might be a European example. *ArcJ* V 1968.
3. e.g. The greensand in south-east England. *SASRP* 2 1950. For survey technique see *PPS* XXX 1964. 200.
4. Verteszöllös, *CA* 6 1965, or Cresswell Crags, Armstrong, A. in Linton, D. (ed) 1956.
5. Olduvai Gorge: Leakey, L. 1965. Torralba: Howell, F. 1968. 86–9. Meiendorf: Rust, A. 1937.
6. Star Carr: Clark, J. 1954. Kalambo Falls: Clark, J. D. 1969. Dolní Věstoniće: Klima, B. 1963.
7. Star Carr. (loc. cit.).
8. Orlogessalie: Howell, F. (ed) 1968. 109, and *PPACP* 1952 gives some idea of the size of the problem. Ismalia: *SA* 205 No. 4 1961.
9. Star Carr. (loc. cit.). Downton: *PPS* XXV 1959. 224.
10. *AmAnth* 4 1939. 189; *PPS* XXI 1965. 74f; Dyrholmen: Mathiassen, T. 1942.
11. Palo Seco: *YUPA* 50 1953.
12. For problems of shell-middens see *APAO* II/3. 1967 and *AmAnth* 4 1939. 189.
13. Forde, C. 1964 pt. I.
14. Kalambo Falls: Clark, J. D. 1969.
15. Ipiutak: *APAMNH* XLII 1948. Cape Denbigh: Giddings, J. 1964.
16. Kostienki: *Anthropologie* 1962. 562.
17. Dolní Věstoniće (loc. cit.) is a good example of excavation. Also Witòw: *PIM* (S.A. 6) 1961.
18. Dolní Věstoniće (loc. cit.).
19. Kalambo Falls, Clark, J. D. 1969.
20. Torralba (loc. cit.). Solutré: Combier, J. 1956.
21. On butchery techniques see *AmAnth* 17 1953. 189, and 19 1954. *PPS* XXXI 1965. 74. Mathiassen, T. 1942.

H

22. Heizer, R. and Graham, J. 1967. 63–4. For examples see: La Colombière: *PMB* 19 1956. Abri Pataud: *AmAnth* 68 2 1966. Combe Grenal: Howell, F. (ed) 1968. 136. Grotta dell'arma: *RSL* XXVIII 1962. Sandia Cave: *SIMC* 99:33 19.
23. e.g. Asprochaliko: *PPS* XXXII 1966. 10f.
24. The Haua Fteah: McBurney, C. 1968. For generalised comments see *SAM* 1945.
25. e.g. The Niah Caves (Sarawak).
26. e.g. Mount Carmel, Garrod, D. and Bate, D. 1937.
27. For the presentation of a cave survey see *SS* I, Pts 2 and 3, 1965.
28. For the significance of cave sediments in prehistory see Schmid, E. in Brothwell, D. and Higgs, E. (ed) 1964. 123. Also Wheeler, S. *AmAnth* 4 1934. 48.
29. e.g. Zeuner, F. 1952. 111–34.
30. As on Mount Carmel, Garrod, D. and Bate, D. 1937.
31. For a discussion of these problems see *AmAnth* 4 1938. 48 and *BNSS* 27/2 1965. 55.

## CHAPTER VII

# Problems in the Excavation of Isolated Dwellings, Farm Buildings, Fields and Roads

'Primarily the house of an English gentleman is divisible into two departments, namely that of the FAMILY and that of THE SERVANTS. . . . As outdoor departments or appendages, if any, there are the STABLES and FARM OFFICES. . . .

The FAMILY DEPARTMENT may be subdivided thus:
The Day-rooms. The Sleeping rooms. The Children's rooms. The Supplementaries (cloakroom, bathrooms and water closets). The Thoroughfares.

The SERVANTS' DEPARTMENT may be subdivided in this manner:
The Kitchen Offices. The Upper Servants' Offices. The Lower Servants' Offices. The Laundry Offices. The Bakery and Brewery Offices. The Cellars, Storage, and Outhouses. The Servants' private rooms. The Supplementaries. The Thoroughfares.'

R. Kerr. *The Gentleman's House; or how to plan English Residences from the Parsonage to the Palace.* 1864. p. 71

These problems are considered together because they are relatively simple ones and some of the solutions will be necessary to the excavation of all more complicated sites. This chapter should therefore be read in advance of and in conjunction with parts of Chapters VIII–XI.

## ISOLATED DWELLINGS

Dwellings are here distinguished by their permanence from the tents and shelters already described and although some may belong to hunters, gatherers or fishers, most will belong to farmers or to those dependent upon farming. They may vary from a simple one-roomed hut to a rural palace and be made of many materials, but all will have the same basic problems in excavation and only the scale of planning and execution will be different. All must be regarded as a unit of excavation, of which every part must be examined, for all rooms or related buildings must be excavated before the whole can be understood. This is best seen in a large house (Fig. 19 and 33) where the scale of the establishment gives each small part of the household its own quarters,[1] but in essence the same events take place in the one-roomed hut, and the excavator should recover from each as much evidence as possible.

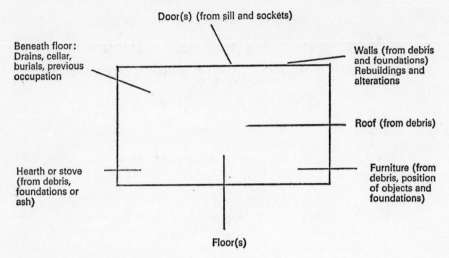

Fig. 18 Problems of excavating a room.

A dwelling of this kind will consist of living, sleeping and cooking quarters, perhaps with the addition of store barns, animal shelters and stockyards, religious areas (shrines and cemeteries) and industrial areas (threshing floors, mills and presses, smithies, weaving-sheds). This may mean that a series of grids will have to be laid down. In sites occupied for many generations, great depths of deposits and many superimposed building periods may be encountered, and this must be taken into account in the planning (Fig. 22).

LOCATING DWELLINGS

In irregularly cultivated areas, especially marginally useful land with little or no vegetation, surface indications of settlements may remain for millennia, and these areas in any part of the world will be particularly worth searching. The slopes of mountains, high plateaux, or areas of grassland or forest (especially after burning) lying fallow or waste are particularly likely areas.[2] When located, the surface indications are rarely completely comprehensible from the ground and 'shadow' aerial photographs may help. Direct recognition from aerial photographs in these kinds of country is also possible without preliminary ground surveys.

In cultivated country, above-ground features are unlikely to survive, and surface scatters of debris, potsherds, stone artifacts, bones and building materials found after ploughing or in casual excavations (e.g. ditches and stream-banks) will be the best guide.

These may be supplemented or even located through soil or cropmarks on aerial photographs, but much more care and long-term planning must go into their acquisition, than is necessary with shadow photographs.

In forested country or conurbations aerial photographs are, for the most part, useless. The discovery of sites must wait upon chance clearances (e.g. fires, road or railway clearance in forest) or constructions (e.g. building programmes). Recorded casual finds from earlier periods may be useful here.

In only a few cases does a preliminary air or ground survey give sufficient information on which to begin an excavation. A settlement area once located must be further tested by resistivity, magnetometer, probe or auger surveys or by a combination of them (page 28). These should provide a detailed pattern of features and will allow the logistical problems to be assessed before digging begins.

## EXCAVATION

Total excavation of the dwelling area should be envisaged. If the surveys have been successful it should be possible to lay down a grid of 15–30 metre squares over the whole area; separate grids within individual huts and rooms should come later. If the limits of the settlement have not been located by survey, the grid will have to be extended, preferably in an intermittent form before the main excavation begins, until the limits are found.

In any region the excavation of the settlement will resolve itself into the excavation of a series of buildings or rooms used for special purposes (Fig. 19).

*Living Quarters.* These may be connected complexes of many rooms, or one or more single-roomed huts scattered about a large compound;[3] each room or hut should be excavated as a separate problem (Fig. 18). Most regions will have their own styles of architecture, and an excavator must be familiar with the local idiom and building materials.

Huts built of *wood*[4] may often be recognised above ground by the remains of the non-timber footings which had supported the timber walls. These are often low (up to 1 m. high) and of stone or clay. They may survive as lines of tumbled stones or low banks of weathered clay, and when they appear through horizontal scraping, their regularity in plan should show their function. The surface debris will be less with walls of this kind than with complete buildings of stone or clay. On their exterior faces, the walls should be related to the original ground surface and drawn sections of the relationship preserved. This can be done if the whole external area is not cleared, by a series of short trenches dug at right angles to the wall and separated by substantial baulks. If, at the level of the old ground surface, the hut is defined only by a trench, this will mean either that the foundations were set below ground level or that only the robber-trench dug by later

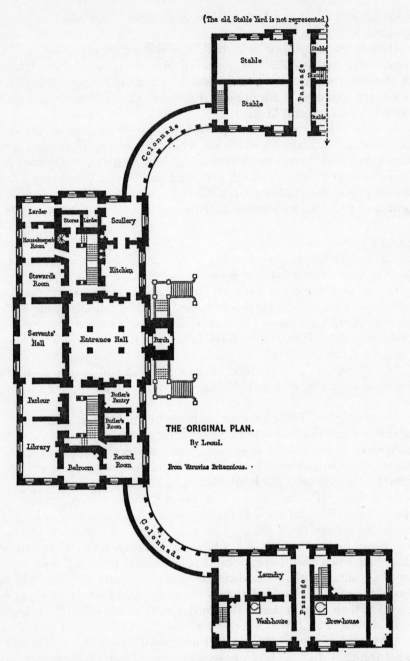

(The old Stable Yard is not represented.)

Stable

Passage

Stable

Stable

Stable

Stable

Colonnade

Larder

Stores

Larder

Scullery

Housekeeper's Room

Stewards' Room

Kitchen

Servants' Hall

Entrance Hall

Porch

Parlour

Butler's Pantry

Butler's Room

Library

Bedroom

Record Room

THE ORIGINAL PLAN.

By Leoni.

From Vitruvius Britannicus.

Colonnade

Laundry

Passage

Wash-house

Brew-house

Fig. 19 (*above and opposite*) Plans of a large country house. (Latham Hall, Lancashire.) To be studied as excavation problems; the use of individual rooms is particularly interesting.

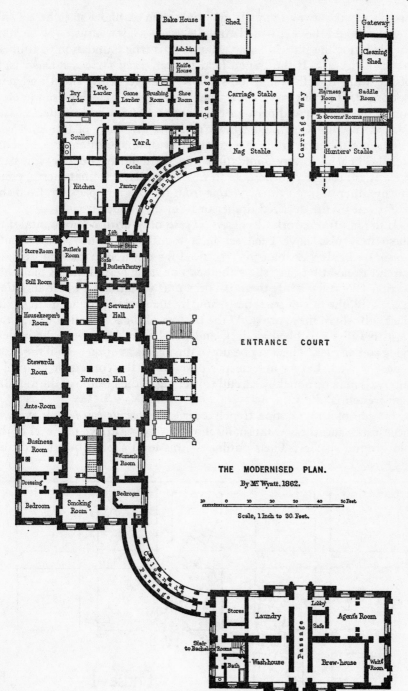

Bake House
Shed
Gateway

Ash-bin
Cleaning Shed

Knife House

Dry Larder
Wet Larder
Game Larder
Brushing Room
Shoe Room
Carriage Stable
Harness Room
Saddle Room

Passage
Carriage Way

Scullery
Yard
To Grooms' Rooms

Nag Stable
Hunters' Stable

Coals

Kitchen
Pantry

Passage
Colonnade

Lift

Store Room
Butler's Room
Dinner Stair
Safe
Butler's Pantry
Safe

Still Room
Lift

Housekeeper's Room
Servants' Hall

Steward's Room
ENTRANCE COURT

Ante-Room
Entrance Hall
Porch
Portico

Business Room

Women's Room

Dressing

Bedroom

THE MODERNISED PLAN.

By M.r Wyatt. 1862.

Bedroom
Smoking Room

10  0  10  20  30  40  50 Feet

Scale, 1 Inch to 30 Feet.

Colonnade Passage

Stores
Laundry
Lobby
Agent's Room

Passage
Safe

Stair to Bachelors' Rooms
Bath
Wash-house
Brew-house
Wait.g Room

people to take away the wall material survives. Short stretches of this trench should be excavated and its cross-section drawn at regular intervals, for the fill will show whether it is true foundation or robber-trench (Fig. 24). If the trench held the *horizontal foundation-timber* (sill) of the wall, it will usually be shallow, near-vertically sided and flat-bottomed. The fill may show the packing (stone, clay, sand, etc.) round the timber, and perhaps the wood itself will show, in decay, as a darker in-filling with nails still in position. In-filling of this kind will look quite different from that of either a drainage ditch or a robber-trench. The fill of any foundation trench should be treated with care since it is necessary to be able to say with certainty that sherds, coins or any other dating evidence came from the original packing, from the cavity left by the decayed timber or from the robber-trench.

If the hut framework was of *vertical posts* only, with no horizontal sills, these may also have been set in a foundation trench. This would normally be deeper than that required for the horizontal timber, and careful excavation may show the posts or their holes in both plan and section (Fig. 65a–b). If there is horizontal variation in the foundation trench fill, the line of posts may show by the packing round them or the dark soil where they rotted. At the bottom of the foundation trench the posts may have rubbed against, and polished or hardened, the under-lying soil or rock. This may be noted during excavation even if the posts have decayed. Larger and deeper posts set at the corners or at special intervals may be noted by careful trowelling of the bottom of the founda-tion trench (Plate v).

Instead of a foundation trench a series of *separate post-holes* may have been used, and these will usually show in plan or above the level of the old ground surface. Their outline at this level should be studied and

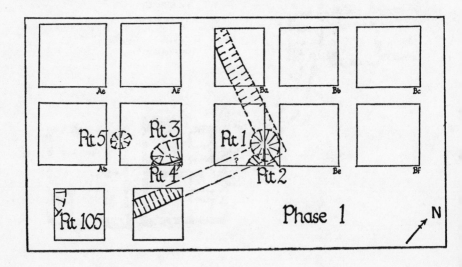

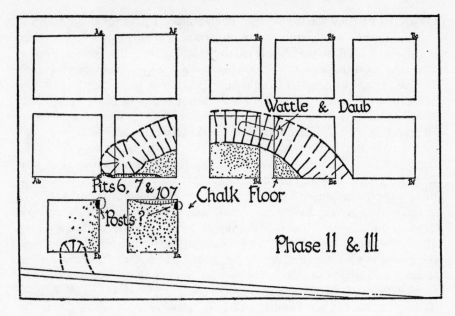

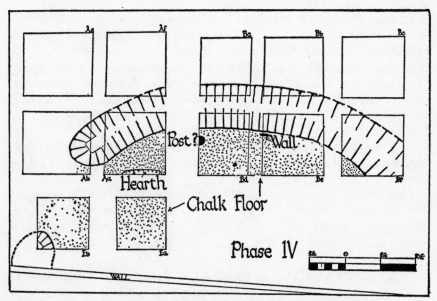

Fig. 20 (*above and opposite*) Plans of successive enclosures, Cambridge.

drawn before they are excavated. Their shape in plan may show, and if it is very irregular the possibility of several successive and intersecting post-holes should be studied. If so, the most recent one might show as a discolouration through the others.[5] Post-holes may be very large (up to 2 m. diameter) and, apart from their regularity in plan, only the nature of their filling can confirm that they are not ordinary pits (Fig. 25 and Plate v). All post-holes should be half-sectioned[5] and drawn. The following questions should be answered. Can the outline of the post be seen? What is its size and shape in cross-section? Did it rot in position or was it removed? Was it packed round with stones, clay, etc.? Even if nothing shows in the infilling it may still be possible to recognise the compression caused by the post-base in the bottom of the hole.

*Walls above ground.* Evidence of these can only be found in the stumps of walls already mentioned or from the scatter of material lying inside above the floor or on the old ground surface outside. Only careful recording of the stratigraphy found above the walls before they were located will give the information (Fig. 63). It should be possible to reconstruct the whole collapse of a building from the wall debris. Traces of the timber beams, wattling, grass or reed panels may be found with the plaster (lime, clay, pisé, etc.). The following questions are to be answered. Is the wall debris missing? If so was it taken away or merely scattered (e.g. by ploughing)? Does all the debris lie on one side of the foundations suggesting the way the wall fell? Did the whole wall fall at once or only sections of it? Was it burnt first? Does the debris suggest one or more storeys?

Lumps of plaster, especially where many lie close together, should be studied *in situ*, for both the smoothed facing surface and the rough back are instructive. The facing-surface should be studied for traces of painting, moulding or incising, and if these are found the whole group of related fragments should be raised together. From the back of the plaster, impressions of wattling, etc. showing the structure of the wall, may be recovered. Samples should be taken of the materials used in the building.

At some stage in the excavation, after the planning and photographing, standing stumps of walls should be sectioned and their construction noted.

*Chimneys:* Areas of burnt plaster among wall debris should be noted and if possible linked with burnt areas or fireplaces on the floors. These may indicate wall-flues or the chimneys of open fires, and both should be distinguishable from the shape and surfaces of the fragments.

Although the problems to be solved in *dry-stone-walled dwellings* are similar to those in wooden ones, a different excavating technique is required.[6] The first indication of a building will probably be a mound

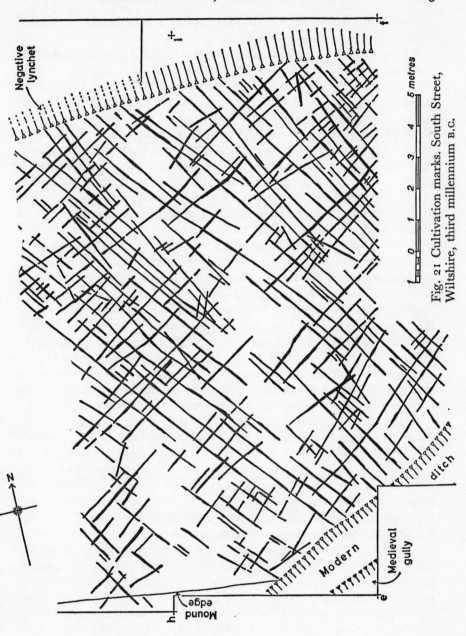

Fig. 21 Cultivation marks. South Street, Wiltshire, third millennium B.C.

or scatter of stones. This should be completely uncovered and studied before any part of it is moved (Plate x).

A heap of stones should then be dug like a burial mound (page 213) until walls are found. Since no mortar was used, the walls can only be recognised by the regular arrangement of the stones, especially those of the facing stones on either side of the core (Plate xvi). Careful horizontal removal of the stones beginning at the apex, should show this regularity in plan. If the faces are plastered, then this will also help define them. The total amount of stones found should be recorded since it may give some indication of the height of the walls. Once walls have been located excavation should proceed as for wooden walls. The stumps of stone walls will commonly survive and should be sectioned to show details of construction; types and sizes of stone; degree of shaping and method of arrangement.

Blocks or bricks of softer but still unmortared material, *clay*, *peat*, or *turf*,[7] are more difficult to recognise but should be treated in a broadly similar way to stone ones. The first indication of them may well be a low mound of weathered material which should also be excavated as a burial mound. Careful horizontal trowelling from the apex should show the edges of individual blocks of material, and the regularity of those laid for the walls should show.[8] Experimenting with brushing in different degrees of humidity and with different kinds of brushes may be necessary before the blocks can be separated. If their faces were plastered this should help define them. The amount of debris and the nature of the construction should be recorded as for stone huts.

A grid should not be laid down until the wall stumps are located. These should be more easily recognisable in plan than any of the other huts, for the regularity of the bricks, the straight faces of the walls and often the mud plaster on them should reveal them to careful trowelling. This may be enhanced by vigorous sweeping with a medium stiff broom which throws up the jointing of the bricks. Once walls have been established excavation should proceed in the general way described. The pattern of wall collapse and the size and construction of the walls should be recovered from the debris. Among the facts that must be recorded are the size and shape of the bricks, the kind of mortar used and the method of laying them, and the size and shape of foundation trenches. When planning and photography have been finished the wall stumps should be sectioned to show this. Alterations and additions will often show in plan at this point as changes in wall construction and angle, or in 'straight joints'.

*Mortared stone or brick* naturally make the most durable kind of buildings. Their excavation is broadly similar to that of unmortared stone, but there are a number of special problems.[9] Their special hazard is that the material is often deliberately removed and re-used by later peoples. They are more complicated to excavate than the others, for they are so durable that they stay in use over longer periods and may have been altered and adapted many times[10] (Fig. 22).

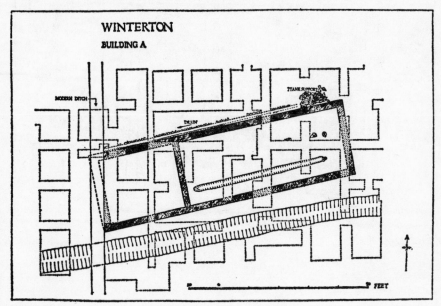

Fig. 22a

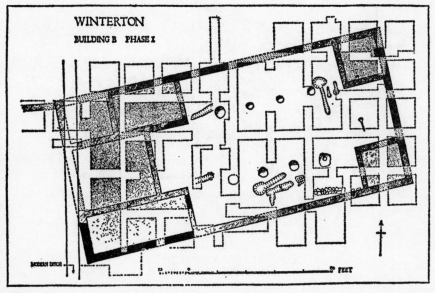

Fig. 22b

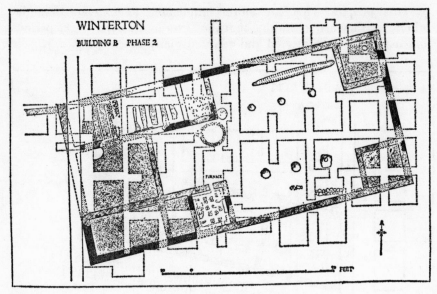

Fig. 22c

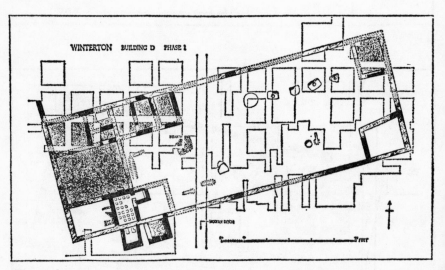

Fig. 22d

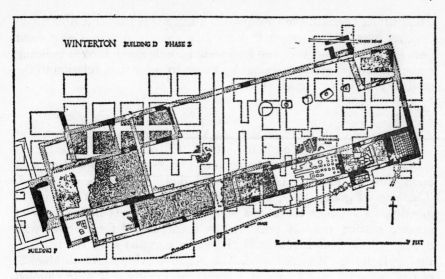

Fig. 22e

Fig. 22 Plans of successive rebuilding of a Roman masonry house, Winterton, Lincs.

Normally foundation trenches will be dug first and may be deeper and wider than in any other kind of construction, depending on the height of the building. Even in single-storey buildings they may well be 1 m. wide and 60 cm. deep with near vertical sides and a flat bottom. On this a layer of stones may be dumped, levelled, possibly at the ground surface, and rammed; the wall would then be set on top of this (Plate IV). Alternatively the wall might be built from the bottom of the trench. It will usually be set nearer to one face than the other and be packed round with stones, clay, earth, etc. Drawn sections of the foundation trench and its fillings should be made at intervals along the wall. The size and shape of the bricks, the composition of the mortar (sampled and then analysed later), the method of laying bricks, tile courses, etc. should be recorded in sectioning the walls. As already mentioned, variations in brick size and laying technique may help to distinguish different building periods. Standing and horizontal wall surfaces should be examined for plaster, possibly ornamented, and for panels of foreign stone. It is particularly important to locate *in situ* the position of fallen plaster fragments.[11] Chimneys and wall flues are particularly likely in houses of this kind.

The trenches dug by wall *robbers* may be considered here. They are the result of systematic digging along the walls, are either narrower or wider than the original foundation trench and have irregular edges, sides and bottoms. The lowest course of the wall or the footing may be found intact beneath the robber-trench since it is the most difficult to remove. The robber-trench is often at a slightly different alignment from that of the true wall, and its fill will include much broken building material. Drawn sections should be made to show it in relation to the original foundation trench (Fig. 52b).

## ROOFS

These may be of many materials, and various combinations of roof and wall construction may be found. Roofs will only be identified from debris found above or round the walls and floor and so will depend upon care in the recording before the dwelling itself is recognised. *Thatchings* of grass, straw, reeds, leaves, etc. are the most difficult to identify, for in most conditions none will survive. At best a layer of organic matter, possibly preserved in a carbonised form above wall debris, will be found. It should always be sampled since its structure may indicate the material used. The negative evidence of an absence of roof material might suggest a thatch, especially if it were coupled with a drip-trench 20 cm. or more from the outside walls. A drip-trench would normally be a shallow, narrow, V- or U-profiled, ditch with a naturally silted infilling. A row of stones found lying along and just outside the wall might also indicate that weights held down the thatch or turves. In some areas the roof may have been covered with a layer of sods of *turf* or *peat*. This will be difficult to identify unless actual fragments survive, for the remains will be similar to thatch. Local conditions and traditions might indicate which was the more likely. *Tiles* are the most easily recognisable, for the fragments will survive.[12] They may be of stone or baked clay and will be found as a layer above the walls and floors and surrounding land-surface. As soon as the layer is recognised it is important to plot the density, angles of rest and distribution of all the fragments and later to show in section their relationship to the wall debris. This will enable the following questions to be answered. Did roof debris lie under the collapsed walls? Was there a concentration of roof material just outside the walls? If so, do the angles of rest suggest that the debris slipped down? (If it did then the roof probably decayed whilst the walls were still standing.) Were different parts of the roof covered with different materials? Can this be linked with different kinds of wall construction?

The details of the tiles found should be noted; their method of hanging (wooden or metal pegs, tying, ledges, etc.) and all varieties of size and shape. It may be possible from this to reconstruct the ridging, gabling, etc. of the roof.

Houses of many kinds will have rows of *posts* or *pillars* inside to support the roof.[13] These should be recognisable at floor level and easily distinguishable, by their arrangement, from furniture supports.

*Wooden* pillars will be set either in post-holes (which should be excavated in the way described and checked for replacement) or set on stone or earth bases. Large stones (possibly shaped), piles of stones (mortared or unmortared) may be laid on the floor. If they have to bear much weight then the foundations of the pillar will probably be reinforced. A pit several feet deep and several feet across may have been dug, filled with stones, levelled and perhaps tiled before the pillar was erected. Such elaboration might be one indication of upper storeys. The shape of the pillar may show in the top of the base or post-hole. *Stone* pillars in more elaborate buildings may be shaped. If column drums are found their surroundings should be studied *in situ* for the rest of the collapsed column and its information about the collapse of the building.

## FLOORS

The floor of a hut or room will normally be the most revealing part of it, for the objects found will more often show how it was used than will the plan or the construction. If walls are still standing, a grid should be laid down inside the room on its axes as soon as the wall stubs have been recognised. The profile of the strata which accumulated with the room will then be recorded (Fig. 22 and 36). With the study of roof and wall decay this should show the nature of the last occupation and the subsequent history. When the highest floor level has been reached the whole floor should be cleared and the surface checked for features.[14] When these have been studied this floor should be removed to see that no earlier ones exist beneath it. If others are found the same processes should be repeated.

Floors can be of many materials, and after being studied and photographed they should be sectioned and the construction noted. The simplest are of *earth*, and will be recognisable by a hard surface crust, or perhaps some change in colour, or by sherds, bones and other objects lying flat. Sherds broken *in situ* and then not disturbed are an excellent indication of a surface. Floors of earth may be reinforced with straw or dung, or with specially imported material (ants' nests, clay, etc.). Contemporary ones are often patched, levelled and renewed regularly. They may be from 1–60 cm. thick. In the latter case they may represent many successive, possibly annual, renewals.[15] If this is the case they should be removed successively, special care being taken to record objects found sealed between them.

Other floors may consist of *Stone or Ceramic Slabs, Cobbles, Gravel, Tesserae, Sherds, or other materials* and may be laid with or without cement. They should generally be treated as the earthen floors but will be easier to recognise.

Some uncemented ones will require regular renewing like earthen ones; cemented ones are normally only made by advanced societies and are the easiest to recognise.[16] The methods of construction, perhaps with beddings of cement and gravel, should be carefully noted; also variations in the size and composition of the tiles, etc. Tessellated floors are perhaps the most elaborate type. If found intact, their cleaning, photographing and protection require special care.[17] They should be drawn through a 20 cm. wire grid and photographed in colour as well as monochrome. The greatest difficulty lies in raising them intact. Loose tesserae should be plotted on trench plans as they appear, since disturbed floors can be reconstructed from this evidence.

*Wooden* floors which were on or raised above the level of the ground are the most difficult to recognise, for most of the evidence will be negative. If the stump of the wall still stands then the slots for the ends of the joists may be seen. It is also possible that the floorboards or the joists may survive or show as a pattern of discolouration. If rows of post-holes or small stone or tile pillars are found these may have taken the place of joists (Fig. 23). Negative evidence suggesting wooden floors might be the unevenness of an earth floor, and an absence of hearths and other features (Plate xix).

### WINDOWS

These are difficult to recognise unless standing or collapsed walls are sufficiently intact for the actual openings to be seen. If the wall was of stone or brick the windows may have had special frames, and fragments of bars, mullions, glass and leading should be looked for. All glass fragments, especially coloured ones, should be carefully plotted, since it may be possible to reconstruct window patterns from them.

### DOORS

Doors can often be located by their sills at ground level or by gaps in standing walls. When only foundations below ground exist there is more difficulty, since the footings may have been continuous. Doorways can sometimes be shown from outside: a path crossing the foundation trench, but not the wall itself, might indicate an entrance.

### THE USES OF HUTS OR ROOMS

The uses of particular rooms can be suggested from the objects found lying on the floor and the permanent features (furniture, hearths, etc.) found in the floor when it has been cleared. Although sleeping, eating, washing and cooking may well take place in the same room it is convenient to consider the evidence of each activity separately (Fig. 28).

*Sleeping Areas:* Separate bedrooms may possibly be distinguished by the absence of cooking and other domestic debris and by the presence of built-in beds and bedding.[18] It is more likely, however, that an area within a room used for many purposes may be distinguished. *Beds* built up above the ground or resting on it may be found. If built up, there may be a platform of stones or earth against the side of the room, or post-holes and foot-impressions of the bed legs. If bed legs were of stone or metal these may also be found. If laid on the floor, curbs of stone or wood may have retained a pile of bedding (rushes, straw, heather, etc.), and the area should be sampled and sections taken from inside.

*Living Areas:* Separate day-living rooms may possibly be distinguished by their superior finish and decoration.[19] The walls may be plastered and painted, the floors better laid and the doors and windows carved. Evidence of furniture may also occur. If this was of wood then only from fragments found on the floor (especially metal handles, locks, nails, etc.) can this be suggested, but if the walls still stand or the furniture was stone- or earth-built more will survive. Cupboards may have been made in the thickness of the walls, and stone slabs used as tables. Around the walls solid earth or stone benches may survive, and on the floor fragments or impressions of mats or carpets. Fireplaces in temperate or cold climates are usually indoors and should be recognisable from the reddening of the earth or stones in and around them, and possibly by charcoal spreads on the floor nearby. The surface may have been smoothed over with clay and many times renewed. They are likely to be either in the centre or against a wall and may be linked with a chimney flue or louvre (Plate XIX). After the exposure and recording of the surface it should be sectioned and its construction noted. This should indicate if a pit was dug to prepare for it, if it had a foundation of stone or clay, and if it had a special edging. The edges of the hearth should be closely examined for post-holes and, if these are found, an attempt should be made to work out their function and relationship from a study of their angles and fillings. Those with similar fillings may go together to support chimney-pieces built out into the room from one wall, or an elaborate structure in the middle of the room.

Some elaborate buildings in temperate and cold climates may have the floors raised on pillars to enable hot air to circulate beneath them. This *hypocaust* system is usually sunk into the ground and may be recognisable because of this.[20] There will be floor supports—usually a series of low pillars not more than 1–3 feet apart, and the stoke-hole through which the fire which supplied the heat was fed. Charcoal spreads often reveal this stoke-hole. Excavation involves sectioning the stoke-hole and the passages between the pillars and establishing the nature of the floors above. Special attention paid to the infilling of the hypocaust may show the kind of floor that fell into it. It may also show whether this was the result of destruction or a collapse after deliberate abandonment. Objects from the in-filling should be treated with reserve, for they can rarely be used as more than a *terminus ante quos*.

*Cooking Areas and Kitchens:* Many societies at the present keep their cooking areas separate; this may be due to family organisation, religious necessity or fear of fire. From excavation it should be possible to identify these areas and also to recreate the whole cycle of food preparation.

Depending upon climate, cooking may be done in special huts, rooms, verandahs or open yards.[21] The uncovering of the floor of these areas may produce quite different debris, internal features and plans from sleeping-huts or huts used in other ways. Hearths, stoves, ovens, drains, food-grinding or pounding areas, store-bins, platforms and middens are to be anticipated. If one or more is found the others should be looked for.

*Hearths and Cooking Hollows:* The excavation of fireplaces has been discussed above, but hearths used for cooking should be especially checked at their edges for post or stake-holes which by their angling and filling might belong to spits, dipods and tripods. Samples of the fuel and samples for a magnetic examination of the clay (page 92) should be taken. *Cooking hollows*, pits in which charcoal was packed round food or pots, may also be found. These should be distinguishable from other kinds of pits but should be sectioned in the same way.

*Ovens* may be above or below ground. Those above ground will rarely be intact and will first appear as mounds of partly fired clay. These should be sectioned on the mound technique (page 124) until the stubs of the walls, recognisable from the smoothness of their inside surfaces, appear. The roof will normally have collapsed, and as the fallen lumps are removed they should be kept for an attempt at reconstruction or at least an estimate of the size and angle of the roof. The floors and walls will usually be fired hard by the heat of the wood burnt inside. When the door has been located the area in front should be examined for the stoke-hole, often in a shallow pit full of charcoal. Samples of the fuel and of the clay (for magnetic examination) should be taken. After planning and photography, the construction of the oven below its floor should be recorded by sectioning. It may well have been set in a pit filled with clay, have been stone-lined, and often repaired. If it was in an open yard the area round should be searched for post or stake-holes belonging to a shelter over it.

*Stoves* may be permanent or portable. Permanent ones will usually be of clay fired hard by much heating, and any heap of burnt clay found on a floor should be exposed and then sectioned with this possibility in mind (Plate XIX). Most of the remarks made about ovens apply here, but some kind of a flue and upper seating for vessels are to be expected. All fragments should be examined for smoothed exterior surfaces, for reconstruction may be possible. Portable stoves or braziers, of pottery or metal, should be expected and looked for.

Below-ground ovens will resemble cooking hollows, but will differ in the intense reddening of their sides and the possible linings of clay or stones. Collapsed roofs of clay should be looked for. They should be sectioned like pits.

*Grinding or pounding areas* will normally be recognised only if grindstones or pounders were used. If so, then the lower stones (either nether quern-stone or mortar) may be found *in situ* in the floor, and upper quern-stones, rubbers or pestles lying nearby. Broken and discarded stones also may be found. The area, especially if it contains any drains or runnels, should be carefully searched for grains and seeds. If it is in the open, stake or post-holes should also be searched for, since some kind of shelter is likely.

*Storage bins and platforms* either for grain or water may be found in a kitchen if there are no separate store huts. The platform will only be recognisable through post-holes or low earth or stone accumulations with revetments. If the containers were pottery, the sherds (probably large and coarse) and possibly impressions of the bases of the pots on the bench surfaces may be found. Wood, basketry and earthenware might also be used.

## DRAINS

These may be found in or under floors. Channels cut into floors are easily located and should be excavated as ditches (page 227). They should be traced outside the hut to see if there is a soakaway, and their fill carefully collected and examined for food debris.

A drain under the floor can only be attributed to its proper floor level if the entrance to the drain is carefully excavated. It too should be traced outside the hut and its fill carefully sieved. In elaborate buildings drains may be lined with stone or cement or carry wooden pipes. These features should be preserved in temporary cross baulks so that they can be drawn and photographed.

## LAVATORIES

Washing and excreting habits vary greatly, but the provision of special rooms and areas should be looked for.

*Bathrooms* might be distinguished by drains or a built-in bath. The floor may well be dished towards the drain and water jars or their impressions in the floor may survive.[22]

*Latrines* may have been provided in or near the house and, if pits were dug, may be distinguishable in shape (often rectangular) and depth from other pits. The edges should be examined for timber slots, and large samples (5 kgs.) of the fill taken.

Sampling of latrine sediment has been a much-neglected aspect of field work, for much nutritional and environmental evidence might be recovered from it.

## FARM BUILDINGS AND FIELDS

Preparations for excavation of farming units must, more than for any other kind of site, be made in the light of ethnographic evidence. All excavators should have considered the pattern of questions posed by ethnologists when reporting on farming[23] and have studied those ethnographic reports which are relevant to their local conditions.[24] In areas where simple subsistence farming, either nomadic or settled, still exists, farms and villages should be visited and their layout, construction and economy studied. Known but deserted sites of such settlements should also be visited and perhaps trial-trenched so that their appearance in decay is known.[25] In lands where subsistence agriculture no longer exists there may be published accounts of it in the reports of visitors.[26]

The aim of excavation will be to recover the complete pattern of life (daily and annual); the details of the economy and equipment; the date of foundation; the succession of events and the date and nature of the abandonment. To do this, the general traditional methods of excavation are insufficient, for it will not be enough to uncover, with great care, the main buildings. Throughout the excavation, the possibility of interpreting the buildings, pits, yards and fields through the evidence of plant, insect, mollusc and animal remains must be in the forefront of the excavator's mind.

### PLANNING

Since farming settlements can be very extensive and the field systems connected with them much more so, planning must be done particularly carefully. If the settlement is a small one, total excavation, or if large, selective excavation must be envisaged, but in either case provision should be made for work on the fields and stockyards, as well as the buildings. Whatever the settlement, a number of campaigns should be anticipated (Fig. 27).

The problems may be considered under two headings:

(i) *The Farm buildings:* the dwelling house or houses, the produce stores and animal shelters and the industrial areas (Fig. 28).

(ii) *The Estate:* the fields, roads, outlying produce-stores, animal-pounds, watchtowers or other buildings (Fig. 29).

The dwelling house has already been considered, and in a farm either near or actually joined to it the buildings and enclosures connected with agriculture and/or stockbreeding should be located.

Fig. 23 (*opposite*) A Roman granary and subsequent tile kiln, South Shields, Durham.

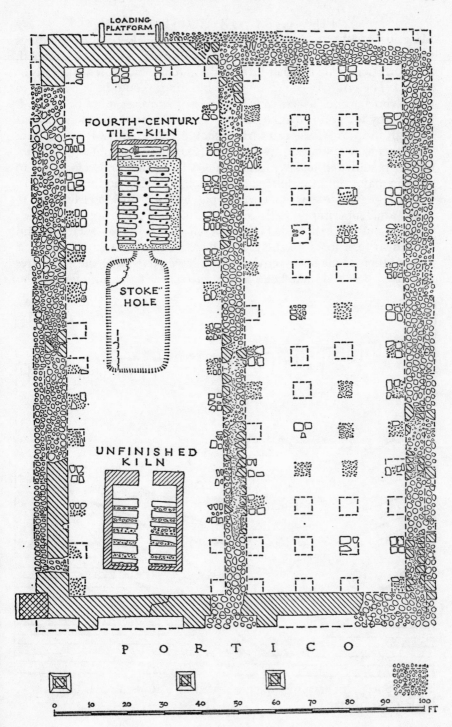

LOADING
PLATFORM

FOURTH-CENTURY
TILE-KILN

STOKE
HOLE

UNFINISHED
KILN

P O R T I C O

0  10  20  30  40  50  60  70  80  90  100
FT

## THE YARD OR COMPOUND

Most farms will have one or more yards, either enclosed by its buildings or adjacent to them (Fig. 27). These may be extensive and be bounded, for protection against beasts or men, by ditches, banks, fences, walls or hedges. The grid of trenches over the buildings should be carried up to this perimeter and, in test trenches, beyond it; care should be taken, if need be by temporary baulks, to preserve and record complete sections through the yard. The yard surface should be recognisable either from reinforcements of stones, gravel or sand (sometimes thickest at entrances, doorways and well-heads); from changes in texture and colour due to organic matter and trampling; or from objects lying horizontally on it. Parts of the yard may well have been patched or resurfaced from time to time, and superimposition, perhaps with objects trapped between surfaces, must be expected (Fig. 24). Each surface should be cleared and studied in turn for domestic and industrial features may be found on them. Much of the farm activity would have gone on in the enclosures and many post and stake-holes (some perhaps for tethering), foundation

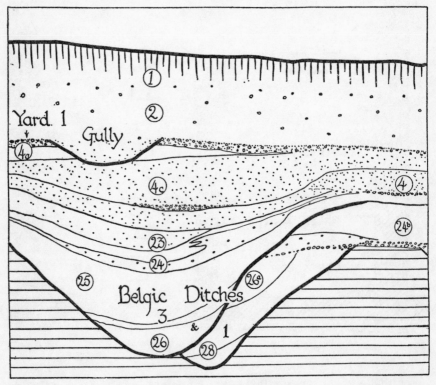

Fig. 24 Successive enclosure ditches, sealed by a Roman yard. Cambridge. Scale 1:27.

trenches (sheds), pits (rubbish and storage) (Fig. 25), wells, ditches, fences and ponds must be expected. The *post-holes* and *stake-holes* should be excavated as described on page 122. From their infillings and shape it may be possible to pick out groups which are so similar that they go together, and perhaps to recognise some of the structures as pens, drying or storage racks, threshing areas, industrial or cooking shelters. The *pits* (excavation discussed on page 212) may also from their shape and infilling be recognised as quarry, storage, latrine or rubbish pits. In some cases their relative chronology may be established. *Wells* should be dealt with as pits.

*Ditches* (excavated as on page 227) may by their intersections show a relative chronology and whether, by repeated cleaning out, etc., they were long-established drains and boundaries (Fig. 24).

Since much cooking is done out of doors, special care must be taken to search for outdoor kitchens under verandahs, along enclosure walls, or in separate shelters. A yard surrounded by buildings should be examined especially carefully for domestic evidence.

In an isolated farm many industrial processes may be carried on in the compound. Special huts, rooms or areas may be set aside for them, and this possibility should be kept in mind when unusual features or complexes of objects are found. Potting, spinning, weaving, smithing and leatherworking are the most likely to leave traces. The characteristic debris and hut or room layouts of these occupations are discussed in Chapter XI. The more distinctly farming processes of *Threshing, Winnowing, Drying*, etc., will leave other traces and can be discussed here.

Any hard flat area, especially if its surface is dished and exposes the surface of bedrock, should be studied with a *threshing* or *winnowing floor* in mind.[27] If it is circular a search should be made for a central tethering post. In a large store building, a hardened area of this kind, especially if between two doors, might be for threshing or winnowing. Excavation should be on the quadrant method and samples should be taken.

*Drying racks* might exist but will be difficult to recognise since pairs, triangles and rectangles of post-holes cannot certainly be claimed as these. If sets of post-holes of similar size and infilling are found, the possibility should be considered.

*Crop-drying kilns* should be more easily recognised, especially if they are partly sunken into the ground.[28] The stake-holes, floor supports and circulation channels may survive. They should be excavated like a hypocaust system (page 131) and special care should be taken to search round post-hole groups or on floors for carbonised grain. The channels may well be revetted with stone or clay and, when cleared and recorded, should be sectioned to show the construction and to search for dating evidence in the foundations.

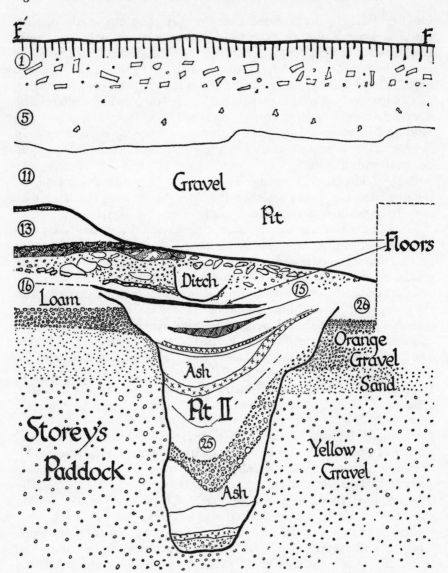

Fig. 25 Roman rubbish pit with house floors above, Cambridge. Scale 1:27.

The foundations of *presses* may also be found and should be distinguishable. Oil or wine is the most likely harvest and the press might be hand- or animal-worked.[29] Circular or rectangular foundations of considerable strength are likely, and the base of the press may well have been raised on a solid earth or stone foundation. The whole may therefore survive as a mound, should be excavated as such (page 214) and may show itself by the exterior wall of the base and the central post-hole. A path might surround it and a building of some kind, located by extending two opposed quadrants of the grid, be found. A careful watch should be kept for pips or seeds, and soil samples should be taken for analysis.

*Animal-, water- or wind-driven mills* may be used on a large farm, but are more likely to serve an area. They should be recognisable by the size of the mill-stones and the nature of the superstructures.[30] Animal-driven mills might be distinguished by the path worn by the animal in rotating or pulling them and, like wind and water mills, are elaborate structures normally serving more than a single farm.

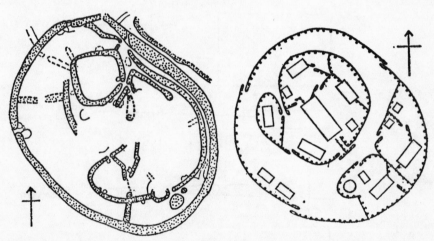

Fig. 26 Ground plan of a palace/shrine, Zimbabwe, and a ground plan of the Lyangamba of the Paramount Chief of Barotseland, Lealui, for comparison showing the planning of stone and reed walling, and the necessity of knowing the ethnographic evidence.

*Store huts* are difficult to recognise[31] unless special constructions were used to gain protection against damp, insects and rodents. These may take the form of a raised floor supported by a pattern of post-holes, low parallel walls, or pillars similar to those described for hypocaust systems (Fig. 27). The absence of domestic debris, taken in conjunction with the other evidence, may also be significant. Large clay or wooden bins, or baskets, may have been kept inside the stores, and fragments or impressions of them or of the platforms, or the depression in the floors on which they stood may be found. The area of the store should be searched for carbonised plant-fragments, and rodent and other bones; soil samples should also be taken (for details of sampling see page 91). Some crops, especially grass, may be stored on raised circular or square *platforms* of earth or stone *c.* 1 m. high.[32] Similar platforms might have been made of wood and would leave post-holes; careful study of the post-hole fills, particularly at the bottom, may show traces of carbonised plants and pests (see Chapter V). *Storage pits* may be used in dry areas or where the crop is parched before storage. They vary greatly in depth but may have quite small mouths. Sometimes they may be distinguishable by being well finished inside with smooth walls and a flat bottom, or by being lined with stones or wattling[33] (Plate XIII).

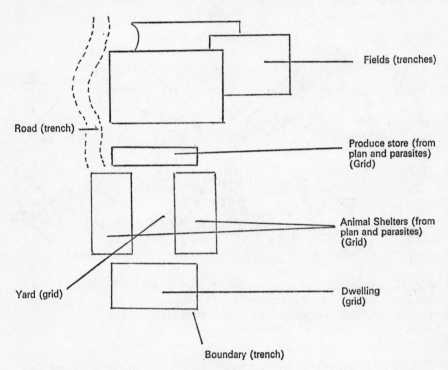

Road (trench)

Fields (trenches)

Produce store (from plan and parasites) (Grid)

Animal Shelters (from plan and parasites) (Grid)

Yard (grid)

Dwelling (grid)

Boundary (trench)

Fig. 27 The problems of excavating a farm.

*Animal shelters* may be part of the same building as the human living rooms or be separate constructions, and any room or hut without domestic debris might have been for stock (Fig. 27). They should be excavated as dwelling houses. *Byres or stables* for large animals may have separate stalls and mangers recognisable by post-holes or stake-partitions. The floors may also be dished, reinforced with stones at the entrance, or provided with drains so that manure may be collected.[34] Samples of any drain sediment should certainly be collected and examined for dung fragments, parasite eggs, insect remains etc. If a byre is suspected and the doorway located, the area immediately outside the door on either side should be examined for a *dung heap*.[34] This may appear merely as extra organic blackening, in which case samples should be taken, or as a walled or revetted area. Sherds and other rubbish are likely to be thrown into it.

*Stockyards:* These may be distinguishable by the fences round them and the trampled and dung-enriched areas inside.[34] They should be sectioned on the quadrant method, their full extent determined, and the soil within sampled.

*Pens, sties and runs* for smaller creatures (goats, sheep, fowl, pigs) may be more distinctive and include a small hut and run. Samples of the floors should be taken for distinctive dung and parasites.

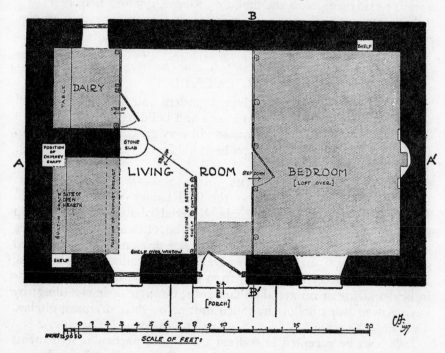

Fig. 28 Plan of a deserted peasant farmstead, to be considered as an excavation problem. The stippled area is ceiled—or vaulted; the rest open to the roof. Llain-Wen-Isaf, Wales.

## THE FARMYARD PERIMETER

This may be defined by an edge to the yard metalling and the occupation debris, but more usually by a ditch with bank, fence or wall (Fig. 20). Once its existence has been established, it should be excavated as a separate problem, the technique being that described for similar military defences (page 230).

If a ditch is found a search should be made for a solid causeway across it (Fig. 20), and efforts concentrated on the entrance and on intersections with other ditches and banks. Especial care should be taken to look for signs of recutting or cleaning out (Fig. 24) and traces of walls, fences or banks which have collapsed suddenly or silted slowly into the ditch (Fig. 38). A grid should also be excavated over an area on the inner lip of the ditch, preferably on either side of the entrance to search for a bank, wall or fence. A bank, even if it has been deliberately levelled, will probably leave some trace. A wall or fence might be an alternative or complement to the bank and might survive as a series of post or stake-holes or a wall stub. A hedge may only be suggested by negative evidence unless the mollusc or insect remains help here.

The entrance and causeway, gridded in the usual way, may give evidence of metalling and gates.


## THE ESTATE

This is here defined as the cultivated gardens and fields, pastures and woodlands, with their communications and buildings.

The degree of recognition possible will vary greatly from one area to another, but search should always be made for it (Plate III and Fig 34).

### LOCATIONS OF FIELD SYSTEMS

In areas of marginal cultivation, the field baulks or lynchets of field systems may survive for millennia.[35] Aerial photographs may help locate them in areas of minimal vegetation, but elsewhere other methods, for example surveys of reconstituted forest[36] or examination of buried ground surfaces,[37] may be necessary. Some indication may also come from *roads* or *tracks* leading away from the settlement. These may show in field-walking or on aerial photographs; through their metalling; by having been worn hollow by much use; or by their drainage ditches. They must be traced as far as possible and excavated (page 147).

*Fields* can be accepted as contemporary with particular settlements only if they can be shown to be undoubtedly related to the settlement by the road or ditch systems, or if some absolute method of dating suggests it. In regions and periods where permanent or semi-permanent field systems were set up and cultivated regularly the baulks dividing the fields (lynchets) could become, through the addition of weeds, stones, soil movement, or spoil from drainage channels, up to one metre.[38] If they exist they should be accurately planned with special attention to gateways and roads. Since a system may extend over many acres, and be quite different from the present field pattern,

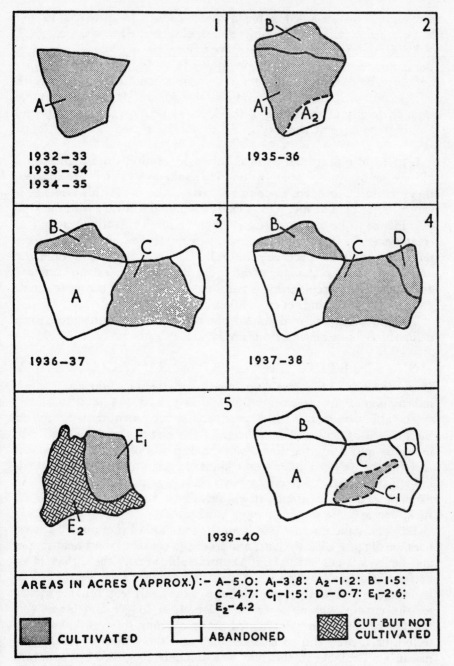

Fig. 29 Plan of a field system, Lamba, Zambia, showing growth, over eight seasons.

any survey must be aided by magnetometer resistivity, probe and auger surveys which can give the courses of ditches, buried roads, etc.

Excavation will have to be selective to solve particular problems; e.g. the intersection of two baulks or ditches to show which was the older and large baulks, ditch-fills near settlement or road intersections which might contain dating or environmental evidence. It may be possible from the study of the shape of the fields in relation to the roads and buildings to suggest the way in which the cultivated area developed (Fig. 29).

If areas of old ground surface buried by erosion from higher up a hillside or by dumping for a mound, bank, baulk, etc., are located, they should be gridded, since in all parts of the world this evidence is rare[39] (Fig. 21). The methods of excavation used will vary with the kind of evidence to be expected (e.g. plough or hoe cultivation, mound or ridge systems). In all cases therefore a general idea of the date of the settlement will be necessary beforehand, since crops and domestic animals have often changed greatly (e.g. in much of West Africa maize and cassava have replaced yams as the main crop, and the agricultural patterns for both kinds of cultivation must be known).

The husbanding of wild animals should also be mentioned here since deliberately built *rabbit warrens* are known.[39]

## INTERPRETING THE AGRICULTURAL ECONOMY

If care is taken in the excavation of the settlement and the estate much information about the economy should be gained.

The ability to gain it will depend, as has been mentioned before, on the general agricultural knowledge of the director and his ability to recognise and bring together many small pieces of evidence. He must therefore be well grounded in the kinds of agriculture and stock-breeding still practised, or likely to have been practised in the region. In *temperate zones*, for example, it will have been based on either digging stick, hoe or some form of plough cultivation.

This can sometimes be told from the tools found (i.e. plough-shares, hoes, or digging stick weights, and from the contemporary field-shapes and surfaces.[40] For example, if a considerable area of the surface of an ancient field can be exposed, it may be possible to see *plough furrows*, and these related to the size and shape of the fields (e.g. roughly square for the cross-ploughing of scratch plough, or longer and larger rectangles for the more complicated ploughs), may show the ploughing technique used.[41] Buried surfaces may also show signs of marling or manuring. Drainage ditches may be found and recognised by the nature of their vegetation and molluscs.[42]

The area under cultivation may be suggested if a large part of the field system has been located. If the size of the field system can be related to the storage capacity of the farm, then possibly crop yields and fallow or pasture provision can be suggested.[43]

The need for protection of the crop during growth might be suggested by watch-towers or shelters on the edges of the fields or by field fences or walls.

*Digging stick, Hoe or Spade* cultivation might leave quite different traces both in the mounding or ridging and in the shape of fields which might well be smaller and less regular than ploughed fields[44] (Fig. 29).

The *crops* grown can only be known if the actual remains of plants (seeds, pollen, leaves etc.) or those of parasites (insects, bacteria and snails) have survived (see Chapter V). These are likely to be well preserved in extremely dry or extremely wet circumstances, but may survive in many less favourable conditions, and samples from likely areas (kitchens, storage huts or pits, drainage or irrigation ditch silts) should be taken as a routine.[45] Additional sources of evidence may be food remains in the bottom of pots and the matrices of seeds, stalks and leaves preserved in pottery or tiles made nearby.[46] A series of pollen samples from nearby ponds or pits which had contained standing water can be important.

Deliberately planted and tended trees or bushes (apple, olive, coconut, etc.) can sometimes be recognised from pips, seeds, husks or fruit stones as well as pollen. Tree boles and horticultural beds may also be recognised,[47] and their purpose perhaps proved by the evidence of pollen.

Additional evidence may come from the methods of *processing and storing* crops.

Reaping methods can only be suggested if reaping tools are found,[48] but preparation by threshing, winnowing and dehusking may leave evidence, as may drying racks, and oil presses (page 138).

Storage may be proved by the discovery of store huts, platforms, pits or clamps, their form depending partly on the crop and partly on the traditions of the community.

*Animal and bird husbandry* can also be studied from a variety of evidence.[49] From a study of the surviving bones, horns, antlers and teeth, of which all fragments found should have been kept with as close an attention to stratigraphy as human bones, it should be possible to estimate the relative importance of husbandry and hunting, the domestic species kept and how they were fed (the presence of haystacks might well indicate hand feeding for example).

Evidence of some degree of movement (*transhumance*) either of stock or people may be recognised both from a study of the settlement and from the plant, animal and bird remains. A statistical analysis of the age and sex range in a herd might suggest movement and slaughtering or castration policy.[50] How and when were they sheltered and the degree

K

of human control might also have been discovered from the excavation of byres, pens, sties, or yards and the discovery of mangers, weaning rings, blood-letting arrows, etc.

The evidence of how and when animals were killed will usually only come from a study of the bones, which can show axe or knife marks and may be able to give the age at death. Concentrations of bones, especially those of articulated and largely inedible fragments (e.g. lower legs and feet, lower jaws) found in excavation may indicate slaughter areas.

Agricultural techniques in the *tropical zones* may well be very different, and the kind of cultivation to be expected in a particular area must have been studied beforehand from ethnographic evidence. Cultivation by ploughing, for example, is much restricted and most will have been by hoe and/or digging stick. These, like the plants themselves in the tropics, will leave little durable remains, and it is only from the old land surfaces and the environmental evidence that the economy might be established.

In some parts of the tropics irrigation is likely and provides in marginal land the kind of evidence already discussed in temperate field systems.[55] Besides the actual channels, perhaps recognisable by their vegetation and molluscs, dams, gates and watering points may be found. Terracing is also often resorted to for irrigation. An examination of the soils from terraces may, like the excavation of lynchets in temperate areas, give some indication of the crop.[55]

As an example of the kinds of evidence to be sought, Yam (*Dioscoreacae*) cultivation may be considered.[51]

Scatters of stone tools, already reported from the tropical forests in all three continents, have been found in West Africa concentrated in areas of several acres.[52] Where these have been found at some depth (up to 10m.) below the present surface they might well be where the lower slopes of hills or valley bottoms have been covered by erosion.[53] This erosion itself might, in some areas, be the result of clearance for agriculture. The buried land surface might perhaps be identifiable from a scatter of charcoal (from forest clearance) or from a scatter of stone tools left after cultivation. Its status as a true soil could be checked by analysis. If it had been cultivated for yams, the mounding-up during growth and the pits dug to harvest the crop might well survive and be revealed by area excavation. Really careful excavation might even be able to distinguish pits cut through the mounds. To carry the study further, not only should the appearance of cooked and uncooked tuber-fragments, the structure and silica skeletons of leaf and woody fragments of yams be known, but the total vegetation pattern at different stages during cropping and forest regeneration should be noted from existing gardens so that the seeds, nuts and pollen of associated crops and local weeds are known. The insect, avian and molluscan pests found in local yam crops should also be known.[54]

In the settlements in the kitchen areas, specialised equipment used in preparing yams—graters, mashers or pounders, earth or clay ovens, pots or griddles—may be found. These, in themselves, will not be conclusive evidence but, if found, will call for intensive study in the areas where they are concentrated. Burnt organic material will need particularly detailed study, for yam fragments and the baked clay from hearths, ovens and walls as well as all sherds of pottery should be examined for the matrices of burnt-out fragments of organic matter.

*Food stores*, special huts identifiable from plans or sitings, clamps or store pits may be found. In *middens*, either pits or mounds, the individual strata of debris, recognised by careful excavation, will need examination for the kind of plant and insect evidence mentioned above.

## ROADS AND TRACKWAYS

Although these may vary from accommodation tracks on farmland to main trunk roads, the principles of location and excavation are the same. All fall into two categories; either they have been worn down by traffic and erosion into a hollow way, or they have survived, usually by deliberate raising and remetalling, above their surroundings. No preconceptions of width or construction should be held about any road and anything from a single pack-animal trail (perhaps as little as 1 m. wide) to a series of multiple trackways (perhaps 400 m. wide) is to be expected (Plates vii and ix).

*Locating problems* may be different for trunk roads and local farm or village networks. Trunk roads of any period will be the easiest to find since they will go from one centre of population or defence to another by fairly short routes and are usually well made.[56] Within the bounds of the Roman and Inca Empires for example, much field work has been done using a variety of field-walking (including the study of commercial cuttings),[57] literary and aural evidence.[58] The long distance routes used by less organised peoples (e.g. the Ickneald Way across Southern England) may be recognisable from the air but will be difficult to locate on the ground.[59] Minor roads, whilst they may be visible from the air, may show only in relation to field patterns, or where they leave farm-yards or settlements.[60]

More detailed locating, especially before excavation, can be done by probe, auger, and other surveys which will locate hollow-ways, metalling, side ditches, timbering, etc. A road can be traced for long distances by this kind of work and occasional trial trenches.

Excavation will be necessary with all roads to recover details of their construction and usage. The *method of construction* will best be shown by trenches at right angles to the long axis, wide enough to expose a good area of surface (2 m. minimum) and extended well beyond the main trackway on either side (Fig. 35). This should show the original road metalling (stone of some kind) or timber (log roads); any renewals; side (drainage) ditches—which may be far from the metalling; and walls or banks. If a hollow way, the same kind of trench might show, on either side of the hollow, the original construction. All details of the metalling should be recorded and samples kept.[61] Corduroy roads (of logs or branches) have been made at all periods in marshy and forested areas. These may survive where the water table is still high or where it has risen.[62] As well as recovering the details of construction, timber samples (cross-sections of all trunks) as well as samples for pollen, soil and molluscan analysis will be necessary (Plate IX).

The *relative dating* of tracks and roads will come from finds stratified in the road surfaces, in features sealed beneath or intersecting with them, or from ditch and banks along them. In the first and last cases finds will be fortuitous, although trenches near settlements are the more likely to produce datable objects. Intersections with other features (especially banks and ditches) should be looked for and trenches be specially sited to solve their relationships.[63] Walls or banks beside roads should be studied for gateways which may show field systems or buildings contemporary with them.

The *uses* made of roads should come from the study of their exposed surfaces. If a wide enough area (at least the 2 m. section already mentioned) is exposed, cart or sled ruts,[64] or pack-animal trails with hoof-prints may be recognised.

On the more important roads bridges, fords, causeways and hill-side terraces may be found. These will also need excavating. Parts of *Bridges* whether of stone or wood may survive in areas where the water-table has remained high or where there has been silting[65] (Plate II). Excavation should be by the grid system with special attention being paid to the methods of construction and repair (Fig. 35a). *Fords* may also survive, if metalled, but only under-water surveys or dredging may show them. *Causeways* especially across marshy ground may be found and should be sectioned like a bank.

## SUGGESTED READING

*History of Technology*★★ Vol. I, Singer, C. et al. (ed) 1957 (for building in different kinds of material) especially 300 and 456.

*History of Building Materials*, Davey, N. 1961.

Huts and hut building among the Bemba, Richards, A. *Man* 1950. 134. 62.

The Reconstruction of mudhouses, Hansen, H. *Kuml* 1961. 128.

Building Interpretation, Taylor, W. *AmAnth* 50 1948. 175.

*Ancient Egyptian Masonry*, Clarke, S. and Englebach, R. 1930.

*The Investigation of Smaller Domestic Buildings*, CBA 1964.

*Prehistoric Europe*, Clark, J. G. D. 1954. (Chap. IV).

*The English Mediaeval House*, Wood, M. 1965.

Excavations in Irish Cooking Places, O'Kelly, J. *JRSAI* LXXXIV 1954. 101.

Weoley Castle Kitchen, *Med Arch* VI/VII 1963. 109 and IX 1965. 82.

*The Desert Fayum*, Caton-Thompson, G. and Gardiner, E. 1934. Chap. 4–14 (for storepits).

Tollard Royal. Wainwright, G. *PPS* XXXIV 1968. 102.

FARMS AND FIELDS

*Notes and Queries on Anthropology*★★, *BAAS* 1962. 248.

*Ancient Fields*★★, Bowen, H. 1963 with good bibliography.

*The African Husbandman*★, Allan, W. 1965.

*Ancient Landscapes*, Bradford, J. 1957.

Lynchets and Early Fields, Fowler, P. and Evans, J. *Antiq* XLI 1967. 289.

*Agricultural implements of the Roman World*, White, K. 1968.

ROADS

*Notes on the history of Ancient Roads and their construction*, Forbes, R. 1934.

*Field Archaeology*, OS 1963 (with good bibliography for tracks).

*History of Technology* I, Singer, C. et al. (ed) 1957. 500.

*Roman Roads in the South East Midlands*, Viatores 1964.

*Roman Roads in Britain*, Margary, I. 1967. Introduction and Conclusion.

## NOTES

1. British houses of the nineteenth century have particularly good examples of subdivision by function. See for example Kerr, R. 1864 and *The Investigation of Smaller Domestic Buildings*, CBA 1964.

2. Dartmoor (England) is a good example: *PPS* XX 1954. 87. See St. Joseph, K. 1967; OS 1963. 8 and Bradford, J. 1957 especially Chapter 4.

3. The artifacts picked up on the surface may give some indication. *Antiq* XXV 1951. 75.

4. e.g. Itford Hill: *PPS* XXIII 1957. 167. Studland: *PDHAS* 87 1966. 142. Hatterboard: *SDAS* 1963. Little Woodbury: *PPS* IV 1948. Enzinge: *Germ.* 40 1936.

5. See Little Woodbury (loc. cit.). If the postholes are too small they should be treated as stakeholes.

6. For general considerations see Taylor, W., *AmAnth* 50 1948. 175. For examples: Jarlshof: Hamilton, J. 1956. Harlhope: *PSAS* XCIII 1960. 174. Keston: *PPS* XX 1954. 87 and Port Godrevy: *Corn Arch* I 1962. 17.

7. Bradford, J. in Singer, C. (ed) 1957. 300.

8. For ethnographic examples see Richards, A. *Man* 134, 1950. 162; for archaeological ones: *Kuml* 1961. 128.

9. For burnt brick see Biggs, M. in Singer C. (ed) 1957.

10. For an example of stone foundations see Winterton: *AntJ* XLVI 1966. 72.

11. For techniques see Wheeler, R. 1936.

12. Their distribution may well show how the building collapsed.

13. Itford Hill and Little Woodbury (loc. cit.). Also *PPS* XIX 1953, 1.
14. e.g. Skara Brae, Childe, V. 1931.
15. e.g. at Glastonbury and Meare: Gray, H. and Bulleid, A. 1911, 1948, 1953.
16. e.g. Fishbourne: *AntJ* XLII 1962. 15 and XLVIII 1968. 32.
17. Wheeler, R. 1936.
18. Skara Brae (op. cit.).
19. Fishbourne (op. cit.), and St. Albans, Wheeler, R. 1936.
20. Discussed in Webster, G. 1966.
21. For an elaborate British example see Weoley Castle: *MedArch* IX 1965. 82. and VI–VII 1963. 109.
22. e.g. Harappa. *AnInd* III 1947.
23. *BAAS* 1962, 160 and 248. For an example of a detailed study, Stefaniszym, B. 1964 Chapters 3–5.
24. Because of sudden changes in crops, e.g. from sorghum to maize in Southern Africa.
25. Or from deliberately built experimental earthworks. e.g. Jewell, P. (ed) 1963, and *PPS* XXXII 1966. 313.
26. e.g. The Scottish Highlands, see Grant, I. 1961.
27. As for example in the Faroe Islands. *Kuml* 1955. 152.
28. *Arch* LXXI 1921, 158. For examples: West Blachington: *SAC* 89 1950. 19. and Beere: *MedArch* II 1958. 123.
29. Presses for oil, wine etc. might be identifiable by flotation and analysis.
30. Watermills: Syson, L. 1965 and *TC* 8.4 1967. 446. Windmills: Wailes, R. 1954 and Freese, S. 1967.
31. e.g. *AmAnt* XVII 1952. 151.
32. As Yorkshire.
33. Fayum: Caton-Thompson, G. and Gardiner, E. 1934. 41. Maiden Castle: Wheeler, R. 1943. Riehborough: Bushe Fox, J. 1949 (IV. 26).
34. Jarlshof: Hamilton, J. 1956. Megiddo: Kenyon, K. 1960. 20.
35. For dungheaps see Allchin, F. 1963, Bowen, H.: 1963, 14, with good bibliography, also Hatt, G. 1951.
36. Infra-red or Stereo-photography might be useful here as well as walking the area. *PhotJ* 101 1961. 211.
37. Under sheet erosion at the bottom of hillsides, for example. Nok might be an example of this. *HSNJ* 1959. 288.
38. Bowen, H. 1963. Chapters III and IV.
39. The Archaeologist and Ancient Fields. Taylor, C. *LRS* 1968 (duplicated) and *Antiq* XLI 1967. 289. For examples see Charmy Down: Grimes, W. 1960, Dartmoor and Figheldean Down: *PPS* XX 1954. 87 and 103, and *AHR* VI 1958. 66. For rabbit warrens see *MedArch* 1966. 139.
40. Bowen, H. 1963. 5, for British agriculture.
41. Gwythian: *WCFC* II. 5 1961. Fifield Down *Antiq* XLI 1967. 289.
42. *Science* 136 1962. 109.
43. A hazardous business, e.g. *Oxon* I 1936.
44. Grant, I. 1961, and Bowen, H. 1963 Chapter 3.
45. e.g. Huaca Pieta. *AMN* 1426. 1949.
46. *PPS* XVIII 1952. 194.
47. Fishbourne (op. cit.).
48. Steensberg, A. 1943 for Northern Europe. These can be untrustworthy for simple farming; see Alexander, J. in Ucko, P. and Dimbleby, G. (ed) 1969. For Roman tools see White, K. 1968.
49. See Hatt, G. in Brothwell, D. and Higgs, E. (ed) 1964 and section on method in Ucko, P. and Dimbleby, G. (ed) 1969.

50. *AmAnth* 17, 1953 and 19, 1954. Evidence of castration should perhaps be looked for more carefully than at present.
51. Alexander, J. in Brothwell, D. and Higgs, E. (ed) 1970.
52. Davies, O. 1967.
53. e.g. Nok: *HSNJ* 1959, 288.
54. A useful introduction to those of West Africa has been published by the Nigerian Department of Agriculture. Research Mem. 50 1963, and 83 1965.
55. For irrigation see *Science* 136 1962. 109. Terrace examination would be especially interesting in the potato growing areas of S. America.
56. Forbes, R. 1934.
57. e.g. in Central England: Viatores 1964.
58. Margary, I. 1967 Chapter 1, and Singer, C. et al. (ed) 1957. 500.
59. Crawford, O. 1953. 60. OS 1963. 144.
60. e.g. in Sussex: *SAC* LXIV, 1.
61. Ditch pollens are particularly important since there may have been much plant movement along the cleared road margins. Salisbury, E. 1964.
62. Somerset: *PPS* 1960 XXVI, 1. Valtherbrug: *BROB* 12–13 1964. 193.
63. Viatores 1964 (passim).
64. As on Stane Street. Winbolt, S. 1936.
65. Singer, C. et al. (ed) 1957. 508.

# CHAPTER VIII
# Problems in the Excavation of Hamlets, Villages and Towns

'Their cottage stood empty on the edge of the common, its front
door locked and soundless. . . . In a year it fell down, first the roof,
then the walls, and lay scattered in a tangle of brambles.'

L. Lee,
*Cider with Rosie*, 1959; 111

Although these settlements vary so greatly in size and complexity that
it may seem strange to consider them together, the problems and
aims of excavating any large settlement than a single dwelling will be
much the same (Fig. 31).

In all the aim will be not only to establish when it was founded and
abandoned, but to recover the whole settlement pattern, including all
the phases of growth, shrinkage, and rebuilding; and to regain as much
as possible of its social and economic life.

Large settlements are the most complicated of all sites, for they will
have all the problems of dwellings with new ones resulting from long
periods of dense occupation, much more material and a proliferation
of elaborate and specialised buildings. There may also be much greater
areas to be investigated. Sites may be further complicated by having
living settlements above them.

In ideal conditions the whole of the settlement area will be available
for excavation and the problem can be studied at length before digging
begins. If the site is still inhabited a whole new group of problems
arises and these are treated below. Planning in either case will have
to be for a number of seasons, perhaps several decades, of work, and
the main necessity, unless time and funds permit complete excavation,
will be to select a series of sites which will answer the problems discussed
below. Much time should go into the planning of these excavations, for
a single well-sited trench may serve the purpose of an extensive grid,
and here more than in any other excavation, resources will need to be
husbanded.

It may be worth emphasising that in spite of their size many thousands
of villages and towns await discovery in all parts of the world. In
crowded England, for example, the discovery of several thousand Roman
and mediaeval villages within the last twenty years, some covering more
than 100 acres, has been the unexpected result of survey programmes.[1]
Similar results have come from intensive surveys in Africa,[2] Asia[3] and
America.[4]

Fig. 30 Plan of Onondaga, New York, U.S.A., in 1615. Compare with Fig. 54. To be considered as an excavation problem.

A distinction may be made here between the location and excavation of small densely settled sites with much vertical accumulation and extensive thinly settled sites.

*Small densely settled sites with much vertical accumulation* will normally be visible as one or more mounds, and after the actual discovery no form of general survey is likely to be of much use in the detailed planning of the excavation.[5] Erosion will usually have so weathered the top of the mound that individual features are unrecognisable, and the sides will be masked by the debris eroded from the top. Only trial excavations, in advance of the main campaign, will enable the problem to be assessed. This might well be done by quite narrow trenches (e.g. 3 m. wide) laid out on the main axes on top of the mound and continued for some way beyond it on these axes at the foot. On top of the mound digging should stop at the first signs of floors, foundations or other stratified remains and be left (or temporarily filled in) until the main grid, laid down on the same axes, is excavated to that depth. If taken deeper at this stage they may make later planning and photography difficult. The trial trenches should not be carried down the sides of the mound but should begin again at the foot of the slope. Here the aim should be to locate the surface of bedrock, to establish the old ground surface, and to find the limits of the settlement (Fig. 60).

*Widespread sites with little vertical accumulation* present totally different problems.[6] Unless conditions and finances are especially favourable, it will not be possible to clear the whole of a settlement which may cover many hundreds of acres. Several seasons' work must be envisaged and selective digging planned. Preliminary work, using a combination of aerial photographs, probe, auger, resistivity and magnetometer surveys, as well as literary and local aural evidence, should be complete well before excavation begins (see page 22). Aerial photography may be of especial use on these sites, and a known site should be watched at all seasons and under different crop cycles, for many years. Preparation should envisage obtaining a plan of the whole settlement. It may not be possible to excavate the whole area, but if all quarters are sampled and, as a minimum, a series of typical dwelling houses and any unusual building complexes in them are excavated, an outline plan will be obtained.

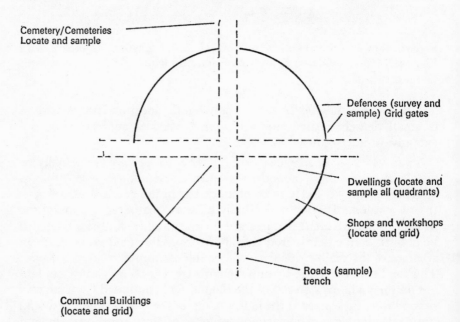

Cemetery/Cemeteries
Locate and sample

Defences (survey and
sample) Grid gates

Dwellings (locate and
sample all quadrants)

Shops and workshops
(locate and grid)

Roads (sample)
trench

Communal Buildings
(locate and grid)

Fig. 31 Problems of a town or village excavation.

The key to any settlement plan lies in its *road pattern*, for if this can be established then areas of excavation can be selected in relation to them. The excavation of roads has been described, and it may well be easiest to recognise them as they approach the settlement through open country and then to trace them to the centre by auger or other surveys (Fig. 34).

The road pattern will often indicate whether a true centre existed, for example at a cross-roads, or whether settlement was scattered on the perimeter of an open space. Once the pattern has been established, areas suitable for detailed surveys can be selected. These will be chosen for lack of disturbance and good preservation (e.g. water-logging) as well as on their location (e.g. near the limits or at the centre, of the settlement). These detailed surveys should show up individual buildings and enable a series of grids to be laid out. If surface indications are lacking and surveys prove useless, then the extent of the settlement may have to be determined by trial trenches or, if conditions are suitable, mechanical stripping.[7]

The trial trenches should be set out first along the main-road sides and should not be less than 3 × 2 m. Each trench should be stopped as soon as an undisturbed level of occupation is reached and new trenches carried on at 20 m. intervals until no more settlement material is found. When the limit of the settlement along the road sides has been found, more trial trenches between the roads will pick up the rest of the perimeter. Defended settlements will of course be much easier to define than unfenced ones, although suburban development will have to be looked for and sampled.

A *main grid* over the whole settlement should be pegged out at the same time as the detailed area surveys are being made. If nothing can be established by surveys before excavation then the laying out of this grid will be the first task.

It should be based on two base-lines intersecting at right angles and extending outside the supposed limits of settlement. The post interval will vary, but 20 m. squares should be a minimum. The framework thus established will relate all surveys and later excavations. Within this, smaller grids can be set out over the areas selected for excavation (perhaps at 5 m. intervals).

## HAMLETS AND VILLAGES

The simplest of these will be merely collections of farms or even one large farm estate and its dependent workers, with communal buildings or specialised establishments added and placed near each other for protection. To a greater or lesser extent (depending on the social organisation of the group) these farms will be similar to the isolated farms already discussed, and the problems of excavating living huts, barns, byres and yards, etc. will be the same (see page 134). Other villages may be composed of the small houses of farmworkers, and these should offer no great excavating problems.

All will have their plan and organisation determined by a variety of factors; by methods of farming (e.g. a collective, or large private, estate), trading, industry or fishing; by social, administrative or religious organisation (e.g. clan or cult); or by defensive needs (Fig. 30 and 34). An established village with its accumulated wealth and cleared land may well have needed more defending than a single farm and have had either a ditch, wall, fence or hedge, or have been arranged so that the houses themselves defended a central area. Once the outline plan has been established and the smaller grids over the chosen areas have begun to be excavated, the following problems will be met everywhere (Plate III).

## THE EXCAVATION OF THE DWELLINGS

In a village, as well as isolated dwellings, compounds housing one or several families, and terraces of single-family houses may be found, and there may be many graduations of size and luxury. An attempt should be made to excavate examples of all existing varieties. If the surveys already mentioned have shown details of house foundations, it may be possible to distinguish the main types without further preparation, and the choice of examples should then depend on the state of preservation. Unploughed areas free from trees should be preferred; areas near the bottoms of slopes may be more protected than those higher up; areas near streams or lakes may have better organic preservation. Where ploughing or other cultivation has disturbed everything to the surface of bedrock, mechanical stripping of wide areas can precede excavation.

Excavation will be on the grid method already discussed in the excavation of isolated dwellings (page 117).

*Terraces of houses.* These are best excavated by a large grid (10 m. squares) until the wall pattern can be distinguished. The uniformity of single-family units should then help to distinguish the terraces. As with isolated houses, all finds and spreads of debris (e.g. daub or roof tiles) should be three-dimensionally planned before the foundations are reached. 'Long' houses may be treated as a version of this type. When the wall pattern is found, the rooms should be excavated separately, internal baulks on the main axes being maintained. In villages it will be especially important to search below the upper foundations and floors for earlier ones.

*Single-family compounds* will be similar to the settlement area of farms and should be excavated in the same way (Fig. 32).

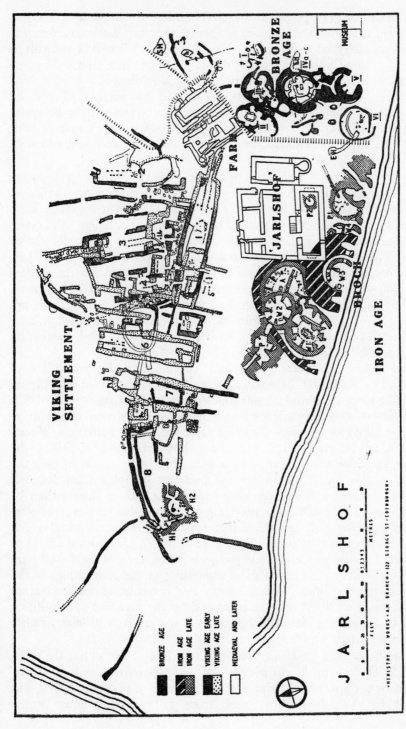

Fig. 32 Plan of successive settlements, Jarlshof, Shetland.

*Enlarged family compounds*, in which a number of related families come together, may have the houses scattered over an enclosure, grouped round a courtyard or joined in a single complex.[9] It will be difficult to recognise these unless there is a ditch, fence or wall round the compound. If this is located, excavation is relatively simple.

The compound perimeter, if not traced by surveys, should be followed by trial trenches and the gateway, which might be quite elaborate, located. If specially laid paths connect the entrance with isolated houses these should be traced in the same way and will help plan the compound.

*Isolated houses* should be excavated as on page 117 and whilst they may vary from single-room huts to palaces, there is perhaps more likelihood in a large settlement of one or more mansions larger, more elaborately planned and more richly furnished than the majority. These will belong to those who by heredity, wealth, outside authority or public choice exercise administrative, religious or financial control. To prove their existence and to excavate their contents is important to the understanding of the settlement, but in spite of their rich finds they lose most of their meaning if, as so often happened in the past, all efforts are concentrated on them and they alone are excavated.[10] Most will be smaller than the great rural palaces (pages 118–19), and excavation will be as for ordinary dwellings.

The following special points may be noted in the excavation of *mansions and palaces*:[11] there will almost certainly be a bank, ditch, fence or wall round the complex; this should be sampled (page 227). Within the compound there will probably be separate groups of buildings serving different functions (halls or areas for giving audiences, offices, shrines, stores, etc.) (Fig. 33). These should be located, failing the probe, auger or other surveys, by a wide grid (10 m. squares) over the whole enclosure. When individual building complexes are located, smaller grids over them will locate rooms, and these should then be given baulks on their main axes (Fig. 22). Function can only be suggested from the plan and the objects found (see below). Special watch should be kept for unusual building materials (e.g. imported stone) or imported techniques and luxury objects more likely to be found here than elsewhere. These may show something of the connections of the settlement with other regions. Even the presence of some external authority in a village may be suggested by the presence of a building built in an alien style (although of local materials) with significantly different pottery or other objects.[12]

The following special features might be looked for within the compound. There may be an *audience hall or open-air reception area*. A *hall* might be set apart by its size and the absence of domestic debris, but might be difficult to distinguish from a large store-house unless

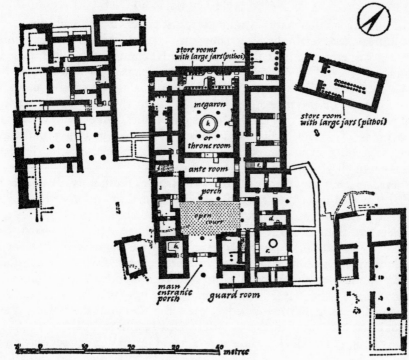

store rooms
with large jars (pithoi)

megaron

k

or

throne room

ante room

porch

open
court

store room
with large jars (pithoi)

main
entrance
porch

guard room

metres

Fig. 33 Plan of a Bronze Age palace.

elaborately constructed and ornamented. It would be excavated like a normal dwelling and should present no special problems. An open-air *reception area* would be more difficult to recognise, but a large space left clear of houses inside the compound, especially near the main entrance, might be significant. The buildings surrounding it should be examined for doors and verandahs opening on to it, and the surface of the area for hardening by trampling, beating or reinforcement by stones, slabs, cobbles or gravel. Other buildings might be *shrines* identifiable by plan or the finds from the area (see page 188 for excavation techniques).

The storage of food-stuffs and other products for the use of the community, or a magnate, or for transmission elsewhere, may lead to the erection of much larger *barns and store-rooms* than those found in ordinary compounds. Their excavation will not differ from that of the smaller stores (page 139), but special attempts should be made to discover what they contained from samples of floor or post-hole fillings or by studies of smashed containers.[13] Some employment of specialist craftsmen within the compound may have taken place, and their workshops may be found as separate blocks of buildings. Potting, smithing and cloth-making are the most likely crafts (see Chapter XI).

## COMMUNITY SERVICES

All but the smaller hamlets may possess some of the following:

*Market-places* are unlikely to show any special features in excavation, but any open space near the centre must be considered with this use in mind. It should be excavated like a yard (page 136) and studied for evidence of public monuments (e.g. statue, altar or cross), places of punishment or produce stalls. The last might show as regular groups of post-holes supporting shelters or display tables. Other evidence might be areas of gravel, strips of cobbling or paving marking pathways between lines of stalls; communal middens, concentrations of small coins, etc (Fig. 34).

*Produce stores* may be built to serve the whole community. They should be excavated as ordinary buildings with special attention to the points already mentioned for granaries and vegetable stores (page 139). Their size alone may suggest their communal use. *Mills* and *presses* (e.g. for flour or oil) may be found near them (see page 138). The water supply might also be communal and *wells, pumps, channelled streams and conduits* may be found outside private compounds. These should be excavated in the ways discussed on page 185. *Fortifications* comprising walls, ditches, palisades or hedges may also surround the village. They should be excavated in the way described in Chapter X.

Although in a village, administrative and judicial processes may often be carried out in one house (since authority may be united in one person), they may be separate and have special buildings or areas set aside for them. This is particularly likely if the village was for some reason the seat of government for an area.

For *administration or legislation* a hall or open place may have been used. This may be near the centre of the village and stand apart from the individual compounds.

A *hall* should be excavated in the same way as a palace hall of audience. No special kinds of finds are likely to indicate its use unless its use as a tax office resulted in the storage of tallies (clay, wood or stone) or receipts (of clay, paper, wood, palm leaves, etc.) An *assembly place* might be a simple open area, either in the centre of the village or outside, or a small arena. The open area is unlikely to give indications of its use unless, when examined by a series of test trenches along its axes, it shows the post-holes of benches and perhaps, at one end, a platform or dais. If the meeting-place is of more than local significance (e.g. a regional assembly) some more permanent structure, perhaps a semicircular excavation into a hill-side (page 174 for excavation techniques) with wooden or stone seats may have been built.[14]

*Judicial buildings* might also be distinct and recognisable, and include a court-house, prison or pound and places of punishment. A court-house would be unlikely to be identifiable on excavated evidence unless

PLATE I General view of a military earthwork taken for publication (Maiden Castle, Dorset). Note the use of the sunrise to emphasise the features.

PLATE II General view of a Romano-British timber bridge as it was visible in a quarry face before excavation (Aldwinkle, Northants). Taken with a telescopic lens from another face of the quarry.

PLATE III Aerial photograph of a deserted mediaeval village (Clopton, Cambs.). Note how evening shadows were utilised. To be studied with the plan in Fig. 34. (West is to the top of the photograph.)

PLATE IV Detail photograph taken during excavation, of a section through wall foundations. Not for publication but to record texture.

PLATE V Detail photograph to show relationship of half-sectioned post-holes to ditch. Not for publication.

PLATE VI Detail photograph of timber-jointing in bridge (see Plate II). For publication. Frosting on the timbers has heightened the effectiveness.

PLATE VII Burial showing mutilation.

PLATE VIII Post-excavation view of timber-lined Romano-British well (Cambridge.) For publication.

PLATE IX Post-excavation photograph of a prehistoric trackway. The Abbots Way, Somerset. Note the advantage of photography over drawing here.

PLATE X Pre-excavation photograph of mediaeval dry-stone wall (El Kab, Republic of Sudan). Note the impossibility of recording this accurately without photography, and photogrammetry.

PLATE XI Post-excavation view of a military ditch section (same site as Plate XII). Note the way bedrock has been cleaned and the angle of the camera.

PLATE XII During-excavation photograph of prehistoric military rampart
(Maiden Castle, Dorset). Note the revetted spoil heaps.

PLATE XIII Post-excavation photograph of a storage pit. For publication (see page 140).

PLATE XIV Near-vertical post-excavation view of prehistoric timber road and huts (Biskupin, Poland). The use of a photographic tower was essential here.

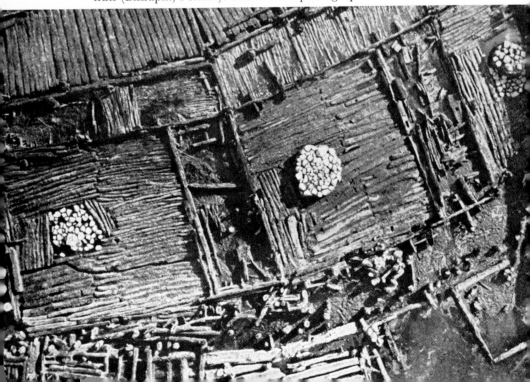

PLATE XV Record photograph near beginning of excavation. Not for publication. Note how the light was chosen to show the shallow excavation.

PLATE XVI Post-excavation photograph of a dry-stone revetting-wall. Note the excellent cleaning.

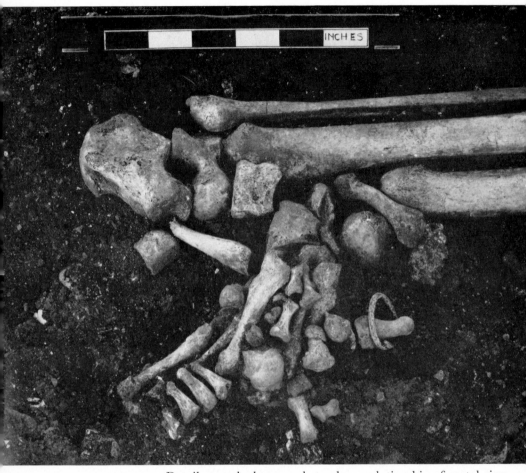

PLATE XVII Detail record photograph to show relationship of metal ring and associated bones.

PLATE XVIII A pleistocene land surface with artifacts in position (High Lodge, Suffolk). For publication. Note the importance of area excavation on a site of this kind.

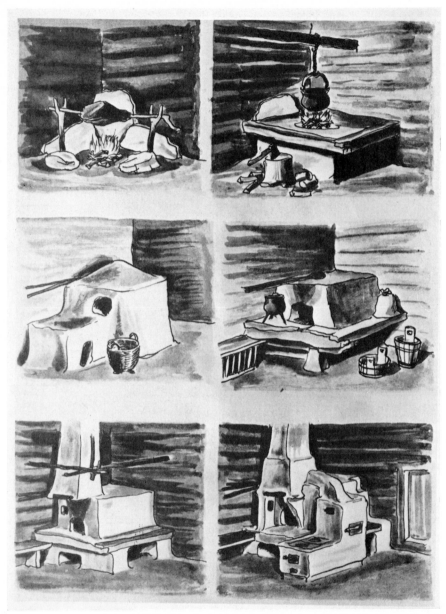

PLATE XIX Sketches of wood and clay cooking hearths and stoves in nineteenth-century Czechoslovakia. To be considered as excavation problems (page 131).

PLATE XX Lithograph of eighteenth-century French glassworks. To be considered as an excavating problem.

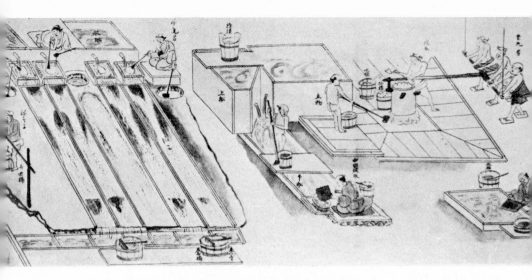

PLATE XXI Painting on silk of a seventeenth-century Japanese goldmine. To be considered as an excavating problem.

PLATE XXII Detail photograph of cart-ruts on a buried road surface. For publication.

prison-cells were attached. Cells might be identified in plan as a row of small rooms served by a corridor, and a guard-room. Fetters or chains, or attachments for them, might conceivably be found in them. Its excavation should follow the general methods used for houses.

A *pound*, perhaps a simple fenced or walled enclosure for strayed or lost animals, might be found in the same general area on the outskirts of the settlement. It would only be identifiable from the pattern of the walls or post-holes.

In any village the commercial and industrial buildings, even where there is no specialised industry, are likely to include shops, craft-work-rooms and inns.

*Shops* may be difficult to distinguish, for trade was often carried on, as it is today, from a room in a dwelling-house. If this is the case, only the objects found (e.g. the contents of a potter's shop destroyed by a fire or house collapse) may indicate them.[15] If the village is a large one and served as a commercial centre for a wide area, specially built shops, similar to those in a town, might be found. They should be recognisable in plan, may well be found in rows and are likely to be near the centre of the village. The finds or the nature of the samples from them may be the only evidence of their use, but some, bakers' shops for example (page 171), may be recognisable in plan.

Practising rural craftsmen are also likely to be present in the larger villages (see Chapter XI). *Smiths* are perhaps the most likely, but *carpenters* (including specialists like wheel-wrights and carriage-makers) and *leather-workers* may also be found. These are likely to be recognised by the finds as well as by the plans (page 273).

*Inns* or caravanserais may possibly be distinguished in plan, or in Britain at least in recent centuries by broken bottles, glasses and crockery.

The *religious sites* will include shrines and burial grounds. These are discussed in Chapter IX (Fig. 34).

## VILLAGE FIELDS AND PASTURES

No excavation of a village is complete without an attempt to locate and comprehend its fields. The problem of relating the fields to the village will, like the farm, be best solved through its road systems, and the methods of study will be similar to those used for the farm (page 142). This may be easier since the roads may have been better defined and better maintained.

A community cultivating the same land for generations will have systems for renewing its fertility (e.g. crop rotation, manuring or specialised land use). Since a system, through centuries of use, may have been firmly imprinted on the countryside, it may well survive beneath any later system and be available for study (the methods of

L

excavating it are discussed on page 144).[16] There are also likely to have been well-established pasture and woodland areas. Local geography and topography may help to indicate the general pattern[17] (Fig. 29, 34).

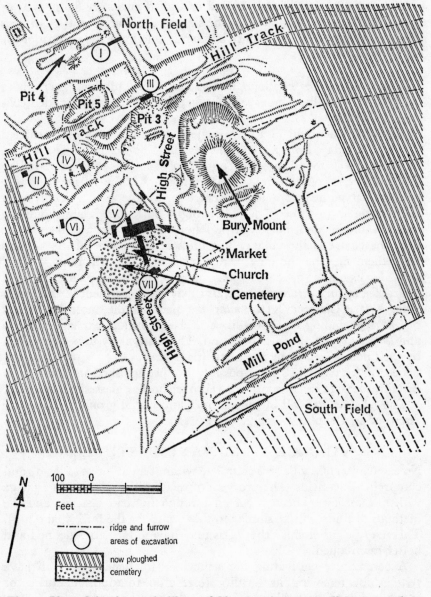

Fig. 34 Plan of the deserted village of Clopton. Areas actually excavated are shown in solid black. (See Plate III for the corresponding aerial photograph.) A very limited excavation has established many of the main features.

Many communities still utilise, during certain times of the year, pastures or fields many miles from their main settlement, for example riverside meadows or coastal pastures in a dry season, areas normally desert after a rainy season, or mountain pastures in summer. The *seasonally used dwellings* at them will vary greatly; some may be small, perhaps with a limited range of specialist equipment (e.g. for cheese-making),[18] but all might show signs of thin annual depositions of debris. The dwellings may have been stone or earthen ones left empty most of the year, or tents or other temporary structures. The traces will be slight but possibly widespread, and only area stripping is likely to explain them.

## PROBLEMS OF SHIFTING AGRICULTURALISTS AND PASTORALISTS

Settlements associated with static agricultural economies will probably have been occupied for a long time and leave much evidence both in the form of rebuildings of substantial houses and in ancillary buildings but the settlements of shifting cultivaters which are occupied for a few months or years, present special problems even if the movement be cyclical rather than linear.[19] They may be larger and more widespread than most permanently settled groups, since a number of families may come together for a season.[20] The cultivated area will be much less easy to recognise than in permanent systems, but the large number of predators under pioneer conditions may, as with many other groups today, have made fencing or some other protection of crops and stock necessary. The actual systems of cultivation may also be different.[21] Houses and stores may well be slighter than more permanent settlements and may have been designed to be movable.[22]

The excavated evidence is likely to be less than that from more permanent sites, there being only thin strata of occupation debris. It is particularly important in a temporary occupation to uncover the whole area. This can only be done by area stripping.

Pollen samples from neighbouring ponds or marshes can be particularly useful since they may show the destruction of the local vegetation and then its slow recovery.[23]

*Settlements of Pastoralists* may be generally similar to those of shifting cultivaters, but will be even more transitory, since cloth or skin tents may normally be used.[24] In areas where recognition is easiest (in deserts and grasslands) settlements have been recognised and excavated like those of hunter-gatherers (page 99).

*Fishing Villages.* Specialised settlement patterns may develop from a concentration on fishing. Sites beside rivers, lakes and seas should be excavated with local ethnographic evidence in mind, and weirs, boat-houses, piers and shell-middens looked for.[25]

## TOWNS

Since these are the product of sophisticated societies, it is unusual for completely prehistoric ones to be found. In most parts of the world something of the nature of the towns of even vanished civilisations is now known, much of it from literary evidence.[26] The director must be familiar with this evidence as well as with the types of buildings and materials still in use or likely to have been used locally.[27]

The location and survey methods to be used have already been described (pages 153-5). By them the road grid and perimeter of the town as well as the depth of deposit in different areas should be known before the planning of the rest of the excavation is undertaken. When these are translated into terms of time and money the director will be able to see how his resources match up to the problems. If they are insufficient, then at least he can restrict himself to solving particular problems and avoid damaging the rest of the site.

### THE PROBLEM OF MATERIAL

In any urban society there is likely to be a great amount of rubbish, especially food debris, excreta and artifacts (mostly of pottery and stone). Since all of the artifacts which survive must be cleaned, and then examined and classified, special arrangements must be made to deal with them. This may have to take the form of processing groups working full time throughout the excavation. If possible the sorting and analysing should follow on at once from the washing and marking, so that the director has a day-by-day review of the material being found in all trenches and levels. The bulk of the material, if all is left to the end of the dig, will be very great and will take much time and expense to transport, lay out and re-study. It must be emphasised that no discarding should take place before each piece of pottery, bone or stone has been washed, expertly examined and recorded. Systems for doing this are discussed on page 63.

### THE PROBLEM OF ACCUMULATION

In urban sites the depth of deposit may be very great (30 cm. a century is not an unusual rate of accumulation in both Europe and Asia). This will mean laying out a large grid, since the trenches will be deep.[28] Mechanical equipment, especially light railways and conveyor belts, would be valuable here, and ladders, ropes, buckets and windlasses may be necessary. Vertical sections will be of particular importance on this kind of site.

### THE PROBLEM OF HORIZONTAL SPREAD

When urban settlement is not restricted by topography or need for defence, it may spread over several square miles and the density of the settlement be very low.[29] Comparatively little rebuilding may have taken place and individual houses and compounds have been large. Deposits will then be shallow and the areas cleared should be large, since only then will the relationship of features be established.

*Safety.* If the mounds are large and trenches deep, provision of revetting equipment and helmets will have to be made (page 43), and special insurance may be desirable (page 32).

## EXCAVATION

In long-occupied sites the main problem, apart from that of the scale of digging and processing involved, is the recognition and disentanglement of the remains of each successive period.[30] The principle that the uppermost settlement should be completely removed before the next is begun must be honoured where possible, but in practice the deeper features (pits, wells and cellars) which have been dug down through earlier settlements may have to be cleared in stages. Detailed recording in each trench is particularly important, and there must be very close supervision of the work. A special difficulty is the general unreliability of dating based on groups of objects found together (e.g. in pits). When so much material of widely differing periods may have been disturbed and reincorporated, a group may contain almost nothing from the time in which it was dug, and only its stratigraphical position will be significant. Wherever possible intermediate baulks should be left through features so that drawn sections supply evidence of its stratigraphical associations.

The complication of the sites will also mean that they are unlikely to be successfully understood if dug by too great a proportion of unskilled labour. Trowellers should form the great proportion of the team, and the inexperienced must be closely watched by the trench recorders.

For the director the greatest difficulty will be making himself familiar with the stratigraphy in each trench. This is a necessity, for his main work afterwards will be to combine the stratified features and finds from each trench into a site pattern for each period. He may be aided in this by the major periods in the history of the town being distinguished by some very obvious layer or junction line between two layers. These will appear in most trenches and in most parts of the town. A very obvious cause of change is a layer of debris from collapsed houses, caused either by fire, earthquake, sacking by an enemy or replanning. Another obvious change is a period of abandonment marked by weathered debris, accumulations of blown sand and soil, a developed soil or an erosional nonconformity.

Within each major period a number of phases are to be expected. These may be visible as alteration to standing structures, rebuildings, or variations in the way an area is used (e.g. houses giving place to a

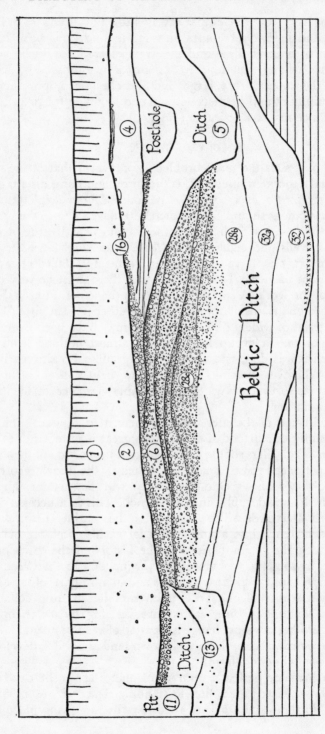

Fig. 35a Section through a Roman road, Cambridge. Note the regular reinforcement made necessary by sinkage above the earlier ditch. Scale 1:24.

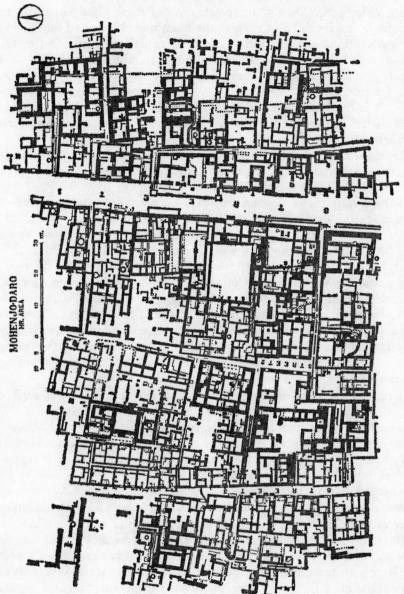

Fig. 35b. Plan of part of a town excavation, Mohenjo-daro, Pakistan. Note the variety of buildings.

road) (Fig. 35a). Most of the correlation of these phases in different buildings and in different parts of the town must be carried out during the excavation, and this must be the continual preoccupation of the director. It is for this reason that the many standing sections discussed below should be adopted. They are necessary for study in all weathers and for reference.

Such is the importance of establishing these successive phases, that areas where these are particularly clearly demonstrated may merit further excavation (Fig. 36).

Sites with settlement over long periods of time will require the director to be familiar with a wide range of features and material and he should have prepared himself for this.

Sites complicated by present-day occupation require different methods from excavation outside them and are even more difficult.[31] Since there will usually be no large areas to excavate, no extensive grid will be possible, and the work will have to be carried out on small sites and by piecing together information over a long period of time. Excavation must be thought of as likely to continue through several decades; it will be dependent on sites becoming available, and must be linked with the regular watching of all casual digging. This can usually be undertaken successfully only by local archaeological groups. It may also involve the use of mechanical drills and excavators and the taking of special safety precautions (e.g. against subsidence in neighbouring houses).

Unless a considerable mound marked the site of a feature, no surface indications are to be expected, for recent building and levelling will have altered the ancient topography. A study of the literary and museum evidence may be of greater use here than in other types of site, since it may record the local topography before building took place and outline the history of the standing buildings.

Discussion with local householders and workmen may be of great use since small excavations, for water, gas, etc., may well be remembered. The areas behind cellar walls and floors may be especially useful.

Trenches will have to be sited in the areas available and not be selected only for their archaeological potential. Permanent open spaces belonging to the community are the most hopeful areas, especially if they have been preserved from pit digging for a long time. If a good case can be made for their excavation (i.e. the solving of an important problem) and if complete restoration of the site is guaranteed, permission can often be obtained from the authorities. Private gardens and yards are other possible sites, and much the same arrangements can be made with landlords and tenants. A third and even more important source of sites comes from the clearance of old houses for rebuilding schemes. A director must keep himself informed of the plans for

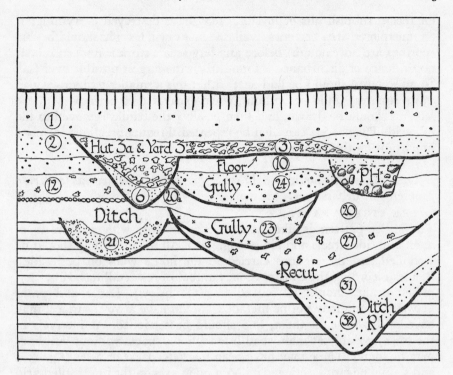

Fig. 36 Section through a town site, Cambridge. Prehistoric and Roman enclosures and huts with 17th century orchard above. Scale 1:32.

large-scale developments[32] and arrange for the excavation of important areas between the destruction and the rebuilding. This can be very difficult to arrange since there may be no time interval between the two.[33] For sites of especial interest a watch may have to be kept from one generation to another for an opportunity to arise.

Areas which are likely to be of especial value are: those in the centre of the town (main cross-roads or river crossing); those beneath banks (e.g. town defences); buildings (churches, castles) where the earlier levels may be intact before a known date; those on the lower slopes of hills where accumulation is likely and the earlier levels therefore less disturbed; and those beside streams or rivers flowing through towns where organic remains may be expected.[34] Areas to be avoided are those with big dumps of recent material (unless mechanical aid is available); areas of known quarrying, and areas honeycombed with cellars (if these go down as far as bedrock).

*The laying out of trenches* will depend on the size and nature of the site more than on archaeological necessities. Grid excavation can be very wasteful if sited blindly without trial trenches or previous knowledge,

for recent rubbish pits or levelling may have destroyed everything. If
an unexplored area becomes available in a town, test pits should be dug
(borings are not enough) before any large-scale work is undertaken. If
no evidence of disturbance is found, then the largest possible grid (say
10 m. squares) should be laid out; within this a smaller temporary grid
(3 m. squares) could be laid out, when excavated to perhaps 1 m. the
sections should be drawn, and then possibly the baulks removed to the
full grid. The process can then be repeated. Frequent sections are most
important on this kind of site.

The following should be looked for and excavated as separate
problems in urban sites:
I. THE STREET PATTERN
The street pattern is likely to be complicated, with a number of
main and side streets and lanes (Fig. 35b). All the main ones should be
sectioned and the sections carried to the house walls on both sides.
Besides recording the construction, number of re-metallings, ruts, etc.,
public drains should be looked for (see below). Lanes and paths
between houses may not be metalled, should have a worn surface, may
have drains beneath them, and should be sectioned. At intervals in
the town, possibly at main road intersections, spaces without buildings
may be found. These may have been markets, parks or assembly areas
and should be cross-sectioned on both main axes on the interrupted grid
technique. If features are found then the grid should be completed.
With them may be linked a public water supply and drainage system.[35]
II. PRIVATE HOUSES
The main differences between town and village houses will be in their
plans. Restricted space may mean smaller rooms, several storeys,
cellars and more elaborate drains and rubbish disposal arrangements.[36]
Greater social distinctions either of wealth or function (e.g. merchants
or priests) may also mean a wider variety in size and plan.

Excavation should aim at uncovering houses of each type present.
Preliminary surveys, especially aerial photographs, may give some
indication of where different types are to be found, but areas near the
centre and the periphery in all quarters should be sampled, choosing
those where preservation is likely to be best (e.g. where mounds are
highest, where there is no sign of robbing, etc.).

In detail the methods of excavation will be similar to those already
described for rural dwellings. Very often a house plan (courtyard,
agglutinative, etc.) will be found to have developed locally and its
variations will need to be studied (Fig. 22). Individual rooms must be
treated as a series of individual excavation problems, with cross-sections
and separate recording, and especial care taken to look for signs of
upper storeys (wall thicknesses, stairways, collapsed walls and floors

from above are especially likely indications of them). The latter, and the objects which were in them, will need to be recognised and excavated before the house plan which lies buried beneath is known. If a mound of debris survives, then excavation in the ways already described (page 124) should enable collapsed walls and possibly the floors to be recognisable from the angles of the fallen material.

Town houses and probably boundaries may remain unchanged for centuries, and phases may be recognised by alterations and rebuildings (Fig. 36). The walls should be carefully examined for changes in construction.

Very large houses may be considered separately as *town palaces*.[37] These are likely to be better constructed, more richly furnished and to remain in use longer than the smaller houses. Their excavation is therefore important, since it may indicate something of the taste and sophistication in material things of which the society was capable. Town palaces should not, however, be regarded as priority excavations for the understanding of settlements, nor should an undue proportion of the resources be spent on them. Their excavation should be the same as that of rural palaces (page 158). Rooms should be excavated as entities, with temporary baulks along the main axes. Besides the domestic rooms, suites of public rooms and courtyards, shrines and perhaps a ceremonial entrance are to be expected. There may also be a number of storerooms and workshops, and the whole might have an enclosure wall and gatehouse. Successive rebuildings and alterations are to be expected and may be distinguished by wall thicknesses, changes in building material, changes in plan, etc. (Fig. 33).

III. COMMERCIAL AND INDUSTRIAL BUILDINGS

Specialised commercial and industrial buildings are more likely to be found in towns than elsewhere and shops, workshops and large storerooms may be expected.

*Shops.* These may well be found in rows with many neighbouring ones all engaged in the same trade.[38] Whilst they will vary in detail, a basic pattern in which a room faces the street and one or more store-, living- and work-rooms are found behind, may be expected. Cellars may also be found under either the street or the house (Fig. 37). Whilst their excavation will be like that of dwelling-houses recognition of the kind of shop may come only from a study of the remains of the stock-in-trade. The most easily recognised will be those selling pottery and metals of various kinds, but under favourable conditions leather, wood, cloth and food merchants may be recognised. If a shop collapsed or was burnt or abandoned, the entire stock may be found. Excavation should try to recover how it was stacked by recording in detail the positions of the objects found. The technique used for a hunter's settlement (page 101) would be useful here, with a 10 cm. grid and collection in 5 cm. spits.

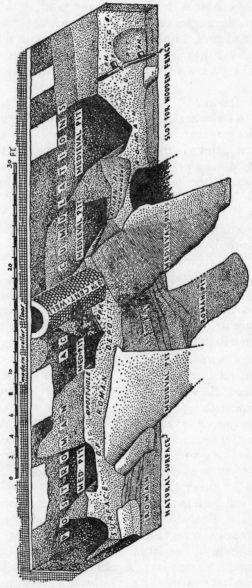

Fig. 37 Axonometric projection of an urban section, London, showing the relationship of Roman deposit to medieval pits and other later features.

*Pottery-sellers* would be especially easy to distinguish and the absence of wasters should distinguish them from manufactories.

*Glass-selling shops* might be very difficult to distinguish from a chemist's or a perfume-seller's and the glass fragments should be collected and studied like those from a pot-sellers. *Metal-selling* (iron copper, gold and silver), *leather-* and *cloth-selling* shops may also be recognised if the stock-in-trade is found. It might also be suggested by the workshops at the rear (see Chapter XI). If the stock is found conservation will be a major problem.

A variety of *food shops* might be recognised either from the surviving stock or, if durable ones were used, from the containers. *Oil-sellers*, for example, might have rows of large pots, either in the shop or the store-rooms, stood on the ground, on low benches, or set in trenches. Samples from the insides of the pots may show their use. *Grain-sellers* might also keep their stock in jars rather than sacks, and these with their contents might survive. Rodent and insect pest remains should also be looked for. *Vegetable-sellers* might in very favourable conditions be located by the survival of seeds and pips, or parasite eggs and spores.

*Store-rooms* will be excavated as large buildings, but might be recognised by their position, contents and floor construction. Granaries and stores designed for cereals, for example, may well have floors raised against rodents[39] (Fig. 23). This may show as parallel stone or brick supports, lines of post-holes across the floor or ramps or steps up to the floor level. Linked with these may be milling or pounding equipment and loading ramps. Samples should be taken from the floor areas, and a careful check made for seeds, husks, rodent and insect remains.

*Industrial buildings* (craft workshops and large-scale manufactories) may also be found often grouped in particular quarters or suburbs of towns. Pottery kilns and tanneries, for example, will normally be on the outskirts of the settlement. Recognition should come partly from plans and partly from the objects found (for excavation see Chapter XI).

IV. PUBLIC SERVICES

These will be the most distinctive feature of a town and if not recognised in the surveys may be identified later. The roads may show more elaborate construction, more alteration and longer use than in the villages, and along the streets drains and water channels may be found (Fig. 35). *Drains* may be discovered beneath the streets and may be stone, brick or wood-lined, and open or covered.[40] Their pattern should be worked out by test trenches at intervals, inspection chambers looked for, and the final outlets from the town discovered. The silt of the drains may well accumulate small lost objects, but these can be of little use for dating purposes unless the date of the building of the drainage system and the time it was in use can be demonstrated stratigraphically.

*Public Water supply.*[41] Whilst it is unlikely that water was brought to many individual houses, central water-points may occur, especially in regions where water is in short supply. In sophisticated societies this may have been piped to fountains or standpipes. Open conduits may be found in the middle or at the side of some roads. They should be recognisable from their regular profile, possibly a stone or wooden lining, and from their route to an open tank or basin. Beneath some of the streets, stone or brick and cement channels may be found, and when these are traced may end at an open basin, trough or tank, or fountain base. Outside the town they should be traced, by test trenches at intervals, to the source. This might reveal aqueducts, bridges and tunnels.

*Tanks, reservoirs and basins.* Open tanks may be found served by pipes or conduits or merely filled naturally by rain, streams or springs.[42] They will be distinguished from ponds by their regularity and linings; revetments and steps are to be expected. Excavation should be carried out as for ponds and unless there is water in them they should be dug with transverse baulks and samples of the sediment be taken. In some areas underground reservoirs may be constructed in bedrock.[43] These will be distinguished from cellars by water-shoots or pipes leading into them. They should, if dry, be dug like ordinary rooms, with baulks on the main axes, and the sediments should be recorded. Objects found, except perhaps those on the bottom, must be regarded as having got there after the period when the reservoirs were in use and will be useful only in establishing a *terminus post quem.*

*Wells.* Large wells in open spaces may be considered as public ones. They should be excavated as described on page 185, and a special search for well-housings be made.

## V. PUBLIC BUILDINGS

Public Buildings may also be found although their position may depend on historical accident as well as town planning.

*Halls of assembly, justice or administration* might be recognisable by size, plan, seating arrangements or finds.[44] Excavation will be as for ordinary dwellings.

*Stadia and theatres,* used for secular or religious spectacles, may be found either inside or outside the town, and may have had standing room or seating for thousands of citizens.[45] The simplest can be a terrace or a semicircular excavation into a hill-side, the stage or area for performance being in the open part. Alternatively a circular or semicircular depression can be hollowed on flat ground, the spoil being piled round the edge. Seats of wood or stone may be provided and there may be buildings in the centre. Excavation will depend on its condition, for if it has been filled, radial trenches must establish its size and structure.[45] The area at the centre should be gridded, and any remains treated as buildings.

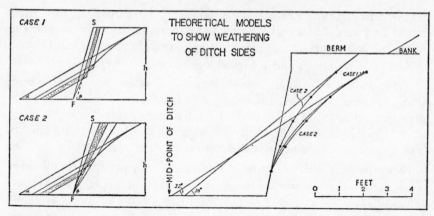

Fig. 38 Theoretical models to show weathering of ditch sides. (Compare with Fig. 24.)

Those built above ground will probably be more ruined; they may be made of stone or wood.[46] Those of stone will be identified by the stubs of the walls or their robber-trenches, and excavation will follow the normal pattern. The area within the wall should be excavated with baulks at 3 m. intervals on the short axis.

*Public bath suites* are an expensive and specialised development of some civilisations.[47] They should be recognisable from their plans. Indoor baths may vary from a single large pool to a series of rooms heated to varying degrees and ending in a cold bath. The heating will usually have been done from beneath the floors and in the walls (see page 131 for excavation methods). Supply conduits, overflow vents and stoke-holes should be looked for. All rooms should be excavated as separate problems, and a complex of other buildings, courtyards, shops, etc. may be associated. Outdoor baths may serve for storing water as well as for drinking and washing. They may be very large (e.g. 10 m. square) and will usually be rectangular and lined; brick and bitumen or clay might be found. Steps going down, into them and supply channels and over-flow may be found. Some of these may have utilised cold or even hot springs.[48]

*Prisons and places of punishment* may also be found. The prisons, if specially built, might be recognisable in plan from the walls, guard-rooms and perimeter wall. Places of punishment with stocks, pillories, gibbets and execution blocks or pits might also be recognisable. *Stocks, pillories and gibbets* would be difficult to identify, although patterns of post-holes might suggest them. Gibbets have been identified by the size of the post or posts and the wear of the heel of the post on the bottom of the hole.[49] Other forms of execution, beheading, impaling, crucifying, etc. may also leave indications.[50] Isolated burials with severed heads or bodies with fractures caused by spikes or poles thrust through them might be found. Heads which had been mounted on poles or piled in heaps, as deterrents or trophies may be found above ground.

Religious buildings and cemeteries are also to be expected.

*Public shrines* will usually be elaborate and often much better built than the other buildings. They may vary from simple halls or spaces to great walled complexes. No special method can be used to locate them unless the religion and the kind of sites chosen for its shrines are known. The special problems of their excavation are dealt with in Chapter IX.

*Cemeteries* may well be found outside the town, possibly on all sides. Their location and excavation are discussed on page 215. Differences may indicate class divisions and their horizontal stratigraphies illustrate long periods of town history.[51]

*Town Defences.* If these existed they are likely to have been substantial and should have been located in the surveys. Two kinds are likely, *perimeter defences* (walls, banks and ditches) and *acropoleis or citadels.* Excavation should be in the normal way for military features (Chapter X). If a succession of defences exist they must be linked stratigraphically to the appropriate building periods of the interior[39] (Fig. 60).

*Docks and Harbours.* If the town was on a sea-coast, lake-side or river bank, then some kind of loading and unloading place for ships is likely. There is most hope of locating these if the sea or river had retreated or changed its course, for the aerial or ground surveys may then show a group of wharves, a mole or an artificially dug harbour as a surviving feature. If not apparent, then the plan of the town defences, with perhaps some special reinforcement, or anomalies in street system where it approaches the shore, may show the most likely area. Underwater work may also be helpful here.[52]

*Wharves and quays* should be most easily recognisable, for they are likely to have been made either by building up and revetting the bank or slope, or by dumping material at right angles to the slope and then revetting it. The former, whether revetted in stone, brick or wood, should be excavated by one or more trenches at right angles to the long axis. These should show any fallen revetting and any accumulations of silt against the face. If it is intended to clear the whole quay, then the trenches should give place to a grid when the revetting is found. If built out at right angles to the shore, the quays should show stone or brick, whether visible before excavation or located by trial trenches. Here the edges should be revetted. Sections should be carried up to the revetting on either side of them and should show silting differences in composition and the rate of accumulation of the silting on either side (i.e. more on the up side in a river, more on the side facing the current in the sea). Sediment samples should be taken. Bollards and ring-holes should be looked for on the wharf edges, and a careful lookout kept for sunken boats and debris.

*Harbours* enclosed by man-made moles or dug into the bank or shore may also be found in the same way as wharves. They should be sectioned along the axes and samples should be taken; sunken boats might also be expected here. The entrance should be gridded and searched for lighthouses and guard-posts. The quays should be treated as above.

*Dockyards*, buildings for storing or building boats might also be found along the banks or the shore. Launching-slots, large sleds, mooring-posts and scaffold-footing might be found, together with stores and tool-sheds. They should be excavated like dwellings.

M

## SUGGESTED READING

*Habitat, Economy and Society*★★, Forde, C. 1964 (Parts II and III) with bibliography.
*Mediaeval England: an aerial survey*★★, Beresford, M. and St. Joseph, K. 1958.
*Houses and House Life of the American Aborigines*★, Martin, L. 1965.
Maya Settlement Patterns in N.E. Peten, Bullard, W. *AmAnt* 25, 355. 1960.
*Rural Settlement in Roman Britain*, CBA 1966.
*Ancient Landscapes*, Bradford, J. 1957.
*The Lost Villages of England*, Beresford, M. 1963.
*Prehistoric Europe*, Clark, J. 1954. 129.
The Use of Machines in establishing village plans, Wendal, W. in Griffin, J. (ed) 1957.
Archaeology and the History of British Towns, Biddle, M. *Antiq* XLII 1968. 109.
Some New Methods in Town Archaeology, Biddle, M., *LRS* 1968 (duplicated).

VILLAGES

*Biskupin*,★★ Rajewski, Z. 1959 and Kostrewski, J. 1938.
*Das Federseemoor*, Reinerth, H. 1929 and 1936.
*The Fatherland Site; The Grand Village of the Natchez*, Neitzel, R. 1965.
*Inyanga*, Summers, R. 1958.
*Mucking*, *AntJ* XLVIII 1968. 210.

TOWNS

*Drevnii Kiev*, Kargen, M. 1958 (Vol. I).
*Colchester*, Hull, M. 1968 and *Winchester*, *AntJ*. XLIV–VII (1964–67). (These are beneath modern towns.)
*Verulamium*, Wheeler, R. 1936; for a plan see *Tikal*, Carr, R. and Hazard, J. 1961; (Part II). (These are free from later building.)
*Jericho*, Kenyon, K. 1957. *Troy*, Blegen, C. 1950–8 (these are 'Tell' formations).

## NOTES

1. Beresford, M. 1963. St. Joseph, K. (ed) 1967.
2. For example, the Wadi Halfa reach of the Nile. Here surveys in advance of the Aswan Barrage revealed many hundreds of new sites. *Kush* XI, XII and XIII 1963–5.
3. S.W. Iran: *PPS* XXXIII 1967, 147.
4. Central America: *AmAnt* 25, 3 1960. 355.
5. For mound surveys: *Antiq* 28 XXV 1954. 24. Surface finds may suggest terminal dating.
6. e.g. in Nigeria: *HSNJ* 2.4 1963. 470.
7. For the use of machines in village surveys see Wendel, W. in Griffin, J. (ed) 1957.
8. In Britain the Roman and mediaeval village patterns have been well discussed: CBA 1966 and Beresford, M. and St. Joseph, K. 1958. 125. See Bradford, J. 1957 for Mediterranean examples and Bullard, W. *AmAnt* 25, 3 1960. 355 for Central American ones.
   For European prehistoric villages: See *Prehistoric Europe*, Clark, J. G. D. 1954. 141; Soudsky, B. *PPH* VIII 1967 and Rajewski, Z. 1959. For North America see Neitzel, R. 1965 and for Africa see Summers, R. 1958.
9. e.g. Benin: *HSNJ* 2.4 1963. 470.
10. A criticism of much settlement excavation, especially in Western Asia.
11. For English mediaeval country houses: Barley, M. 1961, and Wood, M, 1965. For an African palace/shrine see Robinson, K. et al. 1961. For examples in America see Martin, L. 1965.
12. On the values of imported ceramics in dating, see *JAH* IX 1968.
13. Knossos: Evans, Sir Arthur John 1921–36.

14. Yeavering (England) may have an example of a wooden one.
15. The kind of evidence is also suggested by engravings. Goodman, W. 1964. 121.
16. Fields (in Britain): Bowen, H. 1963 with many references. Orwin, C. and C. 1938. Beresford, M. and St. Joseph, K. 1958, 28.
17. For examples in England see Alexander, J. in Munby, L. (ed) 1968 and Taylor, C. in *WAM* 63 1968.
18. In the Scottish highlands for example. Grant, I. 1961.
19. For the study of shifting agriculture see Conklin, H. in *CA* 2.1 1961 with bibliography.
20. This has been suggested for some of the large neolithic villages in Europe, see Soudsky, B. 1967 and *PPH* VIII 1967.
21. *CA* 2.1 1961.
22. Suggested at Köln-Lindenthal. Buttler, W. and Haberey, K. 1936.
23. Dimbleby, G. 1966. 148.
24. Forde, C. 1964. Part III (especially 308). Martin, L. 1965. 113.
25. For examples of weirs see Best, E. 1929.
26. True for the earliest towns of the Ganges Valley (Sharma, Y. 1964), but also for Romano-British ones (Rivet, A. 1965).
27. Singer, C. (et al.) 1957 (456 for brick and stone, 300 for wattle, daub, wood and turf). For general comments *Antiq* XLII 1968. 109.
28. e.g. Jericho: Kenyon, K. 1957, and London: Merrifield, R. 1965.
29. See Kamenskoe: Grakov, B. 1954. Omdurman is an interesting modern example of this.
30. Winchester (interim reports only) *AntJ* XLIV–VII 1964–67. St. Albans (interim reports only) *AntJ* XXXVI 1956–XLII 1962.
31. Good examples: Colchester, Hull, M. 1958; London, Grimes, W. 1968.
32. Through Local Authority architects and planning committees.
33. Grimes, W. 1968.
34. The Walbrook in London is a good example of this. Merrifield, R. 1965.
35. e.g. Mohenjo Daro: Marshall, J. 1931; well summarised in Piggott, S. 1961. For the plan see *AnInd* 3 1947. 58 and 74.
36. e.g. Ur: *AntJ* VII plates 41–2, and Troy: Blegen, C. 1950.
37. For example the palaces at Khorsabad or Persepolis. Frankfort, H. 1958. 75 and 219. Knossos was probably the centre of a town. Evans, Sir Arthur John 1921.
38. For a discussion of evidence from one period (Romano-British) see Frere, S. 1967. 258 and Wacher, J. (ed) 1966.
39. e.g. Harappa: *AnInd* 3 1947. 78.
40. e.g. Mohenjo Daro: MacKay, E. 1938. Lincoln: *ArchJ* CIII 1946. 26.
41. For Roman Britain see Frere, S. 1967. 224 and 401. For a specific example see Dorchester: *AntJ* XX 1940. 435.
42. At Mohenjo Daro one was c. 10.3 × 6.7 × 2.7 m. Marshall, J. 1931.
43. e.g. Israel and North Africa.
44. e.g. at Rome: Gjerstad, E. 1960. Vol. III.
45. These were common throughout the Roman Empire. For Britain generally see Frere, S. 1967. 242. For an example St. Albans. *Arch* 84 1935. 213.
46. Yeavering (*The Listener*, 25 Oct. 1956 and lectures by the excavator) probably had a feature of this kind.
47. Especially in the Roman Empire. For Britain see Frere, S. 1967. 244.
48. e.g. at Bath.
49. As at Caxton Gibbet and Cambridge (England). Personal information.
50. As at Benin. Roth, H. 1903.
51. As at Athens. Desborough, V. 1964.

52. Help may possibly be obtained especially in Britain through sub-aqua clubs. Shipwrecks should be considered separately. See Cape Gelidonya: *TAPS* NS 57, 8 1967, and Zuider-Zee: *AS* 3 1955. For survey techniques see *Antiq* XXXVI 1962. 252 and for photography Townsend, D. 1964.

CHAPTER IX

# Problems in the Excavation of Religious Sites

'Religion is the last resort of troubled excavators.'

Anon

Areas are set apart for non-secular affairs by peoples of all continents and every kind of society. They have been recognised archaeologically in many periods and regions, and the wide fluctuations in the amount and kind of legitimate evidence recovered from them reflects the specialised knowledge required to excavate them.

They are the most worrying of all excavation problems, for the greatest danger to truth lies in the minds of their excavators. If a director knows too little of the kinds of evidence to be expected or is too rash and speculative in his interpretations, loss of evidence or distortion of it can easily result.

No modern ethnographic study of a community would, however, be complete without a study of its spiritual beliefs and practices,[1] and insofar as these leave *comprehensible* material remains they must be interpreted by excavators. The attribution of ill-comprehended evidence to ritual and religious purposes is, however, quite unjustifiable. Since religious customs are among the most conservative and distinctive ones practised by human societies, they can often help isolate contemporary groups or show clan, class or other divisions within a larger entity.

The problems of excavation can be considered under the headings of *places of worship* and (although these are not always separate) *places of burial*.

## THE EXCAVATION OF PLACES OF WORSHIP

Under a variety of names (e.g. shrines, temples, churches, mosques), places revered for supernatural reasons are found everywhere. The religions which many of them served are known, together with the rituals employed and the kinds of buildings used, and if the site being excavated can be linked with a known religion then the excavator must have studied the accumulated literary and architectural evidence beforehand.[2] Even with this knowledge the understanding of individual sites may be difficult, for most will have local idiosyncrasies.

If the site does not belong to a known religion and has to be excavated as a field problem it is much more difficult, for piety can express itself in many ways. In past excavations, buildings of unusual plan and finds have often been attributed to religion, but unless some positive proof can be offered this solution is useless.

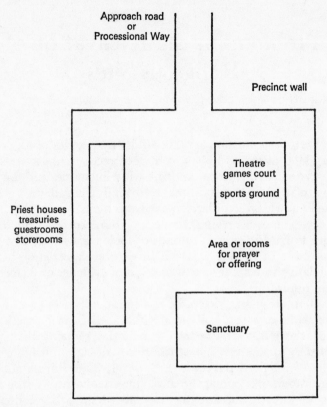

Fig. 39 Problems of excavating a shrine.

LOCATION

Although sites of this kind among settled peoples in historic times may be predictable (e.g. churches and mosques in towns and villages) others may be where manifestations of Deity took place and so are unpredictable to mortals. Even in historic settlements a place of worship can usually be recognised only during excavation by the plan and by finds; there is no certain way of predicting where in the settlement it might be found. Any isolated site, whether a cave or a hill-top or elsewhere, might be that of a shrine, but unless objects with known religious associations have previously been recovered from it, or unless the plan, revealed by aerial photography or other surveys, is of a familiar type, it will not be recognisable as such until excavated.[3] Literary evidence, place names or local tradition may of course point to a particular site having religious associations.

EXCAVATION (Fig. 39)

In all places of worship all or some of the following should be found; *sanctuaries, rooms or areas for prayer, rooms or areas for offerings, priests' houses, guest- and store-houses*. Since the most difficult excavations will be those which do not belong to a well-known religion, they will be first considered.

Excavation should be total, for only then can the significance of the parts be assessed, and the excavation and planning will be therefore similar to that for settlement sites (page 152). All should aim to establish, as well as the chronological information of date of foundation, the phases of occupation and how ended, the features already listed above. The excavation problems of these various features may be considered separately.

## SANCTUARIES

These are the holiest part of every site. It may be possible to recognise them in plan from the way in which other buildings or features are grouped round or lead up to them, or from the finds that come from them during excavation.

No attempt can be made here to describe all kinds of sanctuary (they may for example be a tree or groves of trees, a lake, river or well, a cave, or any kind of building), but some of the special problems of each type of site will be considered later (page 187).

First the features which might be found in any of them will be discussed.

*Altars* of stone and wood may be expected although only the bases of them are likely to have survived. *Stone* altars may well be first encountered as a heap of stones. Any such heap found should be exposed and excavated on the quadrant method (page 213). The individual stones should be numbered and their positions plotted three dimensionally, they should then be brushed and studied for squaring, carving, or inscriptions. When the upper stones have been moved the rest should be examined for regular settings and facings. The sections drawn through the heap should extend well beyond its base. The altar foundation should also be sectioned, still on the quadrant method, to show its construction and to search for foundation deposits (see below). *Wooden* altars are less likely to survive, but rectangular settings of post-holes or timber slots should be looked for in floors (page 120 for methods of excavation). Smoothed clay might have been used to finish them and their surfaces should be examined for traces of burning.

*Cult figures or objects* will rarely be found in place or intact, but all debris lying on the floor of a sanctuary should be examined with them in mind. In particular all unusually shaped rock fragments should be recorded three-dimensionally and their angle of rest noted. Natural, or geometric as well as human or animal shapes should be expected. Metal, bone or wooden objects are less likely to have survived destruction but should be looked for and recorded in the same way.

The basal support of an object is much more likely to survive than the object itself and if no inscription or attached fragment of figure (e.g. feet) remains, will be difficult to recognise. A free-standing base will resemble an altar and should be excavated in the same way; a niche or a wall recess should be sectioned separately from the room, as should any post-holes. Objects of regalia and adornment may also lie where they fell.

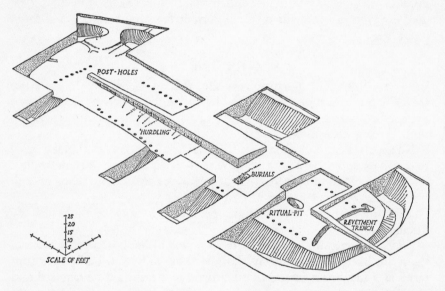

Fig. 40 An axonometric projection of an excavated neolithic long barrow, Skendleby, Lincolnshire.

*Graves* will be found in many sanctuaries and may be dedications, sacrifices, those of specially privileged worshippers, or the cause of the sanctuary and the centre of the ritual. Only the position of the grave and its contents can suggest which. Excavation (method on page 208) may distinguish between these alternatives, perhaps by the superstructure (showing perhaps a shrine;[4] by the grave goods, e.g. a priest's regalia), or by the skeleton (e.g. a bound and decapitated human or a carefully preserved animal).[5]

Rituals of cleansing are often gone through at the entrance to sanctuaries and *lustration areas* should be looked for. Basins and drains set in walls, pools or soakaway pits, metal or ceramic ewers and basins might be found. If the pools are artificial and large they should be excavated like baths.

*Sacrificial areas* might also be found in or near the sanctuary. The pouring of libations will usually leave little trace, but sterile, deliberately filled pits should be checked for pouring-holes and funnels and perhaps sampled for dregs.[6] Piles of smashed cups or rhytons might also indicate libations. Sacrifices of food, especially of animals or birds, may be recognisable from debris. Surface scatters might show the selected (or discarded) portions; pits might also contain portions of an animal (e.g. horn and tail)[7] or all that remained after burning. Plant products would be more difficult to recognise, but all carbonised remains, not merely a sample, should be kept for analysis.[8] The implements of sacrifice (e.g. knives) may also have survived hidden in the area[9] (Fig. 48).

*Votive offerings* may be considered here[10] for dedicated objects might have been laid, hung, buried or sunk in a sanctuary. If *hung*, survival is unlikely, unless they were in a building violently destroyed. If this has happened a search along the base of the walls, both inside and outside, should be made. If *buried*, then they will be discovered when pits are located and excavated in the normal way. The number of objects found in this way may be very great, and if of metal, they may be much decayed so that their excavation will be delicate and lengthy. Unless a conservator is a member of the excavation team, help from an archaeological laboratory should be called in before any removal is attempted. If this is impossible then the whole mass should be freed from the surrounding earth and removed (page 63) to a laboratory. In a large mass, the objects may have to be removed singly, each being first drawn, photographed and described. The description should include details of colour, humidity and angles of rest. If in several parts, the fragments should be boxed separately and numbered on both the box and the sketch. If the objects were sunk in water, recovery will be more difficult. If in deep water, then only a specially equipped team familiar with underwater survey and raising techniques should be used.[11] If the water has since disappeared the whole area of the old silts and muds can be gridded and the objects recorded in their appropriate horizons. Pollen and mollusc samples will be needed through the whole section. If the objects are still waterlogged in shallows or silts, a similar excavation technique within a coffer dam might be possible.

*Dedication or foundation* deposits may often be connected with the construction or dedication of the site. They may be found in pits or under walls.[12] In sophisticated societies their form may be standard (inscribed stones, coins, pottery, etc.), but all kinds of objects, human beings and animals may be found.

*Divination and prophecy* is often practised in sanctuaries, but will leave little in the way of evidence unless some durable material (e.g. bone or shell) is used in the rituals. Stores of these might have fallen from

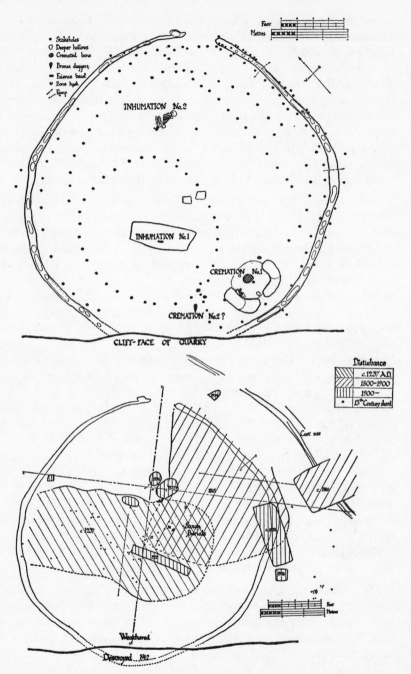

Fig. 41 Plans of a Bronze Age barrow at different periods, Arreton, Isle of Wight. The documented disturbances are: Saxon burials; 1237 a robbing trench; 1810 a road block; 1930 a radio aerial, and 1952 treasure hunters.

cupboards or have been buried. Any collection of identical objects should be examined for inscriptions or scratches.[13]

*Hearths.* These may also be found in sanctuaries and should be excavated like domestic hearths. All carbonised matter should be kept for examination (page 131).

The *particular problems of some of the main types of sanctuaries* may now be considered.

*Caves.* Natural caves are known from ethnographic evidence to be used as sanctuaries,[14] and among the many successive uses of any cave it may be possible to distinguish when it was used as a shrine. Tentative identification might be suggested by paintings, mouldings or carvings, in niches, on the walls and ceilings, or on the floors.[15] The associated objects will naturally vary greatly with the community, but painted or specially shaped stones, figurines, pottery, and metal objects[16] have been found. Those parts of the cave furthest from the daylight may well have been used, and might have to be located by specialised cave exploration techniques as well as by the more usual methods used for cave settlements. Excavation will be by the techniques already described (page 110), and structures, hearths and burials may be found. Fissures and crevices should be searched especially carefully.

Artificial caves, cut into soft rock, are also known[17] and should be excavated in the same way.

*Trees and Groves.* A particular tree or a grove will usually be unidentifiable, but if an open space is found at the centre of a religious complex, trees might be identified by locating the tree boles and by a sampling-grid at perhaps 20 cm. intervals. In an undisturbed soil this might reveal a pollen silhouette[18] and the supporting evidence of molluscs and insects might be conclusive.

*Hills,* either natural or man-made, may be used as sanctuaries and observatories. Natural hills may have had some part of their summit levelled, and buildings, enclosures or cairns[19] made (Fig. 51). Rock and earth will be readily available and may well be used, so that visible remains may help to locate the sanctuary. The natural hill-top should be surveyed and excavated like a settlement, the whole of any levelled area being cleared and gridded and approach roads and paths should be searched for. Man-made hills should be excavated in the way described for tells and mottes (pages 165 and 255). They may well have been used and re-used for long periods and the whole hill may be a series of superimposed sanctuaries.[20] These will need complete excavation beginning from the top downward and will require great resources and much time. Features may be found at the base and on the slopes; (stairways or ramps, terraces and ceremonial gates) and at the top (shrines and observatories). The latter might be identifiable by the orientation of windows or sighting-stones.

*Lakes, Wells and Rivers.* The most sacred part of some sites may well be a stretch of water. This is only likely to be recognised if the plan of the building complex, literary evidence or accumulations of objects found beneath the water[21] suggest it. Excavation will be restricted to the recovery of objects (page 185 for technique) unless some construction was undertaken.

*Built Sanctuaries.* Banked, ditched and post- or stone-encircled enclosures open to the sky and without other buildings have been given the name of *Henges* in Britain but are in fact of many different periods elsewhere and examples of a world wide type.[22] Location has been by aerial photography or by finding existing ditches, banks or stone arrangements. Their size and the position of the bank, which in Britain is normally outside the ditch, may distinguish them from ploughed-down barrows with post circles or defensive enclosures. The detailed surveys which should precede excavation (resistivity, magnetometer, probe, borer, etc.) should establish the full perimeter of the ditches and banks, the entrance causeways, and perhaps locate the position of internal features (Fig. 47).

The excavation of the ditches, banks and entrances should be planned and carried out as for military ones (pages 227–36) and should aim at showing the methods of initial construction as well as alterations and repairs. The most difficult problems will be the size of the features and the safety of the workers.[23] The interior, if there are no surface

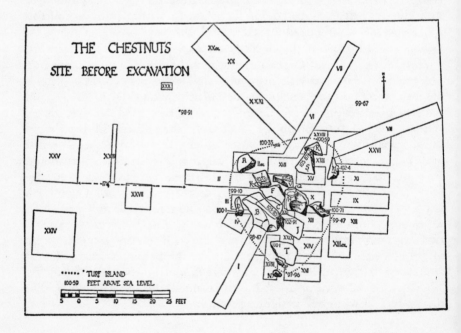

THE CHESTNUTS

SITE BEFORE EXCAVATION

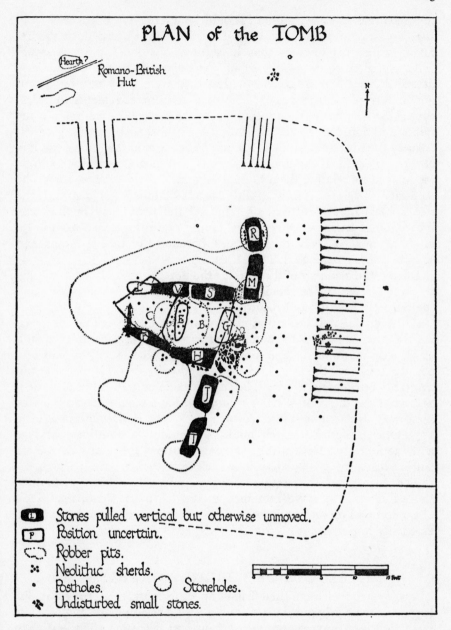

# PLAN of the TOMB

Hearth?
Romano-British
Hut

N

R

M

L V S

C E B G

F

H

J

I

Stones pulled vertical but otherwise unmoved.
Position uncertain.
Robber pits.
Neolithic sherds.
Postholes.       Stoneholes.
Undisturbed small stones.

Fig. 42 (*opposite and above*) A megalithic tomb, before and after excavation, Addington, Kent. The letters on the stones indicate their relative positions; B and C were cap stones.

survivals (e.g. standing stones), should be completely uncovered (Fig. 48); if a large area on the grid, or if small, on the quadrant, method.[24] Features peculiar to them may be settings of wooden posts or stones (Fig. 47). Post or stake-holes should be excavated in the way already described, and it must be shown that they were truly post-holes and not merely pits (page 122). Their plan (e.g. arrangements in pairs) may show whether they supported a superstructure. Stone-holes, if the stones still stand in them, can only be established by probing or extremely narrow trenches (e.g. 50 cm. wide) preferably along the line of the main grid. If the stones have collapsed their true position can be established by relating them to their foundation pits.[25] These should be sectioned as described for megalithic tomb-chambers (page 205). If the stones have been destroyed or removed the holes may be the only indication of their existence. They should be distinguished from other kinds of pits by their packing and perhaps the raising-ramps and support-stakes (page 205).

During the gridding of the interior the debris and tools from shaping the stones or destroying them as well as the features previously discussed, should be looked for and recorded.

*Buildings* used as sanctuaries may vary from specially designed and isolated structures to rooms in extensive building complexes, and as already mentioned, their position in the complex, their plan and construction and the finds in them may identify them. If these are not available beforehand they will be recognisable only during excavation, and until the moment of recognition, will have been excavated in the same way as dwelling-houses constructed of the same materials (page 117). Once recognised, watch should be kept for wall paintings, carvings and mouldings as well as the sanctuary features previously described. Total excavation of the complex is important[26] (Fig. 50).

The main problem during excavation will be that of complexity, for the buildings may have remained in use for many centuries. Much alteration and rebuilding is to be expected and vertical sections will be especially important (Fig. 52b).


## PLACES OF PUBLIC WORSHIP

These may be distinguished from sanctuaries by their provision for large numbers of worshippers, and whilst they may be joined to a sanctuary (as a nave is to a chancel in most Christian churches) they may well be separate from or lack one (as in some Islamic mosques and Christian chapels). Buildings and/or open spaces may be used (Fig. 39).

Locating *Buildings* may be difficult, for they may be anywhere in a settlement and there may be a considerable number of them.[27] If normal pre-excavation surveys give no hint of them then they will only

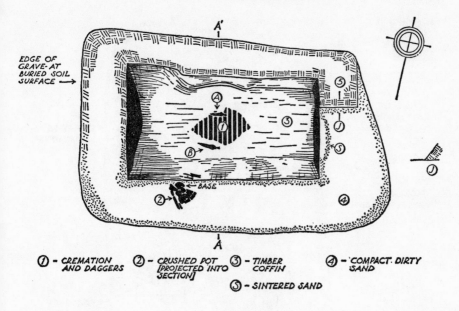

EDGE OF
GRAVE·AT
BURIED SOIL
SURFACE →

① – CREMATION AND DAGGERS    ② – CRUSHED POT [PROJECTED INTO SECTION]    ③ – TIMBER COFFIN    ④ – COMPACT·DIRTY SAND

⑤ – SINTERED SAND

SECTION

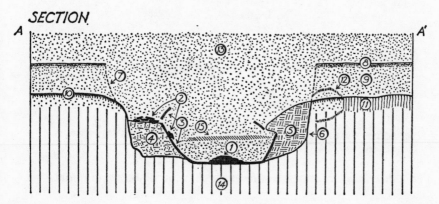

Fig. 43a Plan and section of a Bronze Age grave, Bishop's Waltham. Hants.

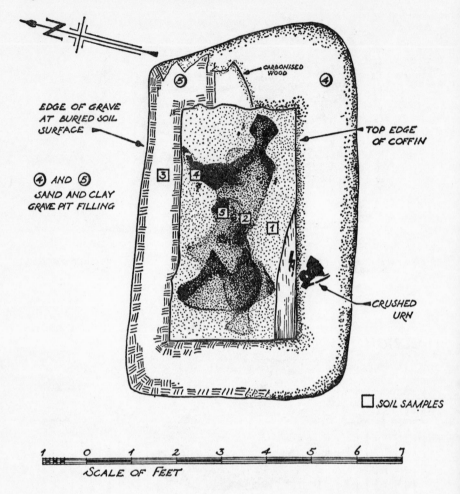

Fig. 43b Enlargement of the same grave showing silhouette of burial.

be recognised during excavation. In either case, excavation will be similar to that of houses and halls of audience (page 117). Recognition may come from plans, and perhaps finds, but usually only if there is literary evidence to support the architectural[28] (Fig. 50, 52).

*Open Spaces.* Although these are well known in the ethnographic literature it is difficult to see how they might be recognised during excavation.[29] If literary evidence suggests it or ethnography offers a local parallel, they may be identified. (Roman army parade grounds with their altars are an example of this combination.)

## OTHER RELIGIOUS BUILDINGS AND AREAS

A large religious establishment or even an ordinary secular community may need, besides sanctuaries and places of public worship, a variety of specialised religious buildings and areas. If concentrated into a single centre which may cover many acres, the problems can be approached like those of a village (page 156), and all the various features be recognised and sampled. If they are scattered through the settlement, little planning can be done unless their plans can be recognised beforehand.

The following features might be found in either circumstances.

*Games-courts and Sports-grounds* have been necessary parts of religious complexes in many parts of the world at different periods.[30] Unless there is literary evidence for them they will be difficult to interpret, but aerial photographs or complete ground plans may suggest their uses. Since they are likely to be large, excavation must be selective and should establish their complete shape and construction, sample any feature present, and if possible suggest the sports which took place. The variety possible and the kinds of problems to be expected may be indicated from some of the better-known types. *Ball-game Courts*[31] may well have carefully sloped and hardened floors and two or more surrounding

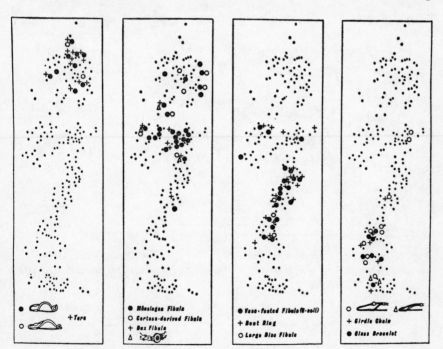

Fig. 44a Münsinger, Switzerland. Linear distribution in a cemetery along a ridge: early Iron Age.

N

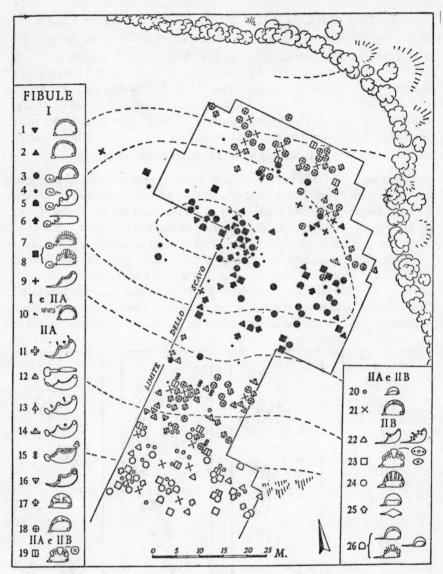

Fig. 44b Plan of a cremation cemetery, Quattro Fontanili, Veio, Italy. The fibulae suggests that burial began at the crest of the hill and spread down the sides. Early Iron Age.

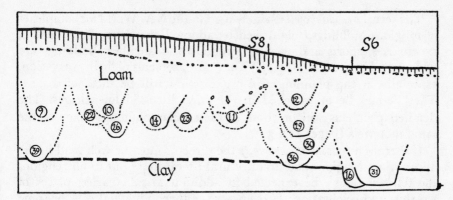

Fig. 45 Section through part of a mediaeval inhumation cemetery, Clopton, Cambs. Scale 1:53. The numbers identify graves.

walls, stone rings set in the walls and stone markers on each side, and stands for spectators. *Foot-, horse- or chariot-racing arenas* might be levelled, have altars, central embankments or statues and be ditched or walled. They might have attached stables, competitors' rooms and entrances, stands for spectators and associated shops.[32]

The *Cursūs* (rectangular ditched enclosures, many miles long) of Britain may be used as examples of possible sports-grounds which, being prehistoric and not yet fully excavated, give no indication of their purpose.[33] One way of tackling the problem might be for the long ditches to be completely surveyed for causeways and then to be sectioned at intervals and at intersections with other features. The interior should be surveyed in a variety of ways (page 28) and then be gridded in selected places. *Theatres for dancing or acting* may also be attached to a religious site.[34] For their excavation see page 174.

*Priests' Houses.* Dwelling complexes for the resident religious may also be found. Individual houses, those of shrine guardians, cult priests, hermits, etc., will present problems similar to those of ordinary secular dwellings[35] (Chapter VII), but, if possible, sections should be drawn connecting them to the sanctuary and showing their stratigraphical relationship to it. Assigning these houses to particular periods of the site will be important.

## LARGE RELIGIOUS ESTABLISHMENTS

These may be found in isolation (e.g. a Christian hermitage or a Mayan ceremonial centre), or in a settlement (e.g. a Sumerian temple), but will always be more than a sanctuary and a place of worship. This will usually be because a community of the professionally religious will be permanently in residence and the establishment will be as a specialised settlement.[50]

The term *ceremonial centre*, widely used in the New World for complexes of religious buildings, might well be adopted elsewhere, for groups of sanctuaries, sports and meeting grounds and ancillary buildings are widespread in the Old World.[36] The main problems of their excavation, especially in the planning and organisation will be those of scale.[37] They should be approached in the way discussed for villages. The detailed problems will be those of the secular buildings made of the same materials (pages 117–30).

If there is a *residential community* the director must be well read in the appropriate religious and architectural literature,[38] but in all religions the following may be expected in addition to sanctuaries, places of worship and celebration: *Sleeping-rooms*, either individual cells or some sort of large collective dormitory, *kitchens*, probably large and collective, perhaps with dining-rooms nearby, *working rooms* for crafts of various kinds, *hospitals*, *meeting-rooms*, *bathrooms* and *latrines*.[39] These might all be recognisable from the kinds of evidence already discussed.[40]

Separate rooms or buildings may be provided as *store rooms and treasuries* for relics, regalia or objects used in ceremonies to be kept in safety. Only if objects are found are these likely to be identifiable. They should be excavated as dwellings.

*Guestrooms*, blocks of small lodgings for pilgrims or suppliants, might also be found. Only their plan might distinguish them and they too should be excavated like ordinary dwellings (Fig. 50).

*The Enclosure.* Many religious establishments will have their perimeters defined in some way. Whilst this might merely be a series of notices, or stone or tree markings, it might also be some combination of banks, ditches, walls and fences and so be recognisable archaeologically. Locating it may be difficult unless aerial photographs reveal it, for it may enclose a much larger area than the actual building.[41] Excavation should be in the way described for military banks and ditches (Fig. 49).

The area between buildings and the perimeter should be carefully surveyed, for field systems, farms, fishponds, cemeteries, etc., may be found.

If *approach roads/processional ways* exist, they may be recognisable from the air or on the ground and should be traced for their full length, which might be many miles.[42] Grids covering both the entrance to the sanctuary and the beginning of the roads, and trenches at points of intersection with other features should be excavated. The processional ways may be between rows of stones or posts, drainage ditches or banks. They should be excavated like roads (page 147). In tracing these the perimeter enclosure may be found and gates, perhaps elaborate ones, might have been built where they entered the sanctified area.

# THE EXCAVATION OF PLACES OF BURIAL

This specialised branch of excavation is concerned with the study of the *burial rituals* of communities. The recovery of well-dated and well-preserved human remains is, to the field archaeologist, a subsidiary labour, since his duty is merely that of careful recovery and recording as a preliminary to study in the laboratory.

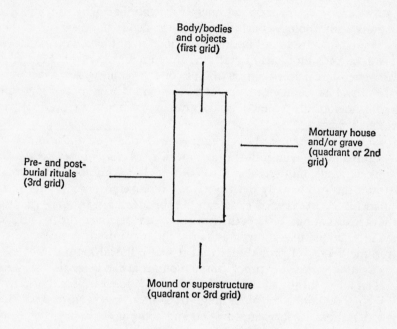

Body/bodies
and objects
(first grid)

Mortuary house
and/or grave
(quadrant or 2nd
grid)

Pre- and post-
burial rituals
(3rd grid)

Mound or superstructure
(quadrant or 3rd grid)

*The problems of a cemetery*

As above for each grave, with in addition:
the perimeter to be established on main
axes (by sampling) and areas of all four
quadrants to be gridded.

Fig. 46 Problems of excavating a grave and a cemetery.

The recognition of burial rituals is most important, for they are among the most distinctive and conservative attributes of a community. They usually consist of a series of acts precisely carried out and are repeated on different sites and on many occasions. They therefore offer excellent evidence of one aspect of the life of a community. Successful recognition of them depends not only upon careful excavation, but upon the attitude of mind of the excavator. Before excavation he should have studied the existing patterns of ritual in his area and any literary or aural evidence of previous ones;[43] be familiar with the kinds of questions anthropologists ask living groups about the disposal of their dead;[44] and have reflected upon those which might have been practised in his area and the kinds of evidence they might have left (Fig. 46).

No general principles can be offered for the *location of burials* either of single graves or cemeteries, for even if mounds were raised or other durable memorials erected, recognition, although simpler, is not necessarily easy.

Burial mounds can easily be confused with other mounds, in Britain for example with windmill-tumps, anthills, haystack-bases, vegetable clamps or castle mottes.[45] In all countries large numbers of mounds exist and more (partially destroyed) are discovered annually in aerial photographs.[46] In very few cases can they be identified as burial mounds without excavation. Where ditches surround or flank the mound or when internal features show in an aerial photograph it can be suggested with some degree of probability that it was a burial mound, but even so excavation is the only proof. Some mounds are so large that they are mistaken for natural undulations in the land,[47] some so low that only a few inches remain after ploughing. In Britain much study has been devoted to their surface appearance and some preliminary suggestion of their date can be made from this.[48]

Of the other kinds of monument, standing stones are the most obvious,[49] but others may include ditches or palisades, which will survive to show in aerial photographs.[50]

Flat graves or those which have lost their mounds will only be located by aerial photographs or by chance exposure. Any human skeleton found in commercial digging should have the area round it examined for evidences of rituals and for neighbouring graves.

Rock-cut tombs have been located by a number of different techniques of which augering, photography and echo sounding have been the most successful.[51]

Once located, two groups of excavation problems face the director: (i) that each burial must be regarded as an entity for which the rituals should be reconstructed; (ii) that if more than a single grave is found the size and nature of the whole cemetery must be discovered.

These will be considered separately.

# THE DEATH AND BURIAL OF THE INDIVIDUAL

The succession of events likely to be encountered in any society may be considered under the headings of Rites of Preparation, of Disposal and of Remembrance. Archaeological evidence of them is only likely to be found if burial forms some part of the rites.

## RITES OF PREPARATION

Many of these take place around the body before the place of burial is reached, and it is only by inference, if at all, that they can be established. Others, notably the preparation of the burial site and of the body itself, leave direct evidence recoverable by excavation.

### (i) PREPARING THE BODY BETWEEN DEATH AND BURIAL

In most societies a number of rites, requiring periods lasting from a few hours to perhaps several years, intervene between death and final burial. The excavated remains whilst they are still *in situ* may show something of them, so that all bodies should be carefully and fully uncovered and no bones should be removed until they have been studied, drawn and photographed.

If the burial was an *Inhumation* it may prove on exposure to be *articulated*.[52] This can be established by showing that all the smaller bones, especially fingers and toes, were present and in position. If this is the case, burial probably took place within a few weeks of death, and study of the attitude of the body may show what happened to it. Was it in an unnatural position with the arms strained behind or legs doubled against the chest? If so this would suggest binding. Was it deliberately mutilated—perhaps with the feet reversed, a hand or head severed, or marks of cuts on the bones? Was it preserved before burial so that the flesh or skin is intact?[52] (Plate XVII).

The orientation of the body should be noted, and whether it was extended—that is, lying on the back, front or side with the legs straight; flexed—a variation of extended but with legs partly bent; or crouched with the legs drawn up to the chest. If the body was buried sitting-up it should be checked to see if the position was an unnatural one, perhaps due to being bound (Fig. 43b).

In all these positions the heads, arms and legs should be particularly studied, the position of the finger and toe bones being especially significant, for they will show whether the feet or arms were crossed and the hands placed or tied together.

If the body was buried incomplete and *disarticulated*,[53] especially if the smaller bones were missing, a longer period, possibly months, if not years, elapsed between death and final burial. Some kind of storage or temporary burial may have taken place and small bones may have been missed when collection took place. Alternatively it may be possible to show that the body had been pushed to one side to make room for later burials, that bones (e.g. jawbones or skulls) had been abstracted by the living, or that animals had disturbed the burial (e.g. broken and gnawed bones).[53]

*Clothes and ornaments.* Still studying the body and its surrounding objects before they are moved, it may be possible to say that it was buried dressed.[54] Any object on or near the body, especially any metal ones, should be examined for survivals of cloth fragments, but it may be possible to decide, even when no fabric or skin remains, that the body was dressed. The position of the objects which may show the presence of clothes should be recorded three-dimensionally and the pins, buckles, studs, toggles, buttons and fibulae may show how they were fastened. Belts or baldricks can be indicated by buckles, studs, belt-hooks, weapons, toilet-objects or pendant purses. Shoes may be shown by nails or studs, and hats by ornaments and clasps. Ornamental plaques and fringes may also show garments. The relative positions of these objects may enable a series of garments to be identified, e.g. cloak, baldrick, tunic, trousers and shoes.[54]

*Ornaments, insignia and amulets* can also be shown to have been worn. Rings can be seen to be in position on fingers, arms or legs, ears, necks or heads. The pattern of necklaces of beads and pendants or amulets may be more difficult to establish, but by recording the position of each object, it may be possible to reconstruct them. If the finds are very numerous it is best to consolidate them and the surface on which they have been exposed and remove the whole intact to a laboratory for study.[55]

Insignia can be suggested by exotic or elaborate objects worn or carried. Maces, axes, head-dresses or especially large and distinctive ornaments are the most obvious examples of this.

If the burial was a *Cremation* a separate series of events before burial may be recognisable. First the presence or absence of the funeral *pyre* will be obvious.[56] If the burning took place on the spot it will show by the reddening of the ground surface and the presence of much charcoal. Careful uncovering of the surface of the charcoal and then its dissection by the quadrant method may show the construction and composition of the pyre. The following should be looked for: a platform of earth, turf, stones or wood which may have been made over a pit or trench dug to act as a flue; the charcoal pattern may preserve the order in which the logs were laid or show how the pyre was held together (e.g. stakes may have been driven in round it or a wall built); the distribution of burnt bones may suggest the position of the corpse and fragments of objects show what was burnt with it. Samples of the charcoal found should be kept so that the wood used can be identified.

If no pyre is found and the cremation took place elsewhere,[57] the heap of bones and/or charcoal which was brought for burial must be carefully uncovered without disturbing it. If it is found in a single heap a container may have been used and the heap may show it in the vertical and horizontal profiles. It should be excavated like an inverted pit and it should be possible to tell from the compactness and shape of the heap and the presence of pins, locks, handles or sherds whether it was deposited in a bag, box, pot or basket or was merely scattered.[58] Wicker baskets can be recognised by the pattern of discolouration, wooden boxes might be recognised in the same way as coffins and pottery or stone containers present no problems of recognition although the details of their interiors need detailed recording. Study may show if they were placed upright, sideways or inverted and were covered or left open. A study of the contents may show the remains of objects burnt with the dead (Fig. 43a).

The later examination of the bone fragments will show whether all the recognisable fragments were collected or only a sample, and whether charcoal was collected as well as bone. It should also be possible to tell if a small pit was made to receive the remains or if it was laid on a flat surface. If the bones and charcoal were scattered the whole surface should be exposed and drawn before any are removed.

## (ii) PREPARING THE BURIAL AREA

This can be an elaborate procedure and may well leave recognisable traces. Areas under mounds are particularly important, since here the pre-burial ground surface can often be recognised and events taking place on it related to the burial.

The marking out of a reserved area may take the form of stakes, pits, posts, ditches, banks or walls and is sometimes connected with the stripping of the top-soil.[59] It may be necessary to extend the excavation well beyond a surviving mound to find the full extent and true shape of the burial area (Fig. 41).

*Stakes, pits or posts* may surround the area, and their circular or rectangular regularity may infer their setting out with a cord either from a central post or round a pegged-out shape.[60] The angles of inclination at which the stakes or posts were set in the ground should be noted, and whether or not they were allowed to rot *in situ* or were removed (Fig. 40). Pits are usually distinguishable from post-holes in profile (page 122) and should be examined for evidence of slow silting or deliberate infilling.

The regularity of *ditches, banks and walls* should also be considered. If they were not laid out with cords they may have been dug or built in a series of short stretches, and this will show in plan and in the varying longitudinal depths of the different segments.[60] Banks or walls of stones or turf may have been erected in the same way. The ditches should be examined to see if they silted up slowly and naturally or whether they were deliberately filled in (Fig. 38). If the latter, evidence of the time gap between digging and infilling should be looked for. This might be confirmed by soil, pollen or mollusc evidence.[60]

The *stripping* of the topsoil from the whole marked out area may have taken place. If this was done, it will probably be recognisable only under a mound. During the excavation of mounds, variation in texture or colour of the soil above bedrock and below the mound should be observed. The absence of an undisturbed soil can be confirmed by analysis.

The study of a surrounding ditch or of post-holes may show the length of time between their being dug and their being filled in or covered over. The silt composition and the molluscs and pollen present may show that they were open for months or even years. Whilst the absence of any silting may suggest almost immediate backfilling.

PURIFICATION AND DEDICATION

Although these are an important part of most burial rites, little material evidence usually survives. Some slight suggestion of them may come from: isolated pits or post-holes either sterile or containing objects and bones, but deliberately filled;[61] from surface spreads of debris; or from fires. To be acceptable evidence, all must be stratigraphically connected with the grave and sealed by later rituals of the same burial. A careful search of the original ground surface round the burial must be made for traces of this kind. Single *pits* or *post-holes* are often noted with burials. Their shape and infilling deserve close attention even when sterile. The infilling can sometimes be seen to be deliberate and may be with clay or soil brought from a distance. Any bones, human or animal, found should be carefully cleaned *in situ* to check for articulation (Fig. 40).

*Fires and Surface Scatters* of objects on the ground surface before the burial took place can sometimes be recognised by their stratigraphical position (i.e cut through by the grave or by later post-holes or sealed by the mound). Fires, to be identified by the reddening of the soil rather than by the presence of charcoal, and scatters of tools, flint-knapping debris and sherds have been recorded.

THE GRAVE-PIT, PLATFORM OR MORTUARY CHAMBER

A special excavation or construction is usually made to receive the body.[73]

If there is a grave *pit* its size, shape and orientation should be noted. Careful trowelling and then brushing of the sides and bottom can show tool marks and so the method of digging it. Lining with timber or

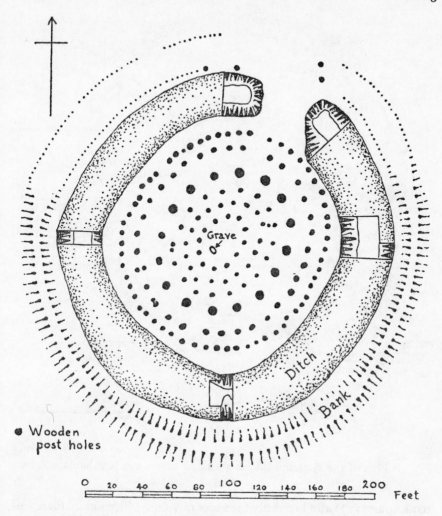

Fig. 47 Plan of Neolithic wooden religious monument, Woodhenge, Wilts.

wickerwork may show in plan or section (page 191); a stone lining will be obvious. The bottom of the pit should be examined for the post-holes of any structure in it or for a laid floor of sand, stones or wood (Fig. 43a).

An alternative to a pit is a *platform* of stones, turf or wood. It should be sectioned on the quadrant method and its details of construction, orientation, shape, etc. noted.

Whether or not there is a pit or platform, a *shelter* or *chamber* may have been erected to receive the body. This may take many forms, for it may be above or below ground, temporary or permanent, and built in a variety of materials. Excavation will be similar to excavating a

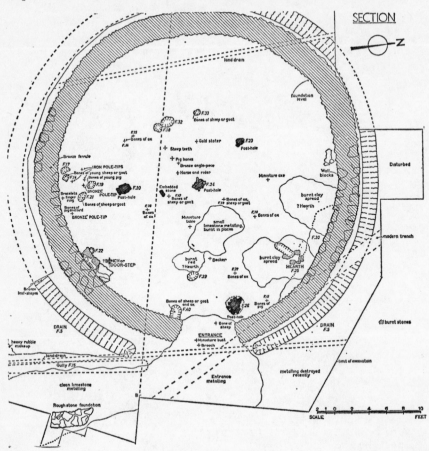

Fig. 48 Plan of the Romano-British shrine at Brigstock, Northants.

room (page 117) and here only the more obviously different features will be considered.

*Wood and Skin Shelters.* If a mound was later raised over a chamber of these materials, traces of posts and of walling may be observed during its excavation. If a number of strata can be distinguished in the mound and if they dip in any spot, this may be caused by the collapse of a chamber left empty of earth when the mound was raised. If any traces of walls or roof survive they will lie immediately above the floor, and the shapes of timbers, wickerwork and skin fragments may show in plan and section as discolouration of the soil. Alternatively the chamber may have been stopped from collapsing by being filled with soil as the mound was raised. If this was done then the vertical impressions of posts and walls may be preserved, and this too will be observed in plan during the excavation of the mound. Confirmation of the finds in the mound should come from the old ground surface. Here the post-holes, stake-holes, foundation trenches or wall footings of the chamber should confirm orientation and plan. Details of the construction may come from a study of the angles at which the stakes were set and from the outline of posts in the fill.

*Stone or earth chambers* are much easier to recognise. *Earth* ones will have walls on which a roof may have rested and will normally be found in plan as a soil change during the excavation of the mound.[65] Particular care should be taken at floor level, to look for roof supports, either post-holes or stone settings on which the posts rested. Laid floors of earth, stone or wood may also be found.

*Stone chambers* will vary greatly in elaboration. Any heap of stones immediately above a burial should be considered as a possible chamber. Its surface should be cleaned without disturbing it and the stones studied for any pattern of collapsed walls. During removal, registers of the stones (numbers, sizes and weights) should be kept so that the original nature of the chamber can be suggested. The final explanation of the heap should come from the lower levels and from the original ground surface where foundation trenches, stone-holes or perhaps intact bottom courses of walls should give the plan and orientation.

Chambers of very large stones (*Megaliths*) will require a different technique.[62] If the stones are standing, excavation will be relatively easy but very dangerous and the chamber should be treated like a room (page 117). Baulks should be left on the main axes and excavation be thin horizontal spits. These should be matched to baulks left outside the chamber. If the stones have collapsed, the heap when uncovered should look like a collapsed house of cards.[63] It should be photographed from as many angles as possible and planned before any stones are removed. If the old ground surface outside and inside the chamber can be recognised and followed up to the stones, their bases can be examined for setting-up pits. If these exist the process of excavation is much eased, and from the study of them and the areas round the method of erection of the stones may become apparent. Approach ramps may show how the stones were dragged into position, and chips and discarded tools how it was finally shaped. Setting-up pits will be necessary for most big stones, and although they are usually shallow in Britain, may be several metres in diameter and depth. When stones are lowered into them either from ramps, timber cradles or slings, lines of cushioning stakes may have been set in the bottom of the pit to stop toppling. The stake-holes may survive and should be looked for. Once in position the stone will need packing and wedging and the material used will be recognisable. All stone-holes should be sectioned and drawn (Fig. 42).

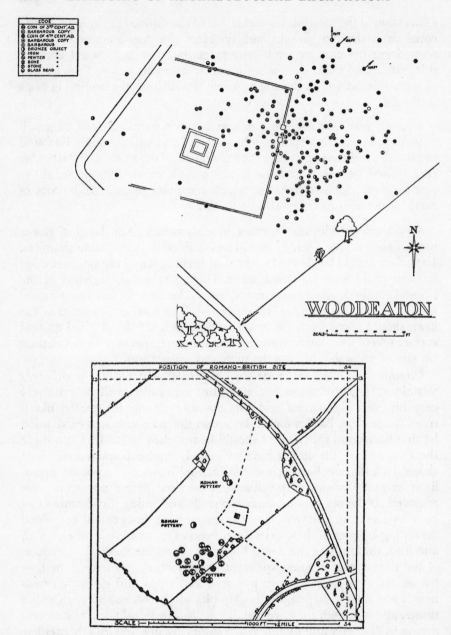

Fig. 49 Plan of a temple at Woodeaton, Oxon. Plan showing the distribution of surface finds in relation to the temple. Romano-British.

If, when examining a scatter of large stones some have setting-up pits and some none, then those which are lying above the original ground surface should, after careful photography and drawing, be removed. Those in setting-up pits should be pulled vertical. Special equipment will be needed; strong ropes, cushioning material round the stones, rollers and either a strong car, a tractor or a gang of men. Pulling stones vertical is difficult, especially if they are to be kept in their true position, but two tractors pulling at carefully chosen angles have proved very successful. Special safety precautions will be necessary if work is to go on round the re-erected stones, and special insurance should be taken out.

As stones are uncovered or moved, great care must be taken not to damage them. Each stone should be recorded separately and this should include photographs, three-dimensional measurements, descriptions of the surface giving details of squaring, dressing, carving, inscriptions and signs of rubbing, and a geological definition. Fresh breaks and missing fragments of stone should be looked for and the latter restored to their parent block. In this way the wall and façade stones will remain and the chamber will be freed for excavation.

Stones found on the surface may well be roofing stones and should be studied *in situ* for the way they fell. Their undersurfaces may show signs of rubbing where they rested on the wall stones. Dividing or blocking stones, shown to be structural by their stone-holes, may be found at the entrance, or within the chamber, dividing it into two or more sections.

*The chamber interior*, as already discussed, should be excavated with cross-baulks until the floor is reached. This may well be of stone slabs, sand or some other special material and so be easy to recognise. If not, then the floor level may appear from the way in which objects (bones, etc.) lie on it. The latter must be carefully recorded.[64] Robbing of the chamber is possible and a watch should be kept for the trenches and debris of robbers.[63]

*The Forecourt.* There may be an area reserved for ceremonies either just outside the mound or revetted into it. Its excavation should be on the grid method with, if possible, 2 m. squares and narrow baulks; the central baulks should be a continuation of that in the chamber (Fig. 42). The main problem will be to locate the old ground surface and then to record all objects found on, or features found in, it.

# RITES OF BURIAL

The precise position of a burial can rarely be established before it is reached by excavation, and there should be no preconception on the part of the director of where it is likely to be found. The shape of the mound if there is one is of little help, for this may have changed since erection and in any case burials are often not at the centre. Careful excavation of the mound or pit is the only method of location. When a burial is located, either in or below the mound, the possibilities of coffined or uncoffined inhumation and of enclosed or scattered cremation must be borne in mind, but in all cases the method of excavation will be similar. The grave pit or burial area should be quadranted and then the quadrants dug successively in not more than 10 cm. horizontal levels. Only by seeing the pit or area in plan and elevation at different depths can features be discerned[65] (Fig. 41).

It should first be distinguished whether or not the remains were buried in a coffin. *Stone or ceramic coffins*[66] are inescapable, offer no particular excavating problems, and care is to be concentrated on their contents. *Wooden or basketwork coffins*[67] are more difficult to recognise. In suitable conditions the actual casket will survive, but usually only the discolouration caused by its decay will show (Fig. 43). Extremely careful excavation is therefore necessary.[65] The vertical sections are particularly important since the thin (perhaps ·5 cm. only) coffin walls may show up better in vertical section than horizontal plan.

Once the presence of a coffin has been established, its construction and shape must be discovered. This should come from the vertical and horizontal exposures mentioned above. It may have been made from a tree trunk or sections of tree trunks, its shape showing whether it was merely hollowed for the burial or was a re-used canoe or domestic trough. If the coffin was made from planks and its outline is preserved, it should be possible to see if it was a box, a cart, a sledge or boat. Coffins made of planks may be nailed together, so that if a nail is found it should be left in position whilst a search for others is made at that level over the pit. If a number are found they should be planned, noting the position of the nail heads and shanks, before being removed and a lower group sought. Coffin handles, corners and side-reinforcing plates may give further indications. Samples of discoloured soil or fragments of the wood should be kept for laboratory identification.

A careful examination round and under the body inside the coffin is especially important, for it may show evidence of bedding or cushions; layers of reeds, rushes, grass, heather, branches, leather and matting have all been reported.[68] Samples should be taken for possible pollen, spore and seed identification.

Where no trace of a coffin is found the body may have been wrapped in perishable material such as skin or cloth.[69] Stains, fragments of organic matter, pins or the position of the body (e.g. the position of the feet in an inhumation or the shape of the heap of bone in a cremation) may suggest it.

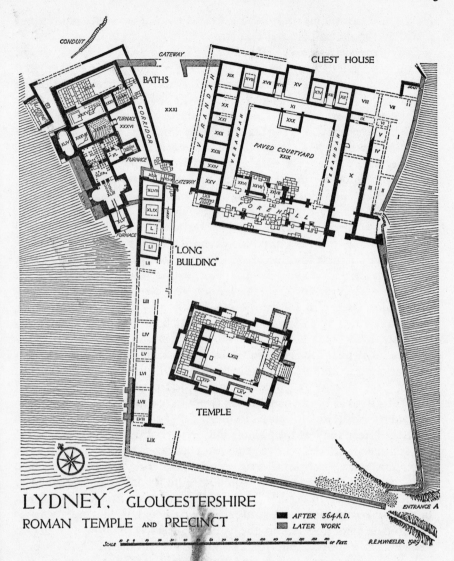

Fig. 50 Plan of a Roman religious complex, Lydney Park, Gloucs.

## OFFERINGS FOR THE DEAD

It is the practice in many societies to leave extra equipment and food and drink with the dead for their comfort in the next life. These can often be distinguished by their position, from clothes and personal belongings worn at the time of burial, and should be studied separately.

o

Horizontal trowelling round the burial should discover these offerings and they should be planned and studied before removal.

*Spare Personal Equipment* might be laid near-by.[70] Weapons would normally be hafted and sheathed, but might be deliberately broken, and study of them *in situ* may give evidence of this. The orientation of the heads of the spears, axes, maces and arrows should give the line of the shaft, and horizontal trowelling might show bindings, ferrules or the discolouration caused by decayed wood, bone or antler. Groups of arrow-heads deserve special attention since a quiver may have been present. Swords, daggers and knives may well show traces of handles or sheaths. Should trowelling define any of these as a staining, either the weapon and its surrounding area should be strengthened and removed intact, or organic fragments should be collected for study. *Household equipment*[71] may also be found stacked for future use, and excavation may expose and record it in functional groups; for cooking, sets of pots, tripods and cauldrons, flesh-hooks and ladles; for eating, sets of plates and bowls; for drinking, sets of cups, coolers, mixers, strainers and jugs; for smoking, pipes, strike-a-lights, pouches. Discolouration may also indicate tents, bedding or hangings. Furniture may show itself by fallen inlays (of wood, bone or metal) or fittings (handles, locks, etc.).

*Spare clothes* may be represented by buttons, buckles and concentrations of organic matter, and study may show if they had been placed in boxes, bags or baskets. *Jewellery* or *toilet-sets* may also be found, and concentrations of beads, ornaments, tweezers, ear-scoops, etc., should be studied for evidence of their containers. The *tools* of their craft may also be placed near the dead. Spinners and weavers might be accompanied by spindle-whorls, loom-weights, shuttles and bobbins; smiths by hammers, chisels, chasers, anvils and tongs, or doctors by surgical instruments.[72] *Conveyances* may sometimes be found either complete or dismembered and stacked.[73] In most cases only the fittings will survive, but their recognition and study before removal is the only way to disentangle and understand the various pieces of equipage. Wheeled vehicles, for example, might be recognised by wheel-rims, hub-casings, axle-pins, yokes, terret-rings and pole-terminals. From these the size and form of the vehicles may be recovered. Sledges may be revealed by their runners and boats by their shape and construction.

### FOOD AND DRINK[74]

If this has been placed beside the dead it may be possible to distinguish it from the remains of funeral feasts. It can often be recognised by its containers if these are of pottery or metal. Meat bones can easily be identified, but care should be taken to see whether groups of them are articulated, for both joints and complete skeletons of food animals may be found. Grain, fruit, flowers or vegetables may survive in a carbonised or desiccated form, and when food deposits are suspected (i.e. on a plate), the earth should be removed for later study. If covered vases or platters are found, it is especially important that their contents should be kept for laboratory examination.

## COMPANIONS

Burials contemporary with, but around, the main burial may be those of animals or humans buried as companions for the dead. The contemporaneity must be stratigraphically certain and recorded with great care, preferably by intermediate sections. They will normally be articulated, and when exposed and studied *in situ* their equipment and position may give some clue to their role. The animals should be studied for method of killing and the position in which they were deposited. The humans, in addition to the details already mentioned, should be studied, for their accoutrements may show them to have been retainers (e.g. soldiers or grooms), or the positions of their arms and legs show them to have been prisoners[75] (Fig. 41).

## RITES OF REMEMBRANCE[76]

Ceremonies at the graveside take place in almost all contemporary societies, and excavators should know something of the wide variety of ceremonies which may be practised. They will rarely leave much material evidence and such as there is will be fragmentary and enigmatic. Excavation must concentrate on the accurate and full recording of all structures and objects, and the report should allow only a minimum of speculation. The evidence is only likely to be found if the original ground surface round the burial has survived intact, and usually this will only be found if a mound was raised later. It must also be shown by the stratigraphy to belong without doubt to the period immediately after burial. The following might be encountered.

### FEASTS, SACRIFICES AND LIBATIONS

A scatter of burnt and broken animal bones and charcoal or actual fires on the old ground surface may be evidence of funeral feasts. The distribution of the bones should be plotted on the plan and samples of the charcoal taken. Hearths, if they exist, should be sampled for possible magnetic dating. The burial in small pits or the piling in small heaps, of selected bones may be evidence of feasts and/or sacrifices. Organic matter may show sheaves of corn or barley, piles of acorns, nuts, etc. The finding of drinking-cups either shattered or intact, perhaps associated with small sterile pits, may be evidence of libations.

### RITUAL SCATTERING, BREAKING, KNAPPING, ETC.

These rites can only be suggested by deliberate scatters of rock (e.g.

sand, quartz, flint, ochre) brought from a distance.[77] These should all be planned and described. Special note should also be taken of the position of any exotic objects found on the old ground surface, e.g. unusual animal bones, shells, or fossils.[78] By modern analogies they may well have been used in graveside ceremonies.

Broken or bent artifacts found lying on the old ground surface may indicate the sacrifice of objects. Associated with them may be scatters of freshly struck flint flakes which by plotting and studying later it may be possible to demonstrate were struck on the site. A scatter of broken pottery, either from a few or many different pots, may also be deliberate.

DANCING

Suggestions of this have been made at some sites from the condition of the ground surface but the indications are difficult to distinguish from those of the builders.[79] Trodden surfaces should certainly be looked for and may show as compacted clay or chalk. When uncovered, depressions should be recorded with plaster casts to check possible footprints. Rings round the burial, paths across causeways in the ditch or entrances through walls or stockades are the most likely areas in which to find this evidence.

COVERING THE REMAINS

This may consist of merely filling in the pit, and so making a flat grave, or in adding a mound (otherwise called a barrow, cairn or tumulus). The covering may be accomplished in several stages accompanied by more ceremonies. In excavating, evidence of these stages will naturally be the first to be recovered.

If no mound exists or after it has been excavated, the first evidence of the grave will be the fill of the *grave-pit*, an area of distinct colour or texture, showing in plan (Fig. 43a). At the edge there may be stones or the sockets of posts which stood round or on the grave. The grave should be excavated by the quadrant method working simultaneously in two opposed quarters. These quarters should not be carried to the bottom of the pit but to perhaps a 50 cm. depth, the sections then being drawn before the other quadrants are removed to the same depth. Then the new horizontal plane can be examined for features. If none are found the process can be repeated at successive 50 cm. depths, the section-drawing being continued down each time unless features (hearths, structures, etc.) make it desirable to interrupt the process. By this method any object found can be given an accurate three-dimensional position in its appropriate layer of fill. The method of filling the pit may be deducible from the tip-lines. It should be possible to tell whether the spoil dug from the pit was backfilled or if new material was brought; whether it was thrown in from one side or all sides; or whether there was a quicksilt at the bottom suggesting that the pit had remained open for some time. [80]

Grave-robbing should also be recognisable as a disturbance of the tip-lines of the fill. A careful watch should be kept for signs of the coffins, objects and mortuary houses already discussed.

When any part of the body is reached the whole of the fill should be removed to this level, so that the whole of the environs of the body and the uncovered body itself can be studied together (page 199).

## THE MOUND

Whilst not all burials are covered with a mound (of earth) or cairn (of stone) it is a very common feature, varying from the small heap of earth left over from refilling the gravepit to great artificial hills of stone brought from far away. The absence of a visible mound (Fig. 40) does not mean that none existed, for continual ploughing or deliberate levelling may have taken place. Excavation can show the presence of mounds even when only 5 cm. of them remain. Recognition will depend on the existence of, and the ability to recognise, the old ground surface. Then, if a stratum immediately below the present soil and above an earlier one exists this may represent the mound. It may show an admixture of bedrock, probably from quarry debris or the gravepit. If this is found its extent should be shown on the plan and sections.

If a mound is present, great care should be taken to record variations in its composition, since these may show its method of construction, the precise stratigraphical position of ceremonies carried on during its erection, and any later disturbance.

The most generally accepted *technique for excavating mounds* or cairns is the quadrant method, since this leaves complete cross-sections of the barrow. [81] Any form of single trench or central pit-digging should be avoided.

From a point at the apparent centre of a round mound, baulks should be laid out, their orientation depending on the siting of the spoil heaps and barrow runs if the mound is well preserved, or on obtaining a section of the most complete part of it if there is much destruction. They should be not less than 1 m. wide (1·5 m. in loose soil or sand). The two larger opposed quadrants should be removed first, so that the complete cross-sections of the mound are exposed, and the other two removed later using the experience gained in the first two. The baulks, left standing until the end, should be preserved for future sampling unless it is necessary (i.e. at the centre) to cut them away. Trenches should be carried well outside the mound, circa 7 m. on each side, so that the ground surface outside can be examined.

Oval/rectangular mounds will need a modified method of excavation but should still be completely excavated (Fig. 40). Of the various methods tried a central baulk along the longest axis with cross-baulks at 2 m. intervals seems most satisfactory.[82] When the chamber or burial areas have been located the excavation methods used will be the same as for other burials (page 202).

Opinions vary on the best way to carry out the actual excavation. Probably it is wisest to begin at the top of the mound and remove 20 cm. levels (which will be of ever-increasing area) until a soil change is reached. The surface of the new layer should be exposed, studied and photographed over the whole quadrant before digging to any greater depth. The process should then be repeated, once more beginning at the centre. Special attention should be paid to possible pits and disturbances (rabbits, moles, porcupines, etc.) and the objects from them isolated. Secondary burials and evidence of ceremonies will be studied during this process and then removed. If a chamber is located intermediate baulks at 1 m. intervals should be left at right angles to all walls found.

As excavation continues, care must be redoubled, for the original ground surface must be established. When located, it should be scraped, brushed and observed, if possible, under all weather conditions. Only in this way will post-holes, pits, etc. be discovered.

Finally the surface of bedrock should be exposed and any pits or post-holes not previously discovered investigated. Pits, including the grave pit, should themselves be quartered or halved so that their fill can be studied in both plan and section.

The restoration of the mound, especially when the baulks are left standing, should be obligatory.

In summary, excavation of the mound may show all or some of the following sequence. A small initial pile of earth, turves, or stones may be found immediately above the burial. Its profile should show if any subsidence took place into the grave or mortuary house, and its surface should be sampled to see if it remained exposed long enough for a soil to develop, or for vegetation to grow. Sometimes a casing of clay or stones may seal in this initial mound.

Over this, perhaps much later, a larger mound of top-soil or of quarried rock may be raised. If this is of soil it should be examined for regular discolourations or changes in texture which might be caused by turves being stacked or basketfuls of earth being tipped. If it is un-weathered, and so probably quarried, then the size and method of depositing the tips should be noted and the source of the material sought (e.g. quarry ditches). During the building of the mound, around its edges, or inside, there may have been revetments of large stones or low walls of turf or small stones, or of stakes and wickerwork. These may have been covered by slip from the mound. The outlines of stakes should also show in the mound material if they were left in position and allowed to rot *in situ*. The possibility of later enlargements, perhaps to cover later burials, should always be borne in mind, and if any indication of two or more complete 'envelopes' are found, samples from the surfaces of the inner ones should be examined for evidence of long exposure (developing soils, vegetation etc.).

Connected with its building may be trodden paths or ramps up which the material was carried. Objects found loose in the mound cannot of course be attributed to the burial; they may be of any previous period and have been caught up with the mound material and brought in from elsewhere.

Stratified within the mound may be evidence of feasts, dances, sacrifices carried out during the erection of the mound.

The kind of evidence left by feasts has already been described (page 211). If this is found stratified on horizontal surfaces high in the mound material it must belong to the period of construction. Dances, suggested only by the puddling or hardening of paths may also be recognised in the mound material.

Offerings or subsidiary burials may also be found.[83] These can only be confirmed as contemporary if there is no possibility of their having been inserted at some later date. They may otherwise mean that the barrow remained in use for generations.

Finally a pole or stone may be set up to mark the spot so that the top of the mound should be checked for stone- or post-holes.

OTHER RITES OF REMEMBRANCE

Most societies commemorate their dead by ceremonies conducted at intervals at the grave-side. These will normally leave few permanent traces, but the surface of the mound, the ground surface round about, and especially the forecourt if one exists, should be examined with them in mind.

The more common rites include offerings of food and drink and the lighting of fires. Animal bones, sherds and fires are often found near burial mounds, but unless stratigraphically related will not be firmly associated with them. The most likely area for evidence of this kind is at the edge of the mound where spill or wash may have covered it.

Secondary burials may also be an indication of continued reverence for a grave. The insertion of later burials in the skirts of the mound can be shown by stratigraphy and grave goods to be successive to the primary burial. The sum of these burials can only be found by a complete excavation of the mound.

## THE EXCAVATION OF CEMETERIES

The common rite, in all parts of the world, of burying bodies near to each other enables much extra information about the communities which practise it to be recovered. If a single grave of any kind be found, the area round should be explored for others, since cemeteries of all kinds of graves are known. Ways of locating them have already been discussed (page 198).

In spite of a few indeterminate groups (e.g. a barrow with a single primary and many later secondary burials), cemeteries normally present a number of problems over and above those already discussed under individual burials (Fig. 46).

(i) *Sociological.* Since many members of the community are represented, legitimate generalisations, impossible to make from a few graves, can be made of the population.[84, 85] These concern: its general skeletal morphology; its diseases, injuries and nutrition; its sex- and age-at-death ratios; and possibly its social divisions. To obtain this kind of information the whole extent of the cemetery and the probable number of graves in it must be known; all or parts of all quarters of the cemetery must be excavated and a large number of bodies (not less than 60 and preferably 150) be recovered.[86]

(ii) *Chronological.* Since most of the burials will be successive it may be possible to establish by grave overlap or artifactal typology the horizontal stratigraphy of the cemetery and to say something of its relative chronology.[85]

# EXCAVATION

Cemeteries will vary greatly in size and density[87] and detailed surveys should be made before excavation begins so that resources can be matched to the problem.

### ESTABLISHING THE EXTENT OF THE CEMETERY

If the burials were in or beneath mounds the most recent of these may be recognisable from aerial photographs or from walking the area. If they were in rock-cut chambers or caves there may be some clue in the natural topography (e.g. entrances in steep slopes) or even if they were in flat graves there may be an existing perimeter bank, wall, ditch or hedge. If the latter exists it should be traced and sectioned in the way already described (pages 227–48). If there are no surface indications the various kinds of surveys already mentioned may be tried (page 26) using a large grid (perhaps 10 m. squares). Depending on the soil-depth and the nature of bedrock, probe, resistivity or gradiometer surveys might show the grave pits. If these are unsuccessful or if the top-soil has been disturbed by cultivation or is otherwise unstratified (e.g. wind-blown sand) the upper level might be removed mechanically. In all other cases selective excavation will be necessary. This should take place along the two main axes of the grid and can be dug on the 'interrupted' method. Excavation should be carried on along the axes

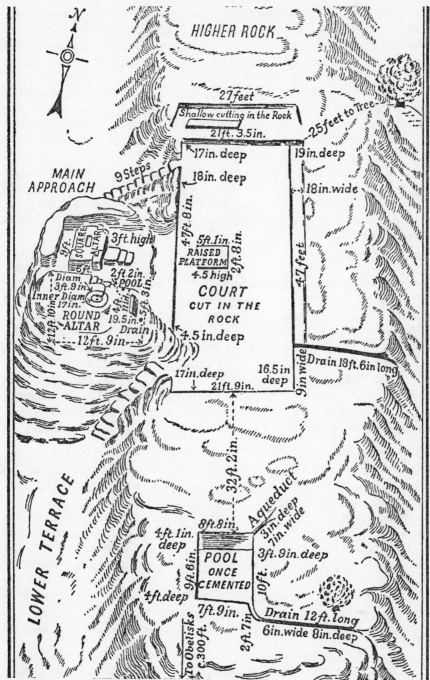

Fig. 51 Sketch-plan of a mountain top shrine, The Great High Place at Petra. An example of useful preliminary drawing.

until no more graves are found. Trenches should be carried down until the fill of the grave pits can be distinguished; further excavation should await excavating on a normal grid. When the full size and density of the cemetery have been established the excavation can be properly planned (Fig. 44a).

Whether all the graves should be excavated will depend upon the resources of the excavating team and the degree of danger to the site. If it is large and not in danger of destruction, then perhaps no more than one hundred and fifty graves chosen from different parts of the cemetery should be excavated.

If the cemeteries belong to living religions or communities, special arrangements will have to be made for their excavation (page 32).

The new problems will be those of organisation and recording, for the excavation of individual graves should be carried on in the ways already described.

The burial practices of many communities can be studied beforehand and the excavation and means of recording can therefore be planned in advance. For example, a Christian cemetery will normally have the bodies laid out east-west without grave goods, and in most burials earlier than the eighteenth century they will be without coffins. Many varying patterns of burial (e.g. near the church on the south side being especially popular, unchristened infants and excommunicants being buried immediately outside the sanctified ground) are to be expected and the whole may well be fenced. Re-use of the cemetery after several generations and the removal of the earlier skeletons to a charnel house is not unusual. Social distinction may show in the existence of family vaults for collective burial among the single graves (Fig. 45).

ORGANISATION OF CEMETERY EXCAVATIONS

On few sites of this kind will there be room for unskilled labour and the work will mostly be by trowel and brush. There will be a special need for skilled trowellers able to clean skeletons and their accompanying objects. Recruitment should therefore be highly selective and limited to a number that can be closely controlled. Not more than two trowellers should be allotted to a grave and they should be allowed to carry its excavation right through. Spoil removal is difficult, for baulks will rarely be in the most convenient places and plank walks or conveyor belts will be useful. Within the trenches a problem will be the disturbance caused by workers moving about. This should be kept to a minimum and restricted to plankways or other fixed routes. Spoil heaps should be

Fig. 52 (*opposite*) Christian church plans. (A) The old Minster, F in relation to the New Minster, G. (B) Also showing foundations and robber trenches, Winchester Cathedral, Hants. To be considered as an example of drawing successive phases.

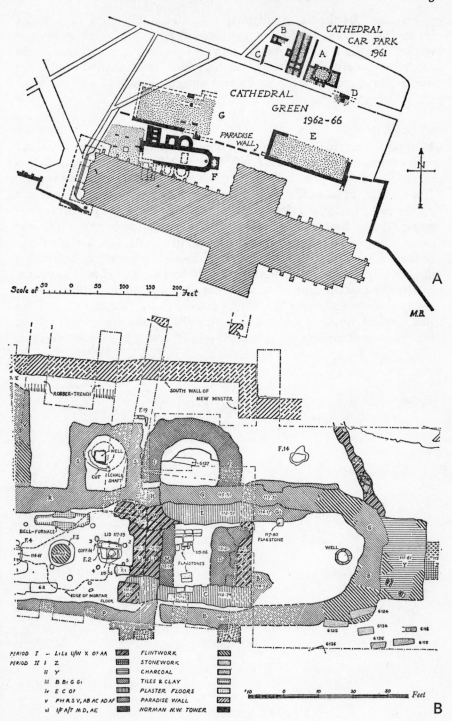

CATHEDRAL
CAR PARK
1961

B
C
A
D

CATHEDRAL
GREEN
1962-66

G
PARADISE
WALL
E
F

N

Scale of    50    0    50    100    150    200   Feet

A

M.B.

ROBBER-TRENCH
SOUTH WALL OF
NEW MINSTER
F.19

WELL
CUT
CHALK
SHAFT

G.127
F.14

113·51
113·57
114·47    G1
117·80
FLAGSTONE
WELL

111·61    115
Y    Z

BELL-FURNACE
F.4    F.3    LID 117·59
114·41    COFFIN
F.2    115·06
EDGE OF MORTAR
62    FLOOR

115·06
FLAGSTONES
112·74

6124
6125    6134
6135    6116
6136    6115

| PERIOD I | — L₁ L₂ U/W X O? AA | FLINTWORK |
| PERIOD II | i    Z | STONEWORK |
| | ii    Y | CHARCOAL |
| | iii    B B₁ G G₁ | TILES & CLAY |
| | iv    E C O? | PLASTER FLOORS |
| | v    P H R S V, AB AC AD AF | PARADISE WALL |
| | vi    I/F A/T M D, AE | NORMAN N.W. TOWER |

10    0    10    20    30    Feet

B

down-wind. In the actual digging a careful watch must be kept for intersecting graves, so that intermediate sections can be set up at once to preserve the relationships (Fig. 45). Depending on local conditions extensive preservation of the bones may have to be carried out on the site.[87] The bagging of the bones and objects (page 63) will also need careful organisation.

RECORDING

Many different methods have been used[88] with success, especially those with preprinted index cards. A criticism of these is that the information recorded is limited but this might be avoided by the following system. If a number of loose-leaf covers are provided (enough for each of the graves being excavated simultaneously to have its own) the strata of the grave-fill and its contents can be fully recorded (page 55). When the grave is finished the pages can be removed to a central file and the cover re-used. Each burial, as it is uncovered, should be photographed with a large label giving its serial number.[89] Plans and sections should be drawn as already described or, if time presses, perhaps photographed by the *photogrammetry* technique. A photographic tower, boom or platform (for vertical views) would be necessary. Especially important will be the drawing of the sections which show intersecting grave pits (Fig. 45).

## SUGGESTED READING

*Notes and Queries on Anthropology*★★, BAAS 1962 (Part II Chap. 7).

*A Guide to Field methods in Archaeology*★, Heizer, R. and Graham, J. 1967 (Chap. 8 with good bibliography. For burials only.

*Digging up Bones*★, Brothwell, D. 1965 (particularly Chap. 6). Good bibliography for burials only.

*A History of Architecture*★, Fletcher, B. 1943 (for a selection of plans of places of worship).

*The Archaeology of World Religions*, Finegan, J. 1952. (For plans.)

*Death, Property and the Ancestors*, Goody, J. 1962.

*The Bronze Age Round Barrow in Britain*, Ashbee, P. 1960.

*Temples in Roman Britain*, Lewis, M. 1966.

The Inner Sanctuary of Feather Cave, *AmAnth* 31 1968.

*West Kennet Long Barrow*, Piggott, S. 1962.

*Libenice*, Soudsky, B. 1962.

The excavation of two additional holes at Stonehenge, *AntJ* XXXII 1952. 14.

*Skorba*, Trump, D. 1966.

*Faras*, Michalowski, K. 1966 (cathedral).

*The Ziggurat and its surroundings* (at Ur), Woolley, C. 1939. Vol. 5.

*Lydney Park*, Wheeler, R. 1932 (shrine and building complex).

*Monastic sites from the Air*, Knowles, M. and St. Joseph J. 1952.

*Pazirik*, Rudenko, S. 1953 (Round barrows). English translation by M. Thompson 1970.

*Trentholme Drive, York*, the Romano-British Cemetery at, Wenham, L. 1969.

## NOTES

1. For a discussion of the kinds of questions to be answered see BAAS 1962 Part II, Chapter 7, and Goody, J. 1962.

2. Christian ecclesiastical architecture, for example, has an immense literature. The regional and chronologically relevant sections of it must be studied before any particular site is excavated. Finegan, J. 1952 and Fletcher, B. 1943.

3. e.g. For Christian sites in Britain see Knowles, M. and St. Joseph, J. 1952.

4. Many Christian churches show examples of chapels or shrines containing specially revered graves.

5. The animal and bird burials in Egypt, or the animal sacrifices in China. e.g. (quoted by Watson, W. 1961. 72).

6. Pits with funnels or flagstones with holes. e.g. Evans, J. 1959. 137.

7. Brigstock: *AntJ* XLIII, 1963. 234.

8. In a different context the burnt remains from Barclodiad y Gawres, Powell, T. and Daniel, G. 1956, show what might be found.

9. e.g. the flintblade in the altar of the western Temple at Tarxien (Malta): Evans, J. 1959. 116.

10. For examples of votive offerings see Hjortspring: Bronsted, J. 1960, and Llyn Cerrig Bach: Fox, C. 1946.

11. e.g. the well of sacrifice, Chichen Itza, *NGM* 120. 4 1961. 540.

12. A common method in all continents. e.g. Anyang: Watson, W. 1961, Ur: Woolley, C. 1934 2, Kastabos: Cook, J. and Plommer, W. 1966.

13. The oracle bones of the Shang Dynasty in China are a good example: Cheng, T-K. 1964.

14. e.g. Elkin, A. 1954. 191 and 232.

15. For ethnographical examples: Elkin, A. 1954, for archaeological possibilities: Ucko, P. and Rosenfeld, A. 1967 Chapter 3.

16. Feather Cave: *AmAnth* 31.i 1968. For ethnographical examples see Elkin, A. 1954.

17. The Hypogeum (Malta) is a good example: Evans, J. 1959. 129.

18. A faint hope perhaps, but worth testing for.
19. e.g. *Mapungubwe*. Fouché, L. 1937 and Fagan, B. 1966. The Great High Place of Robinson (Petra): Albright, W. 1960. 164.
20. e.g. Tell Abu Shahrein: *Sumer* III, 1947. 84 and IV, 1948. 115. Nippur: McCown, D. 1967. (Vol. I). Ur Excavations V: Woolley, C. 1939. Tikal: Willey, G. 1966.
21. Chichen Itza (op. cit.).
22. e.g. Poverty Point: *APAMNH* 46 1956, and *Libenice*: Soudsky, B. 1962. In Britain they date from the Neolithic or Bronze Ages.
23. See Avebury: Keiler, A. 1965 and Poverty Point: *APAMNH* 46 1956. For a recent rescue operation on a large one at Durrington Walls see *AntJ* XLVII 1967. 166.
24. e.g. Woodhenge. Cunnington, M., 1929.
25. Stonehenge: *AntJ* XXXII 1952. 14, and Avebury: Keiler, A. 1965.
26. Good examples of excavation reports are: Nippur: McCown, D. 1967; Skorba: Trump, D. 1966; Faras: Michalowski, K. 1966.
27. In a modern English village the parish church may be well away from the village centre and there may be several chapels scattered through the settlement.
28. e.g. the London Mithraeum: Grimes, W. 1968.
29. Islamic practice is a good example of this; see Garlake, P. 1966.
30. e.g. Central America: 300 BC–1500 AD. Mediterranean: 700 BC–400 AD.
31. e.g. Toltec Chichen. Coe, M. 1966. 125 and plate 72.
32. Rome, Gjerstad, E. 1960. Vol. III.
33. *Antiq* XXIX 1955. 4 and *Dorchester*, Vol. I Atkinson, R. 1951 and Vol. II forthcoming.
34. e.g. Ephesus.
35. Sometimes these are distinctive, e.g. S.W. England: *MedArch* I 1957.
36. e.g. Pangong (Burma) and Delphi (Greece).
37. e.g. La Venta, *BAEB* 170 1959.
38. e.g. Christian religious house plans vary greatly in the different communions and even in different orders. e.g. Evans, Joan 1964; Gilyard-Beer, R. 1958 and Knowles, M. and St. Joseph, J. 1952.
39. Compare the cells of a Celtic house (St. Helens: *AntJ* CXX, 1964, 40 or Norman, E. 1970. 54) with the dormitories of a Catholic one (Fountains Abbey: Fletcher, B. 1943. 384). For excavation see Vale Royal. *AntJ* XLII 1962. 18.
40. For examples see Khafajah (Sumerian): Delougaz, P. 1940; Lydney Park (Romano-British): Wheeler, R. 1932; Winchester (Mediaeval); *AntJ* XLVII 1967. 251.
41. Lewis, M. 1966.
42. Stonehenge and West Kennet Avenues: Atkinson, R. 1960. 66, 75 and 151, and Keiler, A. 1965.
43. In Britain, for example, all excavators should know the succession of rituals employed from neolithic to recent times, for the dates of the burials is often uncertain until excavation is well advanced.
44. see BAAS 1962 Part II, Chapter 7.
45. Grinsell, L. 1953.
46. Nine days' flying in June 1961 located about a hundred sites in North France: *Antiq* XXXVI, 1962. 280.
47. Nutbane: *PPS* XXV 1959. 15. West Kennet: Piggott, S. 1962.
48. Grinsell, L. 1953.
49. As in many Christian and Moslem cemeteries, but also in prehistoric ones as in the recent excavations in Gambia (information from P. Ozanne, University of Ife, Nigeria).
50. e.g. Dorchester: Atkinson, R. 1951.

51. Lerici, C. 1959. At Monte Abbatome and Viterbo more than 4000 were located.
52. Brothwell, D. 1965. Heizer, R. and Graham, J. 1967. 111. Mutilation: *PPS* XXVI, 1960. 298, *WAM* 1914. 616. Soft tissue; Rudenko, S. 1953. 136. Dunham, D. (ed) 1965; Brunton, G. and Caton-Thompson, G. 1924. 19.
53. Disarticulated: Wheeler, R. 1938. Successive: *PPS* IV, 38. 125.
54. Woolley, C. 1934. Rudenko, S. 1953. Glob, P. 1969.
55. Woolley, C. 1934.
56. Fox, C. 1959. Grimes, W. 1960; Glasbergen, W. 1954. For cremation ceremonies. see *Antiq* VII 1934. 58. and Iliad (Book XXIII) Penguin Classics Edition.
57. e.g. Quernhowe. Bones separate: Fox, C. 1959 p. 145.
58. Wickerwork: Fox, C. 1959. 135. Urns: Fox, C. 1959. 52.
59. Laid out: Ashbee, P. 1960. Turf stripped: Landsdowne 6a. Stakes: Fox, C. 1959. 134.
60. *PPS* XXVI 1960, 266.
61. Small sterile pits are quite commonly recorded.
62. Rudenko, S. 1953. 59. *PPS* XXIII 1957. 124. Wood: in general Ashbee, P. 1953 Stone: Piggott, S. 1962. Earth: *PPS* XXV 1959. 15.
63. *ArchCant* LXXVI 1961. 26.
64. Powell, T. and Daniel, G. 1956; Piggott, S. 1962.
65. *PPS* XXIII 1957. 124.
66. *PCAS* XLIX 1956. 12.
67. For general descriptions see Glob, P. 1969.
68. Glob, P. 1969. For spore identification see Bishop's Waltham. *PPS* XXIII 1957. 137.
69. Woollen shrouds were compulsory in sixteenth-century England and the positions of the bodies sometimes suggests them.
70. e.g. Sutton Hoo. Green, C. 1963. Chapters 4 and 5.
71. Green, C. 1963. 73. Hencken, H. 1968. For complete organic survival see Rudenko, S. 1953.
72. e.g. a doctor's grave *PPS* XXI 1955. 231.
73. Rudenko, S. 1953. 233. Lovosice: *RevArch* XI 1959. Honan: Watson, W. 1961. 130. Egypt: Carter, H. 1927 Vol. 2. 54.
74. *PCAS* XLVII 1954. 25. For desiccated remains see Carter, H. 1927. Vol. 2. 189.
75. e.g. at Ur: Woolley, C. 1934.
76. For a description of post-burial rites see the Iliad (Book XXIII).
77. Cairnholy I: *PSAS* LXXXIII 1949. 103.
78. e.g. Endocrines. Grinsell, L. 1953.
79. Fox, C. 1959. 129.
80. *AntJ* XLVII 1967. 224 and *PPS* XXVI 1960. 266.
81. See Ashbee, P. 1960 and Glasbergen, W. 1954.
82. Piggott, S. 1962.
83. *PPS* XXXIII 1967. 336.
84. Brothwell, D. 1965. Chapters 3, 4 and 5.
85. Heizer, R. and Graham, J. 1967. Chapter 8. Examples: Veio (Quattro Fontanili) *NDS* 1965. 53. Hallstatt: Kramer, K. 1960. Münsingen: Hodson, F. 1968.
86. It is estimated that Glasinac (Bosnia) has some 20,000 spread over several hundred acres: Benać, A. 1956; and that Clopton (England) has some 4,000 in one acre: Alexander, J. in Munby, L. (ed) 1968.
87. Brothwell, D. 1965 Chapter I, Sections 9–12.
88. Heizer, R. and Graham, J. 1967. 115.
89. Brunton, G. and Caton-Thompson, G. 1924. Maiden Castle: Wheeler, R. 1943. *ArchJ* CI 1944. 68.

CHAPTER X

# Problems in the Excavation of Military Sites

'Think like a Soldier.'

Anon.

Structures deliberately made for military purposes (defined here as for defence against other men) are common in all continents and most periods. Their excavation poses many problems different from those of religious or domestic sites (Fig. 53), and any archaeologist proposing to excavate one should have prepared himself, in addition to his general training, by a study of military strategy and tactics. Military constructions are usually the product of well-organised and often historically known societies, and unless the kind of weapons available and the nature of the communities involved are known, the sites will not be properly understood.[1] It is therefore necessary that some idea of the date of a site, and if possible its historical setting, should be obtained beforehand.

Two categories of sites may be distinguished: those constructed by professional soldiers for *tactical* (e.g. temporary defences and siege works) or *strategic* (e.g. permanent forts, frontier defences, roads and depots) reasons, and those which may not be the work of professionals (e.g. the defences of domestic sites such as farmyards or towns).

*Professionally built strategic works* are commonly more permanent than tactical ones and connected with the long-term domination or defence of a region. The sites will have been selected with care and expert knowledge and the buildings will be substantial. For this reason there will rarely be much problem in locating them, and especially suitable sites may well have been used many times.

The most elaborate will be *fortresses* (Fig. 60) built by expert engineers.[2] They will often be constructed in stone or brick rather than timber, turf and earth; their excavation is discussed on page 238. Smaller *forts* (Fig. 58) may be control or staging posts, signal stations or supply depots;[3] their position and the finds in them may indicate their role. Earth and wood are as likely in their construction as stone and brick. In both categories separate periods of occupation and restoration will have to be looked for and complexity will be the main difficulty in excavation. *Linear defences* stretching for many miles along political frontiers may be found; ditches and a wide variety of banks, walls and palisades are to be expected.[4] These defences may well be intermittent, joining areas of natural difficulty (e.g. forest, marshland).

*Professional tactical works* will, by definition, meet a particular and temporary military need, and will therefore be less solid and less easily located than the strategic ones.

Most substantial may be the *siege works* protecting the attackers of towns and fortresses.[5] These may vary from long and elaborate sapping trenches, assault ramps and artillery redoubts to perimeter walls or palisades designed to cut off supplies. They will be of earth, wood and stone. The problems of their excavation are discussed on page 227. Also

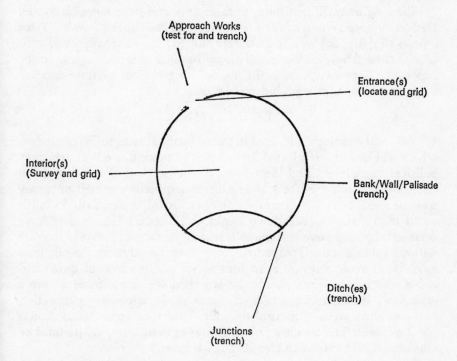

Approach Works
(test for and trench)

Entrance(s)
(locate and grid)

Interior(s)
(Survey and grid)

Bank/Wall/Palisade
(trench)

Ditch(es)
(trench)

Junctions
(trench)

Fig. 53 The problems of excavating military sites.

substantial may be the *campaign camps* (Fig. 59) built by a regular army operating in unfamiliar or hostile country.[6] The simplest will be night camps or laagers set up where a unit bivouacked for a few nights. Although even the most elaborate may only have been used for a few months, they may have been sufficiently well built of earth, stone and wood for much to have survived. *Battlefield works*, the banks and trenches, palisades and breastworks built to meet the immediate needs of fighting, are the least substantial.[7]

P

*Works not necessarily professionally built* will include all kinds of amateur defences as well as those built by architects and professional military engineers. They will normally be strategic rather than tactical, will have the same general features as the professional ones (banks, ditches, walls, gates, etc.) and should be excavated in the same way. *Farm defences* will be the simplest of all and may be more against animal than human predators.[8] In special circumstances the whole farm complex may be planned to be defensible. *Defended houses*, as distinct from farms, will usually be the dwellings of magnates or kings.[9] The fortifications will be more elaborate and often much modified and repaired.

*Village defences* will be similar to farm ones and little more elaborate. Hedges or thorny barricades are as likely as palisades or walls. *Town defences* (Fig. 61, 62) will be elaborate and extensive, usually walls with or without ditches and banks.[10] Towers, bastions and gateways are to be expected. They may remain in use for long periods of time and are likely to be much altered and repaired.

## LOCATION

Whilst local topology will enable many fortified sites to be predicted, others will have been selected for temporary tactical needs or arbitrary political boundaries, and there is no logical method of locating them. Since the remains are likely to be substantial, many methods of survey may be used. Aerial photography may be useful,[11] especially in cultivated land, for ploughed-down banks and filled-in ditches may have been so large and have become so masked that they can be mistaken for natural undulations. Temporary camps, as already mentioned, may have been made anywhere, so that aerial photographs of crop- and soil-marks in any area should be watched for the ditches of large enclosures. Short stretches of linear bank or ditch possibly connecting long-vanished areas of natural difficulty (marshes, forest, etc.) should also be looked for. 'Shadow' photographs of desert, steppe, pastoral or mountainous country can also be most helpful.

A ground survey should also be made of any commanding heights, especially if isolated and overlooking long-settled land, river-crossings or mountain passes, to look for ditches, banks and collapsed walls. Once features have been located, detailed resistivity, magnetometer, probe or auger surveys should establish, before excavation, the complete circuit of the fortifications; a filled-in ditch often being easier to trace than a slighted bank. From it can often be established the existence of features (e.g. angles not explainable by contours) which might indicate enlargements, alterations, or parts left unfinished; and the position of the gate or gates. These are often shown by the presence of approach or interior roads as well as by the existence of causeways across the ditch.

## PLANNING AND EXCAVATING

During the excavation, it being assumed that no literary evidence is available, the following questions should be answered: What was its complete plan? When, why and how was it built? How long was it in use? How did the occupation end?

Two main kinds of problems will be met with: if large areas are enclosed, finds and internal features may be few, therefore, although it is desirable that these sites should be completely excavated, this may involve much unproductive work and it may often be possible only to sample them. Alternatively in the actual fortifications and in the interior of small sites complexity and successive occupations are to be expected.

Since all military sites present similar excavating problems they may be considered together under the headings of *fortifications* (ditches and ramparts) and *interior* features.

## FORTIFICATIONS

*Defensive Ditches* may be very varied in size, from less than 2 m. to more than 35 m. wide and from less than 1 m. to more than 10 m. deep,[12] but will be distinguishable from simple drainage ditches by their position: they will usually enclose an area and have banks, fences, hedges or walls on their inner edge. The main archaeological problems will be: how the ditch infillings accumulated; whether or not they were cleaned out or recut at any time; and their relationships to intersecting features (Fig. 55). Many of these problems can of course be answered without finding any human artifacts. The main logistic problem will be their size and the amount of earth to be moved (Fig. 54).

Trenches should be sited at right angles to the main axes of the ditch and should never be less than 3 m., and preferably 6 m. wide, for light and space will be needed for the interpretation of the siltings near the bottom. The trenches should extend well beyond the visible lip of the ditch on both sides (Plate xii).

In most cases time and money will permit only relatively small areas of a big ditch to be excavated and these should therefore be carefully chosen. The most important areas will be those where objects may have accumulated in the silting. The butt-ends of ditches at causeways leading to gates are those most likely to contain rubbish thrown away or objects lost in fighting. Dating evidence may therefore be easier to obtain here. Any repairing of the defences, especially any partial cleaning out of the ditch, is also more likely to have begun here.

Other important areas which will need excavation are where a counter-scarp bank exists (often spoil from a recutting of the ditch); where there is an intersection with other features (ditches, banks, etc.), or where the ditch profile is well preserved and not mutilated by later events. These will mean that several groups of trenches will be necessary

UPWARD          DOWNWARD

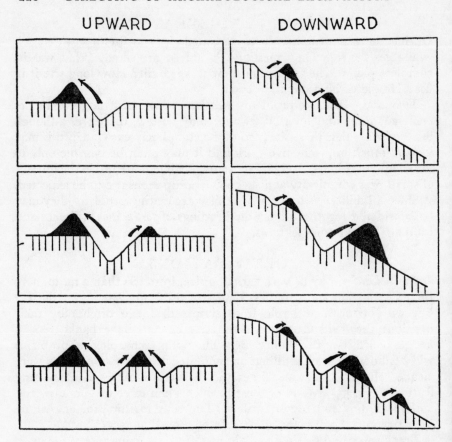

Fig. 54 Methods of constructing defensive banks and ditches. Early Iron Age.

on any site, and on a complicated site in which there are several enclosures, each will need a separate series. The layout of these trenches may be considered separately for different features.

When an entrance has been established, not merely suspected since then the work might well be wasted, a grid should be laid over the causeway and the ditch (as well as the gate) so that continuous sections are obtained through the bank and ditch and the gate and causeway.[13] The size of the grid must depend on the ditch size, but 4 m. squares may often be suitable.

## INTERSECTIONS AND RE-ENTRANTS

Interruptions in the regularity of the ditch and bank, not attributable to natural contours, may have been due to alterations in the plan and deserve careful study (Fig. 55). If no surface signs of an earlier ditch

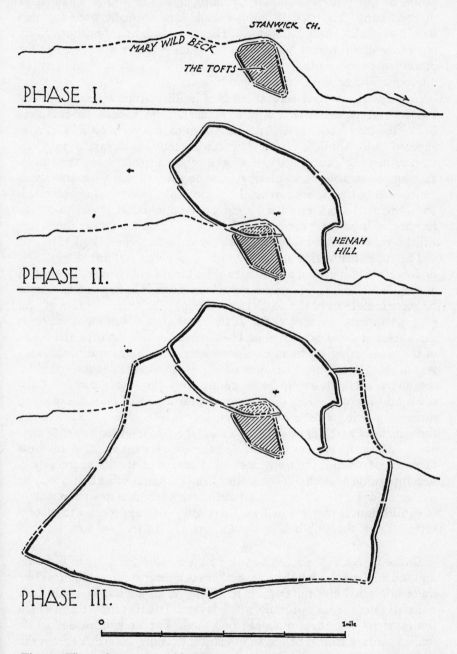

FORCETT CH.

STANWICK CH.

MARY WILD BECK

THE TOFTS

PHASE I.

PHASE II.

HENAH HILL

PHASE III.

0                                                                1 mile

Fig. 55 The enlargement of hillforts. Analysis of the Stanwick earthworks, Phases 1-3. Durham. Pre-Roman Iron Age.

at a different angle are found outside or across the interior at this point, probe or other surveys should try both areas for a filled-in ditch or slighted bank (Fig. 53). If one is found, then specially sited trenches should establish the relationships. They should be at the intersection, especially useful places being where a ditch is under a bank or at the place where two ditches meet, for the silting and profiles may be different. The sections must be published.

Any ditch may have several kinds of infilling from which its history can be reconstructed. Excavation of each layer should be complete before the next is started and the surface of each layer should in turn be exposed and studied. In a big ditch, individual layers may be 1 m. or more thick and it will not be possible to trowel away the whole. Picking, preferably hand-picking, can be used to dig 5–10 cm. levels which will naturally narrow as the bottom of the layer is approached. Inexperienced workers must be carefully watched at layer junctions. Digging will be most difficult at the lips of the ditch where the layers will be very thin, and these should always be trowelled (Fig. 38).

The main distinction noted should be between natural siltings and deliberate infillings, but all changes of texture or colour must be studied *in situ*. *Natural silting* will occur only if the ditch is left open and should be recognisable from the particles in the layer and their angles of rest (Fig. 55b). Primary silts, either at the centre of a V-profile ditch or at the angles of a flat-bottomed or U-shaped one, will often be the result of the weathering of the ditch sides before they became covered with vegetation (Plate XI). They are usually less organically stained than secondary silts. These dip more gently over the whole profile of the ditch and are composed of a series of thin layers of material often of different particle size. Stones, bones, sherds, etc. will normally lie on these surfaces as water or gravity deposit them, the larger, rounder ones collecting at the centre. By studying these layers the relative amounts of material washed in from each side and perhaps its sources (e.g. decomposition of ditch sides or erosion from a neighbouring bank) may be determined (Fig. 63). The amount of silt which accumulates before a state of equilibrium is reached will vary but will rarely approach the ground surface level; a gentle hollow would normally be its final stage.

*Deliberate infillings* should also be recognisable from their particles and the angles at which they lie. Soil or rock thrown into a ditch will be quite ungraded and the fragments will be at all angles; it should look quite different from naturally silted layers. The direction from which the material was thrown should be noted. The finds from deliberate infilling will of course be less significant for dating than those from the siltings (except as a *terminus post quem*) for they may have been brought from far and be of quite different epochs. A common infilling is a

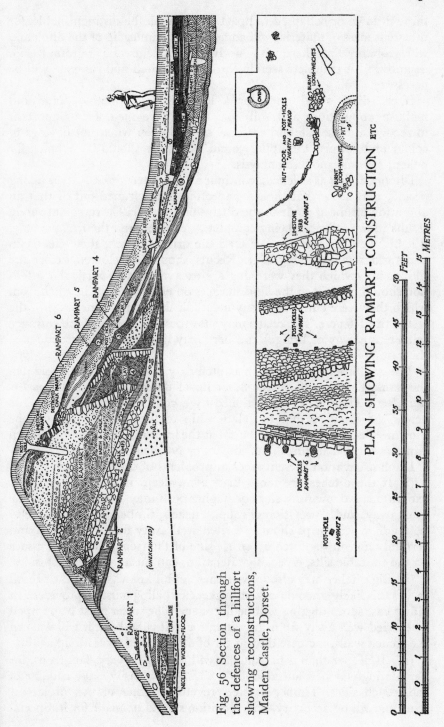

Fig. 56 Section through
the defences of a hillfort
showing reconstructions,
Maiden Castle, Dorset.

PLAN SHOWING RAMPART-CONSTRUCTION ETC

thrown-down or collapsed rampart. This should be distinguishable, for the great mass of material will come from the inner lip of the ditch and will probably link there with surviving fragments above ground (Fig. 24 and 63). A complete section through the ditch and rampart will be necessary.

If the ditch stood open for a long time, distinctive plant and mollusc populations and soils may have developed. It is important to recognise these established surfaces, and even when not obvious in colour and texture, the upper 30 cm. of siltings should be sampled for pollen, soil and mollusc analysis.

Ditches acting as defences, continuously or intermittently over a long period, may show that the silt had often been cleaned out or that an alteration has been made to the ditch shape or size. Cleaning out rarely results in the old sides being completely exposed and the *recutting* may, if it be not deeper and wider than the original ditch, show clearly in plan and section[15] (Fig. 63). Recuts should be cleared before the siltings into which they were dug are excavated, and particular attention should be paid to the land surfaces on either side of the ditch from which they were cut. These may help link them with some stage in the rest of the defences. The recuts may show best at the side of the entrance (either causeway or bridge) and here may link with reconstructions of the gateways.

The spoil from cleaning out the ditch may, if it is not used to heighten the bank, be dumped on the outer lip of the ditch forming a *counterscarp bank*. This should be sectioned by a continuation of the trenches across the ditch so that its relationship to the ditch fillings can be shown.[14] Sections should also be cut at the intersections of counter-scarp banks and other features (e.g. ditches or lynchets).

Ditch excavation presents special problems of organisation:

(i) If the ditches are more than 2 m. deep, mechanical hoists or excavators, barrow runs, steps or staging posts may be needed to get the spoil away, and a provision of ropes, buckets, timber, etc. may have to be made. Spoil heaps should be sited well away from the trench and certainly not on the ditch on either side of the trench; lateral pressure on the unstable silts, especially after rain, can push in the trench sides.

(ii) Big ditches may also be wet ones, and if knowledge of the subsoil makes this likely, then pumps or buckets for baling must be provided. In either case sump-digging will be necessary. The water must be pumped or carried well away from the ditch, for if it runs back it will weaken the trench walls, increase the danger of digging and soon fill up again.

(iii) If deeper than 2 m., ditches will always be very dangerous, for percolating water or unstable lower siltings can easily cause collapse of the trench sides. Timber or steel revetting either of box or lateral strutting will be necessary, and provision should be made for it. Special insurances and perhaps danger pay to employees may be necessary. Extra stability can be given by cross baulks or by having buttresses at intervals. These can be made into staircases.

(iv) If much revetting is done, artificial lighting in the trench bottoms may be necessary and should be arranged for in advance.

(v) If finds are rare, all human artifacts should be recorded by depth within layers. Pottery and other datable objects should be recorded three-dimensionally within their layers, but no reference of the depth to an outside datum is usually necessary. Objects will often lie at or near the junction of levels, and it is most important to locate them accurately here. It may be particularly difficult at the lips of a ditch where the layers will be thin.

Each group of objects belonging together (e.g. spread horizontally on a surface) should be kept together. This will often mean the recovery of intermediate surfaces of accumulation inside a main layer. Evidence of organic objects (e.g. boots, recognisable from staining and the hobnails being in position), articulated skeletons, or collapsed timbering recognisable as patterns of staining, should also be looked for.

*Defensive Ramparts*. These, being above ground, are often destroyed and so less easy to study than ditches. *Banks* will, of course, normally have existed wherever ditches have been dug, the latter often being primarily quarries for them, and will usually be on the inner lip of the ditches. On very steep slopes the ditches may be inside the banks, so the spoil could be thrown downhill[15] (Fig. 54).

Excavation will be concerned with how and when they were erected, whether banks of several periods were superimposed and how they were related to the various ditch siltings. The main practical problem will be the size of the banks which may be very large (e.g. 30 metres wide and 7 m. high). Any trench through them may be a big undertaking (Plate XII).

In assessing, before excavation, what may be accomplished, the man-hours necessary to dig the trench down to bedrock should be worked out (page 38), for much of the most important evidence will come from the lowest levels, and these must be exposed over some considerable area if they are to be properly studied.[16] No trench should be less than 3 m. wide, and if the rampart stands more than 3 m. high it should be at least 6 m. wide. The cutting should extend well beyond the visible bank on each side.

Most of the bank will be archaeologically sterile or will contain only archaeological material brought from elsewhere and so technically unstratified, and since the amount to be removed will probably be too great to dig with trowels, the director will have to control the work closely so that the sterile tips are picked and shovelled whilst tip-surfaces or old ground surfaces are trowelled.

234    DIRECTING OF ARCHAEOLOGICAL EXCAVATIONS

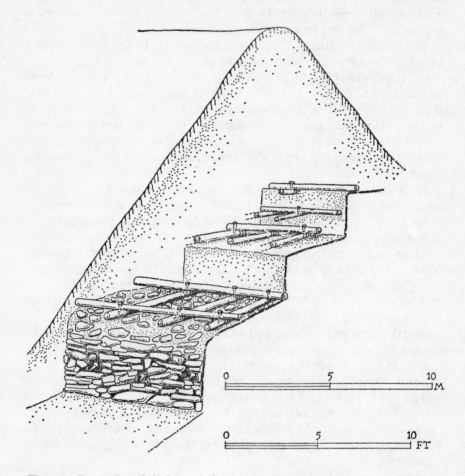

Fig. 57a Examples of timber reinforcements to ramparts. Le Camp d'Artus, Meulogoat, France.

Fig. 57b Successive reconstructions of wooden gates, St Catharine's Hill, Hants.

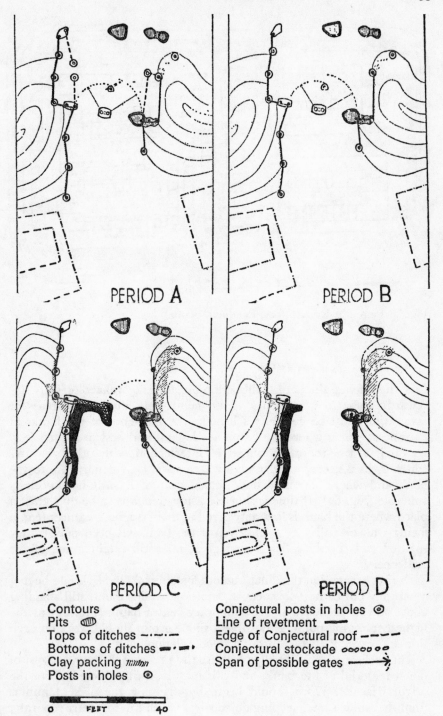

PERIOD A

PERIOD B

PERIOD C

PERIOD D

Contours ~
Pits ▥
Tops of ditches –··–··–
Bottoms of ditches ▰·▰·▰
Clay packing ᶬᶬᶬ
Posts in holes ◎

Conjectural posts in holes ◉
Line of revetment ━
Edge of Conjectural roof ━ ━ ━
Conjectural stockade ○○○○○ ○○
Span of possible gates ━━━➤

0        FEET        40

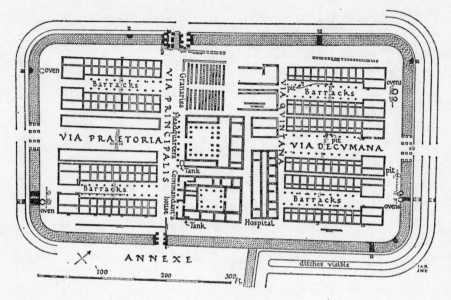

Fig. 58 Plan of a Roman fort, Fendoch, Scotland.

SITING OF TRENCHES (Fig. 53)

Like the ditches, the banks will be too big and too archaeologically un-
rewarding for long stretches to be completely dug, and areas for
excavation must be carefully selected. The butt-ends of the banks at
entrances; places where the banks are highest and best preserved (e.g.
no obvious tree-rooting); places of intersection with other features
(ditches, banks, etc.); and places where settlement came close to the
bank and where slip may have sealed part of it, will be especially
valuable (Fig. 62). If time is short or a test-trench is to be dug, then a
place where the bank is low may give the main original features (e.g. a
facing wall or palisade, etc.). Even if the bank has been deliberately
slighted and is only a few cms. high it may still retain much of the
evidence.[17]

During excavation the inner and outer slopes of a bank should be dug
separately but contemporaneously (unless a wall is found still standing
above the surface), leaving a temporary centre baulk (Fig. 62) at the
highest surviving point. If possible a single group should work on each
side and carry the work through to completion.

The surface of the *outer slope* will usually preserve the angle of rest of
much material of the bank, and this may be quite different from the
original façade. Work should begin by stripping the present humus
from the whole slope, keeping objects from each square metre separate,

for they may have significance later.[18] When the surface of the bank material is exposed, trowelling should begin in 5 cm. horizontal levels at the top of the bank.

If the bank was of dump construction and sterile tip material appears, then picks and shovels should replace trowels and 10 cm. horizontal levels be dug until a change of material is reached. When this happens the surface of the new layer should be exposed from top to bottom of the face before the process is repeated. The surface of each layer should be examined for signs of vertical revetments.

If the bank was faced with a *wall or palisade* this should show, whatever the later history of the bank. Either the wall/palisade will have collapsed and the bank material will have fallen forward, or the wall/palisade will be still intact. If it has collapsed picks and shovels can be used and horizontal 10 cm. levels be dug from the outside towards the centre of the bank (Fig. 56). The most important area will be that sealed under the forward fall, for this should include the fallen wooden (page 239) or stone wall (Fig. 63) and any material which accumulated in front of the wall before it fell. If any of the wall/palisade is intact it should appear in plan. As soon as recognised, the strata on either side of it should be treated differently. Those outside should be removed first, if possible down to the old ground surface so that the wall/palisade can be studied and photographed in elevation. Those inside should be removed later, tip by tip (Plate XVI).

On the *inner slope* of the bank, after the present soil has been removed by trowelling and the bank material exposed, excavation of each tip can be by pick and shovel, beginning at the top of the bank. The surface of each tip must be exposed and studied for revetments, enlargements or a developed soil. On a long-established bank a soil will have developed and this should be recognisable, if not from colour and texture, then from pollen, soil or mollusc analyses. If the bank has been heightened and an established soil buried then this should show clearly in excavation, and dating evidence and any features in it will be especially valuable (Fig. 56, 62).

The *tips* will normally be of sterile rock from the ditch. As many as possible should be distinguished; the directions from which they were dumped; their size and the method of building (e.g. by baskets or wagons), and their likely origin noted. It may well be that they mirror in their materials the digging of the ditch in front of them. Quarry ditches or pits inside the rampart may also have contributed. It should be possible from this information to work out the methods of construction.[19]

As the lowest tips are removed care must be redoubled, since it is most important that the *ground surface* under the bank is exposed intact. At the bottom of the inner slope in particular, slip may have masked the true original limit of the bank and have preserved the land surface of the period. This may well be different from the present one. At the original foot of the inner slope of the bank a drain may be found to take the run-off of water. It should be carefully sectioned (page 230), for it may well show much of the history of the rampart in its successive siltings.

When the bank has been removed the ground surface under it must be studied for wall or palisade foundations, rear revetments, drains and marking-out ditches and posts or banks. The setting out line for the work may well have been given by a small ditch, line of posts or dumps, and this may be found anywhere under the bank or on the berm. The original surface may also give evidence of the period before the bank was erected.

Some of the special problems of organising rampart excavations are:

(i) The back-filling of cuts in standing ramparts should be obligatory, and the siting of spoil dumps should keep this in mind. If the bank is large they should not be on the slopes close to the sides of the trench since they will increase the danger of collapse. They will also be very difficult to remove afterwards, for machines will not be able to reach them. Dumps should be on flat ground if possible and in a position where mechanical conveyor-belts, railways or barrows can take the spoil to them and bulldozers can put it back. If there is no place suitable behind or in front of the trench, then the spoil should be barrowed or mechanically conveyed sideways along the contours to some distance from the side of the trench; duck-boards for barrow runs will be necessary here. Revetted dumps should then be built (Plate XII).

(ii) If higher than 2 m. the sides of the trench will need either revetting, buttressing or cross-baulks. The trenches are only likely to be dangerous if they are narrow and if earth is piled on the sides.

*Walls* of timber, turf, mud, stone or brick may be anticipated (Fig. 60 and 65a). All may be either free-standing or reinforced by a bank, and may have elaborate entrances and towers or bastions. Trenches should be sited where the bank is highest and least disturbed and should carry on across the ditch, since wall material may well have tumbled into it.[20] Different methods of locating and excavating the three types may be suggested.

TIMBER WALLS or palisades are to be expected on the tops of banks (parapet walls); in front of or inside banks (revetting walls); or free-standing (stockades).[21] Defensive ones will normally be larger and stronger than the farmyard fences already discussed (Fig. 65a).

All will be set some depth into the ground, and since the timber will only survive in exceptional conditions, recognition will depend on soil change, either of texture or colour. These changes can best be recognised in plan, and digging in horizontal levels in the way already suggested is therefore essential. Excavation should show how the walls were erected; the kind of wood used; what alterations took place and how the walls fell or were removed. The main problem will be tracing the slight changes in colour and texture which decayed wood will leave, and only careful trowelling and brushing in the bank and on old ground surfaces will show this.[22] Burnt timbers are easier to locate, for the charcoal from them will survive and retain its shape. The surface of any charcoal spread found in or under a bank should be cleaned, drawn in plan and then cross-sectioned. Unburnt rotted timber will show as a discolouration or perhaps as silting in the impression left by the beam. Nails may also be found here. Only a wide trench (3 m. or more) is likely to make comprehensive any complicated timber constructions, and then only if dug in horizontal levels (Fig. 57a). This reinforces the argument for wide trenches already made on grounds of safety.

*Parapet-walls*, here defined as defences on the top of a bank, will be difficult to find unless that top is well preserved. If so, then excavation in horizontal levels should show it almost immediately as a series of post-holes or a foundation trench on the outer edge of the levelled top.[23] When located, the inner limit of the horizontal area should be studied for posts supporting a 'walk' behind the wall. The post-holes or foundation trench should be excavated as already described (Fig. 30). As the bank is removed it should be possible to show the depth of the post-holes and, by temporary baulks, to draw sections of them.

*Frontal-revetting walls* will have been at the original bank-face but will have been buried (after the wall rotted or was removed) in the cascade of collapsed bank material (Fig. 63). The excavation of the forward part of the slope and of the ditch should show, from the angles of the collapsed tips, the approximate position of the wall, and attention can be concentrated there.[24] If the wall rotted, the bottom timbers may have been preserved as discolourations in the bank and something of its structure above ground recovered. Temporary sections should be left if these are noted, so that they can be drawn. It may be possible to distinguish, for example, whether the posts were slotted for tongued planks or whether there was a post and rail fence with a wattle backing and whether it was nailed, pegged or tied.[25] Samples may distinguish the kinds of wood used.

Below ground the foundations will be either a series of post-holes or a foundation trench (Fig. 65a). *Post and rail palisades* will have large post-holes at regular intervals and perhaps, near ground level, traces of horizontal timbers joining them (Fig. 65b). The post-holes which might be as much as 2 m. in diameter and 2 m. deep, should be half-sectioned, and their packing and positions noted. *Foundation trench*

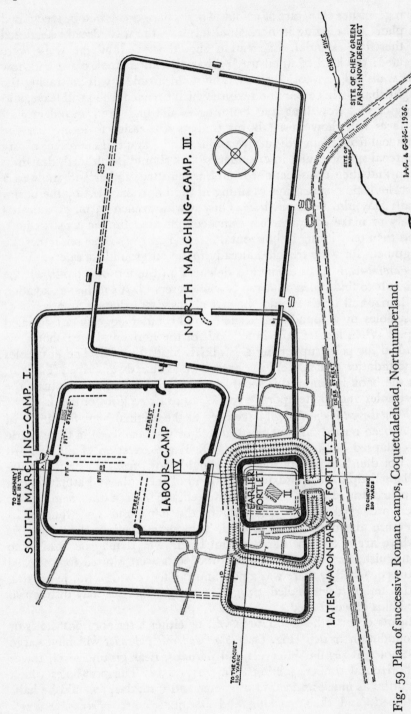

Fig. 59 Plan of successive Roman camps, Coquetdalehead, Northumberland.

*palisades* will have the timbers set in a trench which may be up to 2 m. wide and 2 m. deep. They should be excavated in the way already described. The excavated stretches should not be less than 2 m. long between baulks and should be dug in horizontal levels so that the nature of the packing and the outlines of the closely placed posts can be seen. The final profile of the foundation ditch will be steep-sided and flat-bottomed, perhaps with deeper settings for larger posts at intervals. Intermediate sections should be located to cross-section these, so that they can be drawn. The foundation trench should be studied to see if the timbers were removed or allowed to rot in position.

Whilst some timber walls may have only a simple frontal palisade many others will have cross-timbering through the bank and may even be secured to an inner wall (Fig. 57a). The cross-ties, either horizontal or diagonal, are only likely to be recognised if the trench is wide (more than 3 m.). If, as already suggested, both halves of the bank are dug in nearly simultaneous horizontal levels, the rotted or burnt timbers may show as patterns of dark or softer earth running through the tips. If the bank is of stone these may show particularly clearly.[26] Isolated features (e.g. post-holes or even suspected animal runs) found in the tips should be treated with respect and measured when found, since they may fall into a pattern as the excavation continues. If possible, intermediate baulks should be left across them so that, as excavation continues, they are sectioned in profile. Nails found in the bank should be given three-dimensional measurements, since struts may be located by them. Very elaborate forms of lacing may be adopted (e.g. casemates, where two parallel walls of equal height are joined at short intervals by equally solid cross walls and the boxes so formed filled with soil).

If cross-lacing is found, then the lower area of the inner slope should be carefully watched for a rear-revetting palisade or for the posts to which the struts were fastened. If there was one, then here, as at the front, the bank could have fallen and the foundations may be well inside the present tail of the bank. It should be excavated as was the front palisade.

Refurbishings of revetting palisades will usually have been complete rebuildings, and if, as is likely, the bank had collapsed, will be set upon the collapsed front. They should be looked for high in the forward slope of the bank.

*Stockades* are free-standing, and by definition no bank will be found (Fig. 30). They will be located only by aerial photographs or by uncovering the areas inside the lip of a ditch or round the perimeter of a settlement. The timbering is likely to be similar to the frontal revetting walls already described, and the foundation trench or post-holes should be excavated in the same way.[27] If a stockade is located, a grid of trenches should examine the area immediately behind it, for it

Q

may well have had, 2–3 m. behind it, another line of posts either to support struts or for a rampart walk. The same grid may help to check whether a bank ever existed, for even a levelled bank may have left several cm. of bank material in place.[17]

*Turf walls*, the turves being blocks of earth held together by plant roots, may be found in some areas. They will have been cut as squares and built (without mortar) like a brick or ashlar-stone wall. For a number of years a near-vertical face can be kept on these although they will weather in time to a gently sloping bank.[28] The wall may be very wide at its base (e.g. 10 metres) and will be battered. Any bank which proves to be of soil, rather than rock, should be studied as a possible turf wall. In both plan and section the junction lines between the blocks may be visible, and vigorous brushing of the horizontal surfaces and differential drying when left exposed may help show them up. The weight above will have compressed the turves so that they may be only a few cm. thick, and their colour may vary from black to white.[29] They will not normally be set in a foundation trench.

Also intermediate between banks and walls are *rammed earth walls* made from unshaped earth.[30] The bases are very wide (e.g. 20 m.) and in China the walls were made by ramming thin layers (7–20 cm.) of mud with narrow staves. Excavation should record the number of rammed layers and material (straw, etc.) used to consolidate them. Sherds and other dating evidence may well be caught up in the mud.

*Stone or brick walls*; these should be much more obvious than wooden walls, but like them may be free-standing or may revet banks.[31] They are, unfortunately, liable to be destroyed by having been used as quarries for other buildings. Trenches will not need to be as wide as those exposing the remains of wooden palisades, but since there may be more danger of collapse they should be kept either 2 m. wide and revetted, or made 4 m. wide and buttressed.

If an *embanked wall* has collapsed, the footings will have been buried in the debris or covered by the cascade of bank material from behind, and initially it will have to be excavated as a bank (Fig. 60). The wall, either thrown down or collapsed, should show as a layer of rubble perhaps several metres thick. If of brick or stones mortared together, it will be easy to recognise,[32] but many are unmortared, and any stratum of stones should be carefully studied. The surface should be exposed, photographed and, if any regular building pattern is visible, drawn in plan. As the stones are removed, the search for regular arrangement should continue especially in the bottom layers, which might preserve the facing stones of the wall. Here more than anywhere else, it may be possible to deduce the construction of the wall. If a stone or brick layer is found beneath layers of a collapsed bank then the lower face of it should be treated as the possible wall front (Fig. 63).

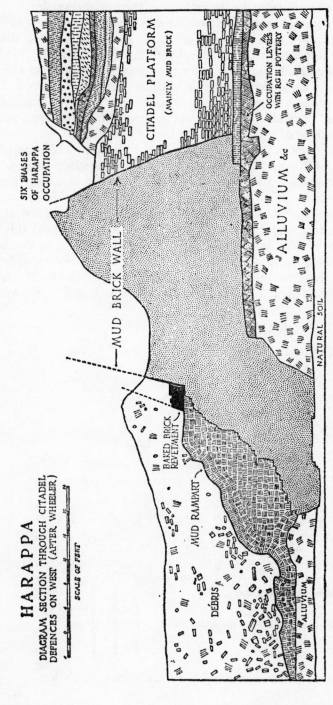

Fig. 60 Section through the defences of a town citadel, Harappa, Pakistan.

If nothing survives above ground, the foundation trench, or if robbed, the robbers' trench, may be the first sign of the wall[33] (Fig. 62).

If a heap of stone or brick is found above ground its surface should be carefully cleaned with stiff-bristled brushes and studied for lines of contiguous stones or bricks. If bound with mortar it should be relatively easy to recognise. If the surface shows no trace of a wall after cleaning and brushing it should be removed in horizontal 5 cm. levels. These should be begun at the edge of the stones on both the inner and outer slopes. The vertical sections should be studied, as excavation goes deeper, for signs of regularity in the laying of stones.

Samples of stones, bricks, tiles, etc. should be kept and examples of those with both typical and exceptional measurements recorded.

Stone or brick walls often attract later peoples who use them as quarries (squared stone is particularly attractive) and when the surface of a collapsed wall of stone or brick is studied before excavation, it may show a shallow trough on its surface. When it is excavated this may prove to be a wide irregular-edged trench driven through the debris to get out the good stone or brick (Fig. 62). It should be cleared before, and separately from, the wall remains on either side of it. If a *robber-trench* is found, then the wall debris on either side of it will probably

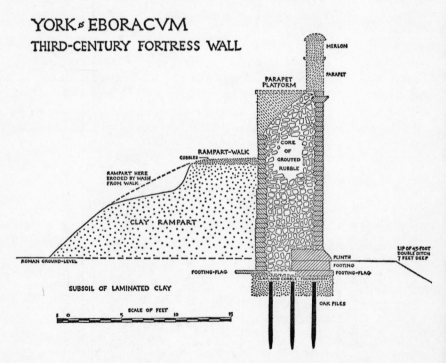

Fig. 61 Schematic section through a Roman town wall, York.

have been heightened by its spoil. The upper strata of the debris should be checked for this spoil and they should be cleared before the wall sealed under them is excavated. The line of a completely destroyed wall may be given by its robber-trench.

The intact *face of the wall* may be found by studying the horizontal surface after every 5 cm. of debris has been removed. As soon as it is recognised, the pattern of the excavation should change. Intermediate baulks at 2 m. intervals should be laid out at right angles to and in front of the wall and excavation should continue between them until the old ground surface in front of the wall is found. The trenches should extend away from the wall to the lip of the ditch or to the edge of the stone fall (Fig. 63). Particular attention should be paid to the lowest lines of bricks or stones above the old ground surface, for here the actual face of the wall may survive and if any shaped stones or special bricks were used they will be found here. From the position and extent of fallen wall debris it may be possible to calculate the height and manner of destruction of the wall (Fig. 61). When the full extent of the debris in front of the wall has been noted and the intermediate baulk sections drawn, the debris can be removed and any remaining courses of wall drawn and photographed. As excavation continues all the fallen wall material should be piled together so that the total amount can be calculated.

Whether mortared or unmortared, the centre of the wall, the core, is likely to be less regular than the faces. It is best to leave the excavation of it until both inner and outer faces are established and then to section it and record its construction.

The inner face of the wall should be located and excavated in the same way as the outer one and will be very little different from it.

Most walls of any size will be set in foundation trenches dug down to a solid bedrock. Even when the wall above ground has been destroyed these trenches and the wall footings in them survive, and sections must be dug through them (Fig. 61). The *foundation trenches* will be vertical-sided and wider than the wall above ground. On their flat bottoms, stones or other hard material will be placed and rammed hard or possibly cemented. At, or just below, ground level the wall proper will have started.

*Dry stone walls*, made without any cement, will be commonplace in any area where stone is common and wood scarce, and a director must be familiar with the local methods of making them. In any excavation report the technique of construction should be described.[34] Possible constructions include:

(i) *Single wall:* This type may be quite thick (up to 4 m.), possibly set in a foundation trench and skilfully built by selecting and laying the stones so that gravity holds them all in place. The stones will not usually be shaped but may be set, for decoration, in herringbone or other patterns.[35] They may be 1 m. or more thick. No special problems occur in their excavation (Plate x).

(ii) *Double wall*: This is merely an extension of the first, with thick 'single walls' on both faces. These might both be more than 1 m. thick with several metres of stone rubble and earth between them (Fig. 62).

(iii) *Treble or more walls*: More rarely extra walls may be found within the core. These may be due to a desire for internal strength or to successive widenings or rebuildings of the wall.

(iv) *Timberlacing*: When intact courses of a thick stone wall have been uncovered they should be studied in plan for timber-slots left through the whole from back to front.[36] If several courses survive these may also show in the vertical faces (Fig. 57a). The timbers, nailed to vertical posts back and front, would have stopped any collapse of the dry stone walling.

If these timbers were set on fire in a strong wind they will have burnt so fiercely that vitrification of the stone near the timbers took place.[36] This should be easy to recognise, and the area, thickness and nature of the vitrified mass should be recorded.

The special problems of excavating dry stone walling are that whilst no special techniques are needed, great care in the removing of stones is necessary if intact courses are to be recognised, especially if the stones are unshaped. If the stones are large, it will be very difficult to preserve vertical sections, and if there is any depth to be excavated the trenches will have to be wide and buttesses should be left for safety. Crowbars, ropes and rollers, and even tractors may be necessary to move the larger stones. The special problems of excavating unfired clay brick walling are discussed on page 124.

*Cemented walls.* Their excavation will be simpler than that of dry stone walling, for once their cemented nature has been discovered loose debris can be picked and shovelled away until solid remains are found. The methods of excavation will then be as for dry stone walls, but a number of special problems may be noted.

(i) Cemented stone walls may well be a modification of the dry stone ones. The outer and inner faces may be of shaped or specially chosen stones with a rubble core set in cement. String-courses of tiles or slabs laid horizontally through the walls at intervals may help to give it rigidity[37] (Fig. 61).

(ii) Cemented baked-brick walls will be excavated like cemented stone walls, but being more regular will be easier to detect. Intermediate baulks, analysis of amount of debris, etc. should be as for dry stone walls (page 244). Methods of laying bricks and brick sizes should be noted.

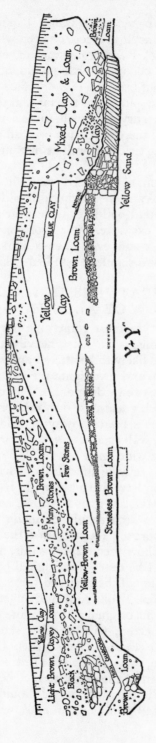

FIG. 62 Section through a Roman town wall and bank with 18th century robber trench above wall, Towcester, Northants. Scale 1:80.

(iii) Cemented unbaked brick walls. If mud mortar has been used these walls can be difficult to recognise even when intact. The walls will usually be much thicker than stone and baked brick ones (e.g. up to 10 m. wide) and a collapsed wall should be excavated like a bank (page 233).[38] Rigorous brushing of the surface of each 10 cm. level may brush out some of the softer mud mortar and show the regularity of the brick-laying. As with a dry stone wall, there may be two facing walls and a rubble infilling and there may have been an external batter (Fig. 60). The method of laying bricks as well as measurements of the brick sizes should be recorded.

The special problems of cemented walls will be recognising later robbing and disturbance and identifying different periods of building by changes in material and building. Unless the cement is mud they will be relatively easy to excavate. Intact portions will still have bricks or stones joined together and, even when collapsed, big fragments of wall may hold together and should be studied (Plate x).

## SPECIAL FEATURES IN FORTIFICATIONS OF ALL KINDS

*Entrances* are usually the most vulnerable part of a military structure and are correspondingly the most heavily defended. For the same reason they are more likely to be altered and repaired. Any excavation must therefore locate and investigate the entrances, for they are likely to be among the most rewarding areas. An entrance will consist of all or some of the following features; outworks or a barbican (outside the main walls and ditches); a causeway or bridge (across the ditch); a gateway through the wall (perhaps two and revetting walls through the bank if the bank is a wide one).

Locating entrances may be difficult if the defences have collapsed in a number of places or have been slighted. If approach roads survive these will be the most obvious indications, and in aerial photographs and ground surveys search should be made for them. If there is no surface sign that approach roads existed then resistivity or magnetometer surveys may show them. Failing this, any causeways across the ditch or ditches must be tested, for original causeways are likely to be solid whilst later ones will be material thrown on to the ditch silting. Resistivity, magnetometer or probe and auger surveys may be able to distinguish between the original and the more recent causeway. If none of these methods succeed, trial trenches should be dug, near their centres, in all the causeways. As these trenches are dug deeper they will, if later than the ditch, show silts and not bedrock. If the entrance cannot be established in front of the ditch, trial trenches should look for road metalling in all gaps in the rampart and should be so sited that they can be extended into a full grid when an entrance is discovered (Fig. 64).

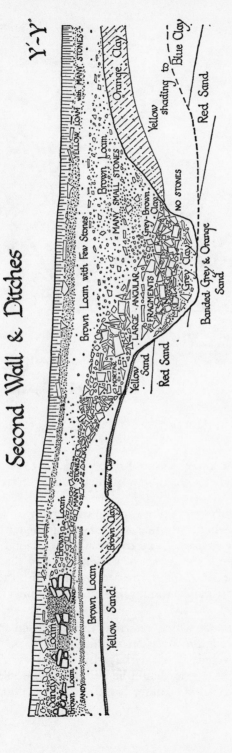

Fig. 63 Section through the ditch of a Roman town defence, with the town-wall collapsed into it, Towcester, Northants. Scale 1:80. Only by planning the fallen wall before it was recognised as a wall, was its composition and structure recovered.

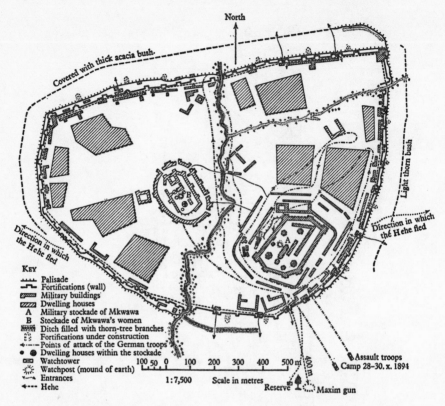

Fig. 64 A fortified East African village, Kalenga. To be considered as an excavation problem.

If it is likely that there was a bridge and no causeway, it may be necessary to establish the gateway first and look for the bridge later.

The only satisfactory method of excavating a gateway will be a grid of trenches over the whole entrance area including the butt-ends of any banks or ditches, the causeway and the outworks. The main axis of the grid should be through the centre of the entrance so that a complete longitudinal section is obtained. Cross-sections should be allowed for at 3 or 4 metre intervals. Baulks should be 1 m. wide, sufficient for wheelbarrow or basket boy walks.

*Outworks or a Barbican* which guarded the approach to the bridge or causeway will be found only on sophisticated sites.[39] The entire plan should be recovered; much perhaps by the surveys already mentioned. If time permits, a grid should be laid over the whole area, but if it can only be sampled, then ditch, bank and wall sections should be dug.

*Causeways* should be completely exposed in the grid and their surface studied. Their shape should be noted (trapeziform, rectangular, etc.), their edges studied for fences and their surface for metalling, cart-ruts, or temporary defences (walls or palisades) made across them.[40]

If it can be established that a *bridge* existed, then the grid over the entrance should be extended over the ditch (excavation technique on page 227). Whilst it is being dug the sides of the ditch must be watched for irregularities (ledges or steps), masonry, timber slots or post-holes. These may be merely at the top of the ditch or may carry on right across as piers or lines of posts. The bottom siltings of the ditch may preserve parts of the actual structure.[41]

*Gateways* may be of wood and/or masonry[42] and alterations may well have taken place from time to time (Fig. 57b). As well as main gates with roads through them, posterns or sally ports (smaller and without roads) may also be found. Water-gates are rarer but should be looked for if the fortification is beside a lake, river or sea. These might well be associated with harbours (page 176).

*Gateways in wooden free-standing walls* may vary from simple ones hung on posts to complicated ones with towers and overhead walks. The grid of trenches over the area should show the post-holes or foundation trenches, and if the site was long occupied there may have been a succession of gates, each a complex of post-holes difficult to disentangle. This will be accomplished only if two things are kept in mind: (i) that excavation in horizontal 5 cm. levels should show the successive surfaces of the roadway and the gate associated with each; (ii) that whether or not these surfaces can be distinguished in plan, all the post-holes should be sectioned and their packing and filling studied (it may be possible to show from the study which belonged together).

Gateposts may be very large (60 cm. square) and post-holes for them of up to 2 m. in diameter are to be expected. Special note should be taken of the kind of gates; for example, a central post-hole may suggest a pair of gates, or several off-centre ones a main gate for wheeled traffic and side gates for pedestrians.[43] *Gateways in stone or brick walls* will be easier to recognise, for the foundations, or if these are destroyed, then the robber-trenches, will remain. The trench-grid may show first a layer of rubble over the whole area and then, as this is removed, the stubs or footings of walls or the robber-trenches. It will be important to recognise the surfaces which relate to each foundation trench. The methods of construction, wall thickness and the existence of different phases of building should be recorded.

If there is a substantial bank, then the gateway will extend through it and have, in addition to the outer gates, revetting walls, and possibly guardrooms and inner gates. The inner gates will present no additional problems to those discussed above. *Revetting walls* will, however, be a necessity and should be found on either side of the passage through the bank and perhaps for some distance along the back of the bank as well. Before excavation they will usually be masked by slip from the bank, but the post-holes or stone foundations should be visible beneath.[44] Excavation will be similar to that of main walls (page 242). The collapsed bank material will have fallen towards the centre of the road, and for this reason the cross-sections will be important.

If the walls were of wood it should be possible to establish their construction (e.g. post, rail and wattle, or tongued-and-grooved planks, etc.) and the way in which they collapsed. If they were of stone or brick, then the collapsed walls may well lie where they fell and their size, building technique and method of destruction may be distinguished.

*Guardrooms* may have been made by revetting small rooms into the bank. During excavation these may show first as gaps in the revetting walls, and the area of the bank behind them must then be removed and the old ground surface studied for foundations and floors.

*The special excavation problems of entrances* will probably be connected with spoil removal. If the baulks can be left sufficiently wide they should be usable for barrow runs and the spoil should be dumped well away from the entrance, perhaps immediately inside the defences since from here it will be possible to back-fill with machines.

Sections along both main axes will be important since the published ones should show the relationship of the road surface to the gates, revetting banks and causeway or bridge.

*Towers and Bastions* may have been made at regular intervals along the walls, at gates or at the angles between alignments.[45] Towers are here defined as standing on the wall or extending behind it, and bastions as protruding in front.

The location of *towers* may be difficult, especially if they were of wood and if no enlargement of the bank was made to support them. Any sudden rearward widening of the bank should certainly be examined, but if there is no variation in the width, only the excavation of a considerable stretch of wall (perhaps 20–30 metres) might show a tower through its deeper or wider foundations or as a change in construction methods. If wider stone or brick foundations or larger post-holes or timber-slots than normal are encountered, four 3 m. squares should cover the possible area of the tower on top of the bank and extend well behind the palisade or even the bank (for excavation see page 233). The rear part might be masked by bank collapse or erosion and would then show only at or near the old ground surface. In all cases the area inside the tower should be sectioned like an ordinary room (page 117) and carried down to or below the old ground surface, for it may have contained several storeys of store or guardrooms, staircases, etc. Study of the tower juncture and wall may show if it was an original or added feature.

*Bastions* may be located as forward projections of the bank, or, if of stone or brick, as an increased amount of debris at regular intervals. Excavation will be similar to that for towers, and the grid should be laid out in front of the wall. Semicircular and polygonal as well as rectangular structures should be expected. Like the towers they should be excavated to bedrock, for they may also have had rooms, perhaps on several floors, inside them. The foundations will be substantial.

At right angles to, or parallel to, the wall, drains may be found on the berm, behind the bank or through the entrance. They should be recognisable from their profile and silting and be treated as ordinary drainage ditches.

*Stairways or ramps* may also be found against the back of the bank. If of stone, the sills of steps, or if of wood, the post-holes of the stair supports may survive.

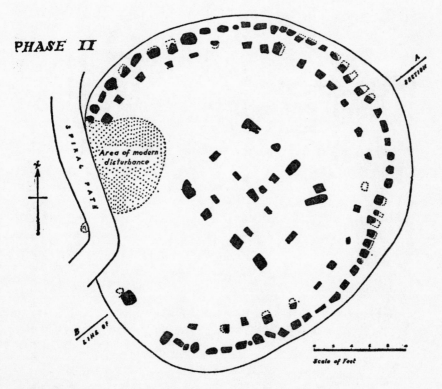

Fig. 65a Plan of a mediaeval wooden castle. Abinger, Surrey. To be studied with Fig. 65b.

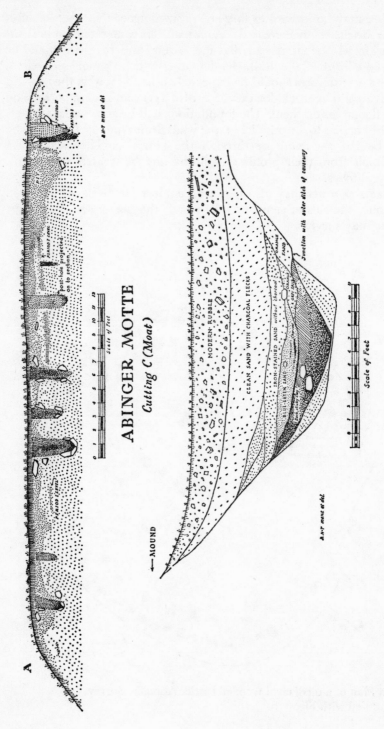

ABINGER MOTTE
*Cutting C (Moat)*

Fig. 65b Section of a wooden castle. Abinger, Surrey.

Some fortresses and settlements have a particular strong point, a *citadel or keep*[46] sometimes the only fortification and sometimes within the main defences. Its excavation is not likely to pose special problems unless it is raised on an artificial mound. This mound, the *Motte* of British mediaeval fortresses, may be of locally scraped up top-soil or of material from a ditch around it and may be 30 m. high.[47] Excavation can be difficult because occupation may not have been restricted to the top, but may have had rooms and cellars inside the body of the mound. Planning should allow for a grid of trenches on the top of the mound and round the base (Fig. 60, 65).

On the top, the grid should cover the whole area and expose either the post-holes or slots of palisades, or masonry foundations. The buildings inside will probably fill most of the area. When these have been studied and recorded, trial trenches should be sunk to check that no earlier structures existed.

On the sides, trial trenches should be cut in steps from top to bottom, since heightenings of the mound may have left earlier structures deeply buried.

At the bottom, radial trenches should check the existence of a *ditch*, a *causeway*, or a *bridge*. If a causeway or a bridge is found, then the side of the motte at that point should be examined for evidence of a passage into the interior or a stairway to the top.

If evidence is obtained from the top or sides that the centre of the mound was hollow, this will have to be cleared. Special provision may have to be made for revetting, spoil removal, etc.

## THE INTERIORS OF FORTRESSES AND MILITARY CAMPS

All fortifications will have signs of dwellings inside them and it is essential that these be excavated if the nature of the site is to be understood. Since a good strategic position may have been occupied many times, each occupation phase must be established stratigraphically and related to its appropriate phase of the defences. The use of the buildings should also be discovered by a study of the plans and the objects found. In this way it should be possible to distinguish the establishments of professional soldiers from those of civilians or even of irregular military forces.

The area of settlement inside a fortification may be difficult to locate, especially if the enclosure was large and was intended to shelter stock as well as humans.[48] If aerial photographs show no internal features, a series of ground surveys (magnetometer, resistivity, auger, probe, or phosphate density) may help, and should be carried out in advance of the campaign. If these fail, then the search by excavation should begin from the entrances (Fig. 53). Here, if roads have been found entering the gates, they must be traced until their routes inside the fortification are completely known.[49] Further search will depend upon the size of the interior. On small or densely occupied sites the whole interior should be excavated, for only then can the meaning of individual structures be assessed. Planning the excavation should take this into account, for a series of annual campaigns will probably be necessary. If the road pattern has been established, grids along both sides of the roads, with especial attention in the areas near cross-roads or immediately inside the fortifications, may show the area of settlement. They should be connected by interrupted grids

The domestic buildings of professional soldiers and of civilians may be considered separately. Those needed by a *garrison of professional soldiers* should be distinctive in plan and may well extend over the whole of the interior. They may be laid out parallel to the roads or be clustered along the inside of the defences[50] and will probably show a regularity in plan and a variety of functional buildings (Fig. 58). Reconstructions and changes in the use of buildings are to be expected.

Excavation will therefore be on a large grid system (e.g. 8 m. squares). In general it will resemble the excavation of a village (page 00). If buildings were built at the tail of the defensive bank, especially if they were revetted into them, these may provide the least disturbed and most archaeologically useful area.

The following buildings should be looked for:

*Barrack blocks* are likely to be large simple buildings, possibly divided inside into dormitories with an occasional room for an under-officer. They should be excavated like ordinary rooms (page 117) with internal cross baulks. Associated with them may be communal kitchens (page 132 for excavation) and latrines and wash-houses (for excavation page 133). Smaller domestic buildings of more complex plan isolated from the main blocks may be officers' quarters and should be excavated as ordinary houses (page 115 for excavation methods).

*Administrative blocks* may be recognisable from their plans and be near the centre at a cross-roads. They should be excavated as dwellings. Shrines, hospitals and stores might be uncovered as separate blocks (page 183 for excavation technique). Stables (page 140) and artillery or wagon parks may also be found. Their excavation presents no special difficulty except that only when excavation is complete may it be possible to recognise them. Parade grounds, well-levelled and perhaps cobbled, may also be found.

*The buildings of civilians* will be less easy to interpret. Unlike the professional garrison buildings, there will be no certain way of linking them, other than by stratigraphical evidence, with the fortifications, and the nature of the settlement may have changed many times. It might have been for example, in succession a small village, the stronghold of a chief, a shrine and a town. The relationship of these to the fortifications will only be certain from the study of a complete excavation. Even the presence of artifacts contemporary with the settlement, beneath, in or on top of the defences, will not be proof of connection between them,[51] and stratigraphical connections between the features will have to be looked for and recorded.

Once the general area of the settlement is located, it should be excavated on the grid system and the plan and finds studied. If it is a *farm, village* or *town*, the size of the settlement in relation to the defences will show whether the ramparts were deliberately constructed for it, or if a small settlement was utilising or ignoring a large and unrelated defence system[52] (Fig. 64). In the first case excavation and interpretation will be relatively simple;[53] in the second it will be necessary to show if the settlement was earlier, contemporary with or more recent than, the ramparts. This must be done by analysing and dating the defences; by studying the objects contemporary with the settlement (e.g. were they found only in the upper silting of ditch or on original ground surfaces in or under the bank); or by finding some part of the settlement in stratigraphical relationship to the defences (e.g. partly overlaid by bank). If it is earlier or later than the defences it is of no further interest here, for its excavation has already been discussed. If it was contemporary then the plan and finds must be studied so that its role can be determined (e.g. as a peaceful habitation between times of crisis, the headquarters of a chief, or as a shrine). It may be difficult to distinguish between the first two unless specialised buildings are found, but a study of the pollen and animal bones, for example, may show that farming was carried on rather than food brought in (page 89). Intermittent occupation might show through the stratigraphy (e.g. sterile layers), a study of the artifacts (e.g. coins) or food debris. Excavation will be in the way already described for settlements (page 117).

If the plan shows one house larger than the others, or a group of houses separate from the others and perhaps enclosed, then a *chief's household* may have been found.[54] It may vary in size and importance from a village-headman's house to a royal palace and should be excavated in the ways already described (page 158). Extensive alteration or rebuilding is to be expected in the larger buildings, and also more evidence of looting and robbing. It may be possible to show whether the chief was living within an existing refuge or whether he erected the fortifications for his own protection.

The dwellings of temporary inhabitants, either those of soldiers or civilians, will leave much slighter and less organised evidence. If not revealed by aerial photography or some other survey, of which the phosphate survey might be the most useful, there will be little hope, other than by complete excavation, of finding them. Huts, hearths and

R

perhaps a thin scatter of domestic rubbish are to be expected. It will be important to establish if they were contemporary with the defence, for *refuges* may well be larger than professionally built military fortresses, since they were designed to shelter the population from a considerable area in time of danger.[55] Their main characteristic will be intermittent occupation, and the problem, apart from size, will be to recognise refurbishings and re-usings of the site. Little occupation debris may be found. Construction may well be in earth or wood as well as stone, and marsh and dense forest might be used in the defence, resulting in gaps in man-made circuit of banks and ditches.[56]

## SELECTED READING

*The Archaeology of Weapons*\*\*, Oakeshot, R. 1960.
*The Art of Warfare in Biblical Lands*, Yadin, Y. 1963.
*The Art of Warfare in the Middle Ages*, Oman, C. 1924.
*The Greek and Macedonian Art of War*, Adcock, F. 1968.
*The Roman Imperial Army*, Webster, G. 1969.
Maori Hill Forts, Firth, R. *Antiq* I. I. 1927.
Some problems of Hill Forts, Rivet, A. in Frere, S. (ed) 1958. 29.
British Camps with Timber-laced ramparts, *ArchJ* CXI 1954. 26.
Heuneberg, *Germ* 32 1954. 22 (hillfort and dwelling).
Manching, *Germ* 39 1961 and 40 1962. 297 (hillfort and settlement).
Rainsborough, *PPS* XXXIII 1967. 207 (hillfort).
Hod Hill, Richmond, I. et al. 1968 (hillfort and campaign camp).
*Isca*, Boon, G. 1960 (fortress and army headquarters).
Inchtuthill, *JRS* LI 1961. 158 (frontier fortress).
The . . . . Defences of Romano-British Towns, *ArchJ* XXII 1955. 20. To be read with
   Frere, S. (1967). 221 and 248.
The Roman Wall, Collingwood-Bruce, J. 1957 (frontier works).
*Offa's Dyke*, Fox, C. 1955 (frontier works).
*The History of the King's Works*\*, Colvin, H. (ed) 1963 Vol. I (fortresses and palaces).
*Norman Castles in Britain*, Renn, D. 1968.
*Der Husterknupp*, Herrnbrodt, A. 1958 (fortress).
Abinger, *ArchJ* CVII 1950 (fort).
Degannwy, *ArchJ* CXXIV 1967. 190 (fort).
Buhen, Emery, W. *NYP* (frontier fortress).
Berwick-on-Tweed\*, *AntJ* XLV 1965. 64 (town wall).
Jericho, Kenyon, K. 1957 (town wall).
London, Grimes, W. 1968. 47 (town wall).
Biskupin, Rajewski, Z.\* 1959 and Kostrewski, J. 1936 (village defences).
Harappa\*. *AnInd* 3 1947. 58 (town citadel).
Masada\*, Yadin, Y. 1967 (fortified palace and siege works).
Rickmansworth, *ArchJ* CXVI 1959. 138 (house defence).

## NOTES

1. e.g. for the Bronze and Early Iron Age Western Asia see Yadin, Y. 1963, or for Mediaeval Europe, Oman, C. 1924.
2. The English royal castles in Wales are a good example. Colvin, H. (ed) 1963. For a similar series in Nubia see Emery, W.
3. The Roman network in Wales (Nash-Williams, V. 1954), or the British network on the North West Frontier of Pakistan (*The Times* 1964) are good examples.
4. e.g. in earth, Offa's Dyke: Fox, C. 1955, or in stone, Hadrian's Wall: Collingwood-Bruce, J. 1957.
5. e.g. Masada: Yadin, Y. 1967. Ystadfellte: *JRS* XLVIII 1958, and L 1960.
6. For regional studies in Britain see *PSAS* LXXXIX 1956. 329, Crawford, O. 1949 and OS 1963, p. 107 and 119. Good examples are Hod Hill: Richmond, I. 1968 and Fendoch: *PSAS* LXIII 1939. 100. Norman, E. 1970. 74.
7. The most remarkable surviving ones are those of the 1914/18 war in France.
8. e.g. Little Woodbury: *PPS* IV, 308, and VI, 30.
9. e.g. Zimbabwe: Robinson, K. 1961. Masada: Yadin, Y. 1967. Jarlshof: Hamilton, J. 1956. Rickmansworth: *ArchJ* CXVI 1959, 136.
10. For a good study of walls see Scranton, R. 1941 (Greek) or (for late Roman town walls), *ArchJ* CXVI 1959. 25 and *ArchJ* XXII 1955. 20. Examples Benin: *HSNJ* 2.4 1963. 470. Jericho: Kenyon, K. 1957.

11. e.g. Crawford, O. 1949. Beresford, M. and St. Joseph, K. 1958, 130.
12. e.g. Maiden Castle and Stanwick: Wheeler, R. 1943 and 1954. Rainsborough: *PPS* XXXIII 1967, 207.
13. e.g. Maiden Castle, Wheeler, R. 1943.
14. e.g. Wandlebury, *PCAS* XLIX 1958.
15. Rivet, A. in Frere, S. (ed) 1958. 29. Maiden Castle and Stanwick (loc. cit.). Great Casterton: Corder, P. 1961.
16. A small area can be misleading. Animal runs can be mistaken for foundation trenches and patterns of beams and post-holes missed.
17. e.g. Wandlebury (loc. cit.).
18. Part might be slip, but part might be bank still in position; it will be impossible to tell at first.
19. Heuneberg: *Germ* 32 1954. 22. For an unfinished example showing construction methods, Ladle Hill: *Antiq* V 1931. 474.
20. Only in these circumstances is the constructional method likely to be preserved.
21. For British examples see *ArchJ* CXI 1954. 26, with good gazetteer.
22. e.g. Manching: *Germ* XLX 1962. 297.
23. e.g. The Caburn: *Arch* XLVI 452; also *Antiq* V 1931. 71.
24. See Wheeler, R. and Richardson, K. 1957.
25. Biskupin (loc. cit.); Heuneberg (loc. cit.); Manching (loc. cit.).
26. e.g. Preist: *Germ* 23 1959 (good English summary in *ArchJ* CXI 1954. 64).
27. e.g. Williamsburg: S. P. 1953. 447.
28. e.g. The Antonine Wall: Robertson, A. 1960. 8.
29. Depending on local soil chemistry.
30. e.g. Paio Chia Chuang: Watson, W. 1961, 62.
31. Good examples of excavated ones are: Stone (freestanding): Jericho—Kenyon, K. 1957; York—RCHM 1962. Stone with bank: St. Albans—Wheeler, R. 1936. Brick with backing: Harappa—*AnInd* 3 1947. 58. Baked Brick and Stone (freestanding): London—Grimes, W. 1968. 47. Unbaked Brick and Stone (freestanding): Buhen—Emery, W.
32. As at Pevensey (England) where great masses of fallen wall still hold together.
33. From personal experience. For robber trenches see *AntJ* XLVII 1967.
34. Rainsborough: *PPS* XXXIII 1967. 207. Jarlshof: Hamilton, J. 1956. Worlebury: *Ant* V 1931. 85.
35. Castell Bryn Gwyn: *Arch Cam* 3 1962. 25.
36. *ArchJ* CXI 1954. 61 and 94.
37. St. Albans: Wheeler, R. 1936; and York: *RCHM* 1962.
38. Harappa (loc. cit.) both burnt and unburnt brick. Buhen: Emery, W. *NYP*.
39. e.g. *Antiq* V 1931. 73. Maiden Castle (loc. cit.). Brown, A. 1964 and Colvin, H. 1963.
40. e.g. Rainsborough (op. cit.).
41. South Mimms. I am grateful to Dr. J. Kent for this information.
42. St. Catherine's Hill: Hawkes, C. 1930 for a succession of gates. Rainsborough (loc. cit.). Degannwy: *ArchJ* CXXIV 1967. 190.
43. e.g. St. Catherine's Hill (op. cit.).
44. e.g. St. Catherine's Hill (op. cit.) in timber. This is found in stone in mediaeval castles, e.g. Northampton. For Roman ones see Wacher, J. (ed) 1966.
45. e.g. Roman: *ArchJ* CXII 1955, 20: with rearward extensions: *PSAS* LX 1957, 161. Mediaeval: Renn, D. 1968. *MedArch* 8 1964. 184.
46. e.g. Harappa (loc. cit.) Mycenae: Mylonas, G. 1966. Troy: Blegen, C. 1950. Renn, D. 1968.
47. Abinger: *ArchJ* CVII 1950. 15.

48. e.g. the Manching hillfort which was enclosed by four miles of walls: *Germ* XL 1962. 293.
49. e.g. Inchtuthill: *JRS* LI 1961. 158. Fendoch: *PSAS* LXIII 1939. 100.
50. Fendoch (loc. cit.). Buhen: Emery, W. Isca: Boon, E. 1960. Caernarvon: Colvin, H. 1963. For parade-grounds *ArchJ* CXXV 1968. 73.
51. The artifacts might well have been incorporated from an earlier period.
52. e.g. Hod Hill: Richmond, I. 1968. Stanwick: Wheeler, R. 1954.
53. e.g. Vucedol: Schmidt, R. 1945. 15. Wasserberg-Buchau in Reinerth, H. 1929. 36.
54. Hod Hill (op. cit.) Heuneberg (op. cit.) Troy (op. cit.) Masada (op. cit.).
55. Stanwick had a circumference of 16 miles, Wheeler, R. 1954.
56. e.g. Wheathampstead: Wheeler, R. 1936.

CHAPTER XI

# Problems in the Excavation of Industrial Sites

'God gave them no sheep but cleverness instead'
A Suk saying quoted by R. J. Forbes *Metallurgy in Antiquity*, 1950

The increasing interest in industrial remains in recent years has been particularly concerned with preserving evidence of the industrial revolutions of the last four centuries,[1] but has underlined how little is known of the industrial sites and techniques of earlier periods. If more research groups should devote themselves to the industrial aspects of earlier communities and search out and excavate industrial sites, a great gap in our knowledge would be filled. Quite apart from any specialised interest, however, all field archaeologists should be able to recognise and record a wide variety of industrial processes and materials. On all sites and in all periods, areas for, and debris from, industrial workings may be found. Directors must also know where to turn for specialised help and advice and must be willing to devote as much time to the industrial problems of their sites as to any others.

The excavation of a *specialised industrial site* will always require intimate knowledge of that industry and should hardly be attempted without it. But this will not by itself suffice. Workers will need to evolve special techniques of excavation, for at present few exist, and in the following chapter suggestions of the ways in which research could develop as well as indications of the kind of work which has been taking place, are offered.

The stages of any industry may be considered under the headings of *Winning* (mining, streaming, collecting, etc.); *Processing* (cleaning, smelting, mixing, etc.) and *Finishing* (making usable objects). The study of the industry will only be complete if all the stages between the prospecting for raw material and the despatch of the finished articles can be demonstrated.

## WINNING THE RAW MATERIAL

Some raw materials (e.g. wood, leather, bone and shell) will usually come as by-products of hunting, gathering, or husbandry; others are obtained through planting or animal husbandry (e.g. cotton, flax and wool) and others again by mining, streaming or collecting (e.g. metal ores or stone). Except for the third group these methods of winning will leave very little archaeological evidence, although the distribution of processing debris may give some hints. Mining, collecting and streaming sites, however, are worth more consideration.

## MINING SITES

Whatever the material being mined, the archaeological problems of excavating the sites will be similar (Fig. 66). All will require that the director has studied the known methods of working that specific material[2] and, if possible, has visited existing mines and has discussed the problems with practising engineers. He should also have visited abandoned mines and have studied their appearance and nature in decay.[3]

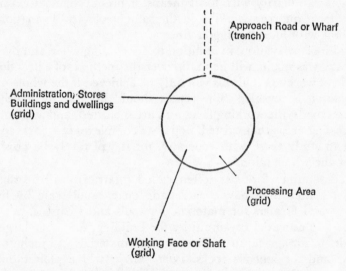

Fig. 66 Problems of excavating a mining/quarrying site.

On *flat ground* sites will usually be recognised by the surviving hollows above pits or shafts and the spoil-heaps near them. The series of hollows and mounds may look like a geological formation, for if a deposit was worked over a long period they may cover many acres. They may be discovered by field walking and by noting concentrations of mined raw material (e.g. ironstone). Aerial photographs may also show filled-in and levelled mines as plough or crop marks.[4] On *hillsides* the scars of pits or the mouths of shafts might be located by the talus platforms and spoil tips. All surface irregularities noted during a survey should be recorded. In some cases sites may be located by petrological analysis of objects found elsewhere. If these are sufficiently distinctive they can be assigned to their possible sources and the actual source located.[5] New sites are certainly waiting to be discovered in all areas by systematic searching based on a study of the surface geology. Workers will have to be familiar with the rocks sought by man and with industrial debris from all stages of processing.[6]

OPENCAST MINES (simple pits of various sizes), will be much more common than deep mines, for only relatively sophisticated societies use the latter. A wider variety of material is also likely to have been won from them than from deep mines, and they are known to have been made in recent times by hunter-gatherers[7] as well as farmers. They may well be quite easy to locate, for the disturbances are much more visible than those of deep mines.

Preparations before excavation should include a study of the local geology, a familiarity with local means of pre-mechanical extraction, visits to local quarries working in the same geological formations and discussions with local mining engineers.

The aim of excavation, in addition to discovering when and by whom the quarry was made, will be to discover the methods of extraction and the scale of working, and this will only be achieved if the whole pattern of extraction is revealed. The report should be able to describe the approach roads, the working faces and areas cleared, and any buildings or processing areas that existed. Separate complexes of trenches will be needed to study these with economy, for it will rarely be possible to uncover the whole mine.

Opencast mines for *stone* (often called quarries), will be the most varied, for they may have been made on a small scale by hunter-gatherers and farmers for materials for tools and weapons, as well as by more sophisticated communities for building, for other large scale industries or for agriculture. Those for tool-materials will include many for flint and for igneous rocks. *Flint quarries* will exploit tabular or nodular strata by pits before the seams become too deep.[8] The kind of flint being mined must be established and processing areas (page 274) looked for nearby. *Igneous rocks* (dolerites, granites, lavas, etc.) which are suitable for grinding-stones (for paint or metal as well as for food), tools, weapons and building materials may also be quarried, and scree-slopes are often utilised (page 275). They have usually been recognised from their processing debris.[9] Quarries for *clay* (for body-paint, pottery, pipe-, tile-making, etc.) may also be found. They may be wider and shallower than other pits and, unless deliberately filled in, are likely to have been full of water for some time; this may help to distinguish them. They also may be recognisable from their processing areas (page 278). Other sedimentary rocks are quarried for building or agriculture; *sands and gravel* as metalling for roads and yards, and *limestone, sandstone, chalk* etc. for building material. Chalk or other minerals may also be dug to improve specific soils (e.g. for lightening or marling heavy soils). These quarries may have been filled and may leave little surface debris. *Metal ores* are also dug in this way and recognition, in addition to the methods already mentioned, will be finding ore fragments and processing areas (page 269).

The main features to be found in any opencast mine during excavation may now be considered.

Although metalled *approach roads* are only to be expected in the more elaborately organised mines, most will have had trackways to them. These are most likely to be located as they descend ramps into the larger pits or follow routes left between many small pits. A suspected road should be sectioned (page 147), for it may give evidence of the methods of transportation (e.g. cart-ruts or pack animal-trails). It must be traced as far as possible both inside and outside the quarry by trial trenches, by probe or by other surveys. Dating evidence may come from its surface, and branches from it may lead to storage or processing areas.

If cut into a hillside, the *working face* may survive although masked by scree or hillwash. One or more trenches at right angles to the face should be dug to expose the junction of the working face and the floor of the quarry. Their width will depend on the amount of slip to be cleared. From the floor and face the method of working may be visible (e.g. boreholes for wedging or splitting or charcoal and thermally shattered stones from fire-setting). Tools (picks, cleavers, wedges, hammers, rakes and shovels) may also be found. In hard deposits the face should be examined for graffiti, official inscriptions and setting-out marks.[10]

Large pits dug into flat ground should be examined for a working face in the same way. Pits, especially shallow ones, should be dug on the quadrant method, so that sections right through the feature are obtained. If the pit is very large a single trench through its centre or quadrants excavated in stages might be used (page 213). Quarry pits will sometimes be more irregular in profile than rubbish pits and will often have steeper sides. Pits which stop at a change in the rock (e.g. at the junction of gravel and clay) are especially likely to be quarries. Excavation should show if they were deliberately filled in (e.g. a homogeneous fill or steep clean tiplines) or whether they silted up slowly (weathered sides, quick silt, standing water, developed soils, etc.). The significance of any dating evidence will depend upon the recognition of the kind of filling.

All the edges of a pit or quarry should be established so that, with its depth, the cubic amount removed can be estimated.

*Ancillary buildings* may be found in or near the edge of quarries and beside approach roads. They will probably be located, and should be dug, as ordinary houses. Their plans and finds may show whether they were living-quarters, stores or offices.

*Preliminary processing* of the raw material, especially if it was stone or metal, may have taken place at the mine, and heaps of raw or discarded material should be looked for. Processing procedures are discussed separately on page 269.

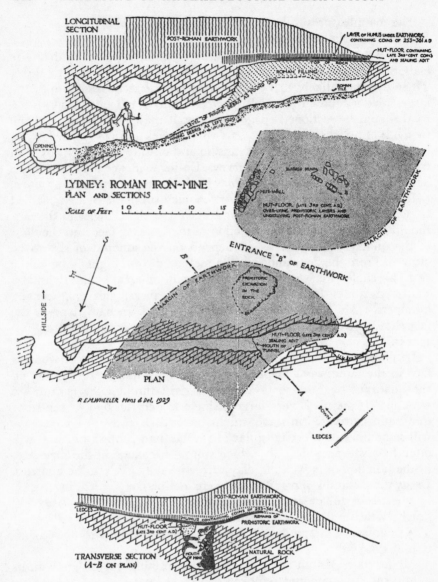

Fig. 67 Roman iron mine: plan and sections. Lydney, Gloucs.

DEEP MINES, requiring tunnels or vertical shafts and galleries, need greater professional skill and determination than open workings. They are therefore more characteristic of elaborately organised societies and are commonly used for metal ores and other especially valued rocks (Fig. 67).

Location will come from recognition of spoil-heaps and blocked shafts, or of the surrounding processing sites. Areas where salt, metals and other desirable rocks occur deserve careful surveys.[11]

Two groups of excavation problems may be distinguished for deep mines; those of clearing and studying the shafts, tunnels and galleries and those of excavating the pithead or tunnel entrance installations.

In the *shafts, tunnels and galleries* there will be special problems of safety, spoil removal, lighting and insurance, and if the workings are likely to be complex, professional miners should be employed to help and advise on techniques to be used. Safety may require elaborate revetting, and a provision of wood or metal struts and shuttering will have to be made well in advance; mining helmets should also be provided. Spoil removal may require a light railway, conveyor belt, rollers or a well-organised basket or barrow-walk. Spoil should be dumped well away from the mouth of the tunnel and will need sieving or screening. Shafts will require windlasses, mechanical hoists or conveyor belts. Artificial lights will be needed if the tunnels are of considerable depth, and cables and a portable generator will have to be provided in advance. In vertical shafts or downward-sloping tunnels in impervious rock, accumulations of water may be a problem and flooding must be anticipated. Sumps may have to be dug and the water pumped out; sludge pumps with filters and long hoses may have to be provided. A director should certainly take out a special insurance for this kind of site.

The excavation of *tunnels* driven into a hillside will resemble that of caves (page 110). It will rarely be possible to lay down a grid of trenches inside, but, if possible, longitudinal as well as transverse sections should be drawn.

When the walls and roof are exposed they should be studied for tool marks and for evidence of fire-setting and explosives. Ledges for, and smoke from, lamps should be noted and there may be slots for timber staging or revetting.[12] Graffiti may also be found. The depth of deposit on the floors will vary with the method of mining, but if little is found and the debris was taken outside, the floor should be searched for grooves or rails for trucks, and paths for basket-carriers or for pack animals. It is at this level that tools, baskets, dung etc. may be expected. If there is much debris on the floor an attempt should be made to distinguish between a collapsed roof and debris left by men after sorting. Sectioning may show a succession of working surfaces with horizontal deposits brought down by fire-setting or explosives. The working-face, when reached, should show the technique of extraction. Drill-holes, pick-marks and tools may be found as well as the nature and amount of the seam worked and the reason for stopping.

The excavation of *shafts* (near-vertical tunnels of relatively narrow diameter), will have to be complete if systems of galleries radiate from the sides and base.[13] If the shaft is wide enough it should be dug like a well, on the quadrant method. If the sections are drawn each time the filling is lowered (say every 1·5 m.), a complete profile will be obtained. It should be possible to say whether it was ever completely cleared, whether it was deliberately filled afterwards or whether it silted up slowly. Dating evidence may also come from this infilling. The walls may show tool-marks, perhaps wear-marks from ropes and the entrances to the galleries. The floor should be studied for evidence of camping (fires, food debris, foundations) and processing (knapping debris, etc.).

If *galleries* lead from the shaft they should be excavated by the methods used for tunnels (see above). Transverse and longitudinal sections at the entrance will be of special interest, and there will be special problems of spoil removal and safety, now as when they were made. The walls and ceilings should be studied for tool-marks and carbon from lamps, and the floor for tools and buried miners.[14]

At the shaft-head there might be evidence of *hoisting equipment*, and the area round should be gridded and trowelled. At the lip of the shaft, grooves from ropes or chains might be found worn into the rock[15] and these would suggest where windlasses or animal hauling-paths might be. The latter might be recognised by a deliberately made path or by a puddling and hardening of the ground. Post-holes may show shaft-head buildings, windlass housings and perhaps processing areas.

Ancient *spoil-dumps* should be recognised, plotted and sectioned so that the means of spoil disposal and the volume of work can be estimated. *Dumps of raw material, processing debris* or *finished products* awaiting removal might also be distinguished (Fig. 68).

## COLLECTION SITES

When outcrops of desirable materials are first discovered by men, they may not need quarries or mines to exploit them. Recognition of these preliminary workings will come only through finding the processing debris in surface surveys of scree slopes, the foot of cliffs, sea shores and river banks.[16] A similar group of sites will develop through the exploitation of alluvial deposits in stream and river gravels and of salt on sea shores and near brine springs. The methods used include panning, washing, hand-sluicing and dredging.

*Salt* may be described as an example. Sites have often been located by the mounds of debris (called red hills in England). One well-documented method of manufacture, based on the Halle-Giebichenstein excavations, would require the construction of clay floors and the erection on them of green-clay evaporating pans; the lighting of fires beneath them; the knocking of the salt from the pans; and the pressing of the wet salt into clay moulds. These processes leave the vast quantities of briquetage (debris from pans, moulds and fires) which make easily recognisable mounds.[17]

Excavation should be by sectioning the mounds on the quadrant method, dating evidence often being found stratified within them. The area round the mounds should be gridded, surveyed and excavated for subsidiary buildings, salt-stores and approach roads. A special survey of the saline concentration in the soil might be of use here.

*Panning, washing and sorting*, to collect nuggets or smaller particles from alluvial deposits, may also be expected to leave archaeological evidence. This kind of winning has been especially practised for scarce metals, and in areas where tin, gold and silver occur, sites should be searched for. Recognition might come from the heaps of discarded silts, sands and gravels; from panning troughs or channels; or from the slag-heaps from processing the ores[18] (Plate XXI).

In the absence of good excavation reports, suggestions of the kind of evidence to be looked for may be made from ethnographic parallels.[19] The working stages of panning and sorting should have needed wide troughs or channels in which the alluvium could settle and then be sieved or picked over. They might also involve a partial damming of a stream. Nearby, the ore might well have been processed into cakes or ingots before removal, and the usual debris (page 272) of slag, ashes and charcoal might be found.

## PROCESSING SITES

Materials of many kinds need more than simple mining to bring them to their most usable state. These processes must be considered by individual materials.

Many mined *minerals* will need refining or chemically changing before they can be further used, and an excavator of a mine or quarry must be familiar with the processes necessary for the raw material from his site (Fig. 68). He must also know the techniques used among communities of varying degrees of sophistication, so that when the general nature of his particular site becomes known (e.g. the casual diggings of hunter-gatherers or the professionally dug mines of an urban community), the kind of processing evidence to be expected is familiar[20] to him.

Whilst no detailed rules for locating processing sites can be laid down, common sense has always dictated that they be as near as possible to

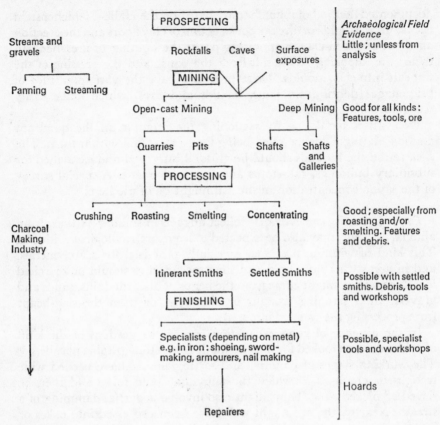

Fig. 68 Stages in a metallurgical industry.

the source. The areas round mines should therefore be searched for the heaps of waste and for the processing equipment. If not found nearby, the nature of the processing (e.g. use of much water or charcoal) or the terminus of any roads or tracks leading from the source might suggest where further search should be made.[21] Walking, especially over ploughed land, may show large fuel concentrations (e.g. charcoal), raw material dumps (e.g. ore) or processing debris (e.g. furnace slag). The field archaeologist must have handled and be able to recognise these. The more common kinds of equipment (e.g. pestles, hammers and mortars, crushing troughs, anvils, kilns and kiln furniture) may also be found. Comparatively recent remains may sometimes be found by a study of field names and pond or road distributions.[22] Aerial photographs may also help on occasion, for slag, spoil or fuel heaps may show as shadow, crop or soilmarks.[23]

METAL ORE PROCESSING SITES will vary in detail for different metals, but they will be generally similar, and iron-processing might be taken as an example of their excavation problems (Fig. 68).

*Iron Ore Processing Areas*, either for roasting or smelting, should be distinguishable even when they are part of the same industrial complex as the mine. In preparation for their excavation, directors should be familiar with the techniques necessary for iron-smelting in their region and should have handled the more typical sorts of debris (e.g. slag, cinder, roasted and unroasted ore), as well as having read the more general accounts of the processing involved.[24] The following are likely to be encountered.

With many kinds of *ore roasting*, heating with charcoal will be necessary to convert carbonates to oxides, and this may be carried on in a special area. The process will include: making the charcoal, breaking up and sorting the lumps of raw ore, roasting them, and screening them after roasting to discard the useless pieces.

The location of roasting areas should come through the discovery of heaps or spreads of lumps of raw ore; undersized and discarded pieces of roasted ore (which will be bright red in colour); and discarded charcoal (which will be in very small fragments). On a specifically roasting site no furnace debris (baked clay fragments, slag or cinder) should be found. Under primitive mining conditions the roasting sites are unlikely to be far from the mine.[25]

The full extent of the area should be planned and the nature of the various spreads or heaps noted. If it is not possible to grid the whole area, then mounds or spreads of different materials should be sectioned on the quadrant method. Four kinds may be found:

*Raw Ore.* Piles of untreated lumps of ore as brought from the mine. No special stratigraphy is likely, but samples shoud be kept and the size and shape and amounts of the lumps noted.

*Charcoal-burning* sites. Charcoal may well have been made nearby, and patches of burnt earth with small charcoal fragments might show the burning floors. Samples from undisturbed burnt earth might be useful for palaeomagnetic dating. Mounds or spreads of very small charcoal fragments without signs of burning might be debris rejected after screening. In either case charcoal fragments should be kept for identification.[26]

*Roasting Floors and Pits.* These should be distinguishable by having a mixture of roasted ore and charcoal. They should be completely excavated on the quadrant method, particular care being paid to the edges of the burnt area. Here the post-holes of a shelter, bellows-nozzles (tuyères) of clay and/or a series of draught slots below or above ground might be found. Palaeomagnetic samples should be taken.

*Rejected Roasted Ore*. Dumps of very fine bright red ore fragments might mark the screening of the roasted ore. They should be sectioned on the quadrant method, a lookout being kept for the post-holes of fixed screens.

Smelting sites[27] will normally be near roasting and mining sites, and here the oxides (whether obtained naturally or through roasting) have been heated to remove impurities. The location or recognition of the sites will be through finding furnace debris, concentrations of burnt clay fragments with slag adhering, slag and cinder. There may also be hollows (indicating furnaces) visible on the surface. A magnetometer survey might well locate the furnaces if the general interference is not too great.

The whole extent of the debris and its mounds or spreads should be planned and, if possible, excavated on the grid method. If this is not possible then any concentration of features should be sampled. The following features might be uncovered:

*Piles of roasted ore lumps*. Sectioned on the quadrant method, these should be recognisable from the size of the lumps (more than 1 in. diameter) and this should enable them to be distinguished from rubbish dumps. Samples should be kept and the amount of ore found noted.

*Furnaces*. Excavated on the quadrant method, these may consist of shallow pits, which, if loaded and fired, might contain on the top, burnt clay with layers of cinder and slag below, or if not fired, alternate layers of charcoal and ore.[27] Such furnaces might well be domed over and perhaps lined with clay. They should be studied for the methods of construction. The edges especially, might show draught slots and bellows-nozzles and further out, the post-holes of a shelter. Samples of undisturbed furnace-walling might show the temperatures achieved, and by palaeomagnetic dating, the age. It is likely that the debris of abandoned and emptied furnaces will be found, in which case the clay fragments should be checked for curvature so that the possible shape and size of the furnace might be recovered.[28]

*Slagheaps*. These, excavated on the quadrant method, should be recognisable in cross-section. The number and size of them might give some indication of the quantity of iron being produced.

The processing of other metals, especially *copper, tin*,[29] *gold*[30] *and silver* could leave a parallel series of events and equally distinct evidence.[30]

*Skin-processing* is essential, and a whole series of soaking, unhairing, drying and tanning processes are usually necessary.[31] Most of them will leave little archaeological evidence, unless the digging of pits was involved. These, depending on local methods, will be necessary for *soaking, pickling* and *tanning*. Any carefully shaped pits, especially if clay-lined, should be studied with this possibility in mind. The filling, especially the bottom, should be sampled for traces of bark or other tanning materials.[32] In a large-scale manufactory complexes of pits of various kinds might be expected.[33]

Other evidence might possibly come from heaps of raw material, lime for unhairing, salt for drying, bark for tanning, and from actual leather fragments.

*Fibre-processing*, although fibres are used and processed by most communities, actual fragments of them are rare in excavations. But evidence of their processing may be found and be the best indication of their use.

Proteinic fibres like *wool or hair* are usually prepared by washing, combing and spinning.[34] The *washing* may be elaborate, with several soaking pits and wringing tables and it may be possible to identify these. The contents, especially at the bottom of possible washing pits, should be sampled for chemical analysis. *Combing* might be inferred from the finding of combs or cards, and *spinning* from the finding of spindle whorls (possibly very large ones) or spinning-wheel fragments. *Felting* might also be recognisable from specially prepared pits or organic fragments.[35]

Bast fibres, like *hemp and flax*, are prepared by *retting, cleaning* (breaking, stretching and combing), and *spinning*. Unless pool-retting, involving the digging and lining of special pits, took place, only the tools (e.g. hackling-boards, skutching blades, roughing-combs and spindle whorls) or organic fragments will be found.[36]

Cellulosic fibres, like *cotton*, need the fibre to be separated from the seeds and the latter might be found lying on the floor. Fragments of separating machines might also be found.

*Silk-processing*, which requires the heating of the cocoons in water and the reeling of the thread, might, if carried out commercially, leave evidence in the form of fires, small ovens and perhaps reeling machines.[37]

In wood-processing where large quantities of wood are used, mostly in settled and elaborately organised societies, intermittent stages between logging and finishing may exist. Sawyers' yards might be identifiable from pits and tools.[38]

## FINISHING SITES

These are here defined as places where the material, raw or refined, is worked into usable objects (Fig. 69). Such sites may fairly be considered separately from the others, for work of this kind is usually done away from the mines or processing areas. Although the degree of organisation in the manufacture will vary, so that it may be carried on either in a corner of a room, camping area, or in a large specialised craft-workshop or factory, the aims and methods of excavation will be similar in all cases. Since areas of this kind may be found in any settlement site, all directors should be familiar with the debris from the native crafts found today or in the past, in their area. They should also, from their general studies, know the kinds of specialised tools necessary in finishing crafts,[39] for only during excavation will the workshops be recognised, and no search for them can really be made before excavation begins.

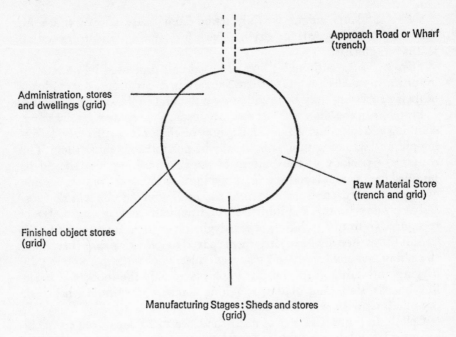

Fig. 69 Problems of excavating a manufacturing site.

Since the evidence will be different from different crafts it may be considered under separate headings, but in all cases excavation should be complete enough to attempt an estimate of production as well as to show all the stages in the manufacture of each kind of object. In some cases a marketing survey of the product may also be considered.

## STONE

Stone-finishing sites are the most varied and widespread of all, for besides the durable nature of the debris, stone tools and weapons have long been used by hunter-gatherers and farmers. Shaped stones for building or sculpting have also been used for millennia by urban and other elaborately organised communities.

*Artifact knapping and/or grinding sites* will usually be fairly close to the source of the material. They may possibly be located by searching likely areas on foot,[40] especially scree-slopes, beaches, cliff-faces and stream banks. Since in most cases the artifacts will have been made by flaking, there will be a great mass of trimming flakes, upwards of 20,000 pieces at a site being not uncommon. These will, depending on the size of the source, be spread over a wide working area, possibly several acres, but big heaps are unlikely except at gun flint manufactories or similar large-scale workings. In desert conditions these concentrations can be located from slow-moving cars or animals.[41]

Excavation should always be on the grid system and 6 m. squares should be suitable for this kind of site. The main problems will be those of vertical and horizontal stratigraphy, since the site is quite likely to have been visited intermittently over a long period. Excavating technique should, at first, closely follow the pattern suggested for hunter-gatherer settlements (page 101). If ploughing has disturbed the upper levels of the site, all the artifactal debris in the disturbed soil should be kept and bagged by 20 cm. squares and (depending on the density of the flakes) in 2–4 cm. spits. When an undisturbed surface is found, possibly identifiable by the angles-of-rest of the flakes and by scattered charcoal and ash, the surface has been completely exposed before any flakes are removed. This surface should show the extent of the working area, since the grid can be extended to find its edges. Later analysis will show any variations in the distribution, and types of flakes or cores lying on the surface, but concentrations should be planned and photographed before any further digging is done. The following may be expected:

In *quartering areas* where large nodules are broken into more convenient sizes, piles of unused, of broken or of rejected nodules may be found. Set among them or near them may be large anvil stones (possibly of a different rock), and broken debris and hammerstones may lie around.[42] Any heaps should be sectioned and an estimate made of the total amount (weight and volume) of debris present. If a number of quartering areas are found this may be a clue to the horizontal stratigraphy of the site.

*Trimming areas* may be nearby, and concentrations of flakes varying in nature from large preliminary to small final ones may be found. Densities should be recorded in 10 cm. squares and 1 cm. depths.[43] All should be kept for later study (page 63) for they will show the detailed processes of knapping. Bone, antler, wood and stone hammers, punches and anvils may be found. All artifacts, finished tools or weapons should be treated as 'special finds' (Fig. 7).

When an individual surface has been studied in this way it should be removed in 3 cm. spits, keeping careful watch for lenses of soil, sand, etc. and for the horizontal bedding of flakes which might indicate new surfaces and a succession of visits to the site. If none is found the process should continue to bedrock where features (post-holes, etc.), unrecognised above, might be found.

*Grinding areas* in which artifacts are ground into final shape may be where suitable abrasive stones occur rather than near the trimming area. They may be recognisable from the grooves worn in stone outcrops.[44] Gridding the area nearby might expose piles of objects awaiting grinding or of broken and discarded fragments. If these are found petrological samples should be taken to identify the source area.

In more recent times manufactories for gun-flints, mill-stones, etc. may have been more permanent and the foundations for huts and stores, as well as large piles of debris may be expected.[45]

*Sites for shaping building and sculpting material* will, for obvious reasons, be near the quarry or mine. Their environs should be examined for the litter of discarded and broken stone which marks a processing workshop. This debris, recognisable as shaped but broken, may also be found by the surface searching of the area. Processing sites of this kind are connected with highly organised communities, and a complex of buildings and equipment is likely.[46]

Excavation should be on the grid system and should expose the ground surface with all its debris left on it for planning and photography. As the debris is removed the amount should be recorded. The following might have been made at this kind of site:

*Ashlar (squared) Blocks.* If these were produced there should be heaps or spreads of part-finished and broken blocks. With them may be the tools for sawing, splitting, pounding and pecking (e.g. saws, hammers, wedges and chisels). Stacks of finished blocks ready for removal may also be found. All blocks should be examined for working lines and graffiti. The sizes and shapes and quantities of the blocks should be recorded.

*Roof Tiles or Floor Slabs.* These will leave debris similar to, but different in shape from, ashlar blocks but should be excavated in the same way.

*Blocks for sculpture.* It may be possible to distinguish these from the other two from the size and shape of the blocks or from the rough hewing of statues in the quarry.

On all sites approach and service roads and ancillary buildings are to be expected.

# LEATHER

Leather-working was probably as widely practised in time and in as wide a variety of societies as stone-working, but is much less easy to recognise. In all sites, the finishing processes of thinning, cutting and sewing will probably also have been carried on, but only when the actual leather survives can much of the detail be worked out.[47] Usually only the tools will survive for study, and these will vary greatly with the nature of the community.

In *hunter-gatherer settlements* areas may have been set aside for skin-working. Although not elaborated in any way, they may become recognisable during excavation by concentrations of special tools. If of stone, these might be scrapers or knives (there may also be

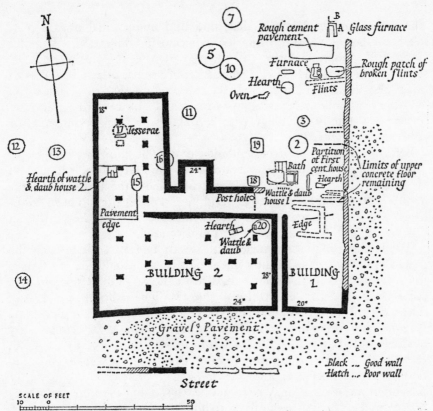

Fig. 70. Plan of the Roman glass factory at Caistor by Norwich.
To be considered with Plate xx.

concentrations of sharpening spalls); if of bone, these might be needles
and thong-softeners.[48] If conditions favour the recognition of stake-holes,
pegging-out stakes might be found. Any fragments of leather should be
studied for their production techniques as well as for their purpose and
source animal.

In *farms and private compounds*, rooms or huts may have been set aside
for leather-working. The processing pits already discussed may be
nearby (page 272), but the huts may be distinguished by tools similar
to those already mentioned (but here perhaps of metal), or from leather
fragments found on their floors. If the tools suggest leather-working the
floors might be sampled for salt concentrations.

In *villages and towns* might be found the workrooms and yards of
specialist leather craftsmen. Tools and leather scraps will be the only
ways of recognising them, but here specialised equipment and the
debris of different kinds of leather-working, e.g. shoe-makers or saddlers,
might be recognisable.[49]

## CLAY

The making of fired bricks, tiles, pots and many small objects (e.g. tobacco-pipes or figurines) may be expected in communities of many kinds.[50] The manufactories will vary greatly in elaboration, but all should have the same general succession of events. Sites with areas of burnt clay intact may be suitable for palaeomagnetic dating (page 92).

Pottery manufactories will vary from small sites used intermittently to supply a family or village with containers, to large commercial or government plants.[51]

Before excavation a director should not only be familiar with general potting techniques and the appearance of the materials and debris at every stage in the making, but must also know the traditional local methods of potting. Once the general period of his site has been established, he should have studied any local collections of the pottery of this period and know the forms and fabrics used.

The location of manufactories will usually be from walking over the sites. On cultivated land the typical debris can usually be recognised from the plough furrows but casual disturbances, rabbit scrapes, tree roots, drain-trenches, etc. will also show it. This debris will consist of burnt clay from kiln linings and sealing, kiln-furniture, and wasters (broken and distorted pots discarded after firing). It can be very obvious and may have given a name to the field (e.g. in England, Redlands). Charcoal dumps, coming from the clearance of stoke-holes, may also be found, and even piles of raw clay awaiting use. Clay pits, often water-filled, may be found nearby so that the whole area may be covered with low mounds and hollows. Once generally located, precise planning of the workings may be done with a magnetometer or gradiometer (page 29). Auger surveys may also identify charcoal, clay and waster dumps.

On small sites a grid of 4 m. square trenches might be used to cover the whole area of working. On large or ill-defined sites an interrupted grid should supplement the survey and locate the limits of the debris.

During excavation the following features may be expected:

*Dumps of raw clay* ready for use. When sectioned these should show as sterile, homogeneous, featureless mounds. Samples should be taken both to confirm that the ceramic objects were made from the same material and to help locate the source of the clay.

*Refining and tempering* may have been done nearby. Refining will be difficult to recognise unless grinding took place, when the stone mortars and rubbers may be found. Heaps or scatters of temper (possibly identifiable from that in the completed ceramics) may also be found; they might be of crushed stone, shell or sand, and the heaps should be scetioned in the usual way. If grinding took place the mills[52] or the hardened and dished floors of the grinding areas might be found. The edges of the latter should be examined for shelter foundations—either post-holes or wall footings.

If wall footings are found they might also belong to *shaping areas*. On ethnographic evidence shaping is often done under shelter, and the sheds might be identifiable from their internal features. The floors, perhaps merely hardened earth, might also show the equipment used and the foundations of benches and wheel-sockets, water-pots sunk into the ground, burnishing pebbles, pots containing paint or colouring matter (e.g. ochre, chalk or magnesium) and clay wheels should be looked for. If conditions favour organic survival, wheels, paddles, smoothing spatulae, incising knives, combs and stamps may be found. All pots need *drying* before firing, and separate shelters or verandahs may have been provided for the purpose. They are likely to be un-walled, and post-holes or column bases may be the only evidence they leave.

*Kilns and firing areas* will leave the most permanent traces, but may well be at some distance from and to leeward of the main manufactory.[53] If the site was long used, there may be many successive kilns, and if possible all should be excavated, planned and sampled, since some may have been left loaded or have been filled with rubbish, and only excava-tion will disentangle the horizontal stratigraphy and the sequence of operations. If selective digging only is possible, kilns (preferably loaded) should be selected at intervals through the whole area. Since the firing-area will usually be recognised before the manufacturing one, any paths found between kilns should be traced away from the firing-area in a search for the making-area. The path might be located by its relation to the stoke-holes.

Firing may be done in a wide variety of ways, from simple open fires to elaborate kilns, but a director should know from his preliminary studies the general nature of the kilns to be expected.[54] Excavation, having begun on the grid system already described, should change when the kiln has been located to the quadrant method, and one of the axes should pass through the stoke-hole. During excavation the following should be expected:

(i) The kiln walls and floor may well be covered by collapsed roof. This will probably have been of wood, stone and clay, and from a study of the fragments the size of the dome and its construction may be recovered.

(ii) When the original ground surface is reached the bottom courses of the kiln walls may well be revealed and can be planned and examined for the method of construction.

(iii) The chamber should show, as it is cleared, the methods of firing and stacking. It will become obvious if a 'pit' or platform construction was used; where and how flues, stoke-holes and dampers operated;

whether the kiln was of the 'open flame' or 'muffle' kind; was 'up'- or 'down-draught' and was for 'continuous' or 'intermittent' firing.[54] Methods of stoking should show from the construction of the firing platform and the presence of 'saggers' or fire-bars.

The debris in the stoke-hole should show the kind of fuel used, and samples of the wood, coal, dung, etc. should be taken. Samples of the walls and floor, taken at intervals over the whole area and recorded three-dimensionally, might on later examination show the temperatures achieved. One of the drawn sections should be through the stoke-hole and the interior. Samples for palaeomagnetic examination should be taken.

The debris in the interior of the chamber, especially if the last firing was a failure and the whole load was left *in situ*, can show the types of pot being fired together and the methods of loading. Other piles or scatters of debris may be found near the kilns. They will consist of wasters, broken kiln furniture (bars, walls, etc.) and fuel. The dumps should all be planned, representative ones sectioned, and the total amount of debris calculated.

*Stores and other Ancillary Buildings* may also be expected. The finished products might well have been stored under cover, and stacks of pots or piles of broken but undistorted fragments should be studied with this in mind. Other buildings, such as dwellings, stables and offices might also be found. Linking them, the working areas and the outside world there should be *service and approach roads*. These should be sectioned for methods of transportation and dating evidence, and should be traced as far as possible from the site.

Specialised manufactories (e.g. for tobacco-pipes or figurines) present no special excavation problems but call for considerable pre-excavation research on the part of the director.[55]

Brick and tile manufactories will vary from small establishments set up for a few months to serve a particular building need, to large ones operating for centuries (Fig. 23). Location and excavation techniques will be generally similar to those for potteries, but the following differences may be noted.

*Bricks* will be made in much the same way whether sun-dried or fired. After cleaning and tempering the clay in the ways already described for pottery, the shaping, if not done by hand, will probably have been in wooden moulds. The bricks will then have been laid out in rows or stacks to dry.[56] These may survive or may have weathered into heaps, but should be distinguishable in cross-section from the heaps of raw unshaped clay brought in from the quarry. They should be sampled for source identification. In areas with a regular rainfall the edges of a heap or stack should be examined for roof supports, since some form of shelter will have been necessary. *Firing stacks* will naturally have left the most permanent traces. Although details will vary, the bricks must always be piled, and the fuel so arranged, that the air can circulate. Some system of parallel rows of bricks, possibly with troughs dug between them or on low platforms, should be looked for. When located, the grid should be laid at right angles to the rows, or if located too late for this, then temporary sections should be kept across the whole stack. The lowest course of the stack may well be heavily overfired and vitrified. Much fuel, possibly charcoal, will be found nearby; examination should show how it was arranged (e.g. in a stoke-hole or piled at intervals), and analysis will reveal its nature. Sampling for palaeomagnetic dating should be carried out.

The standard sizes of bricks and their relative numbers should be noted throughout.

Ancillary buildings will be similar to those of potteries. Stacks of finished bricks ready for delivery should be easy to recognise, and equipment stores, offices, etc., as well as access and service roads, may be found.

*Tiles* will always be fired and will be recognisable by shape. The manufactories will be similar to those already described for bricks and may produce a wide range of sizes and shapes of products. *Floor* (usually large and thick), *chimney* (various forms of box or cylinder), *wall* (flat and possibly ornamented or keyed for plaster), and *roof* (slope or ridge), tiles may be made. This elaboration may mean several different sizes and constructions of kiln[57] and in large scale works whole batteries of them may be found. The quantities of each size and shape of tile should be noted (Fig. 23).

## METAL

*Smithies*, whether for iron, copper/bronze or precious metals, will be generally similar in equipment and layout although they will vary greatly in elaboration and scale. Ethnographic studies suggest that most smiths work under shelter of some kind, although some operations, perhaps those involving a fire, may be done outside. Buildings and yards should therefore be excavated together.[58]

All smiths will need to heat their metals and usually have a carefully constructed fireplace and bellows. These may be the most obvious surviving remains. Any charcoal-filled pit should be considered with this possibility in mind and its edges studied for bellows-nozzles (tuyères) and draught slots; bellows bag-settings with wood or stone clappers may be found nearby. A stone or brick-built platform may be a more elaborate form of this and have supported the fire and bellows. It should have a burnt upper surface or burnt inner compartment with draught holes and a chimney. Quenching pits may also be found.

The excavation grid round the pit or platform may uncover the walls of a building or verandah, and if the fire is near a wall, a chimney flue should be looked for. The floor might show other evidence of the techniques used, and in all cases discarded or stored raw material and objects might be found. For example:

If the metal was *moulded*, congealed splashes of metal, fragments of ingots, dross, risers, crucibles, mould-fragments (of sand, clay or stone), tools (e.g. hammers, tongs, files and ladles) and grinding stones might be found.[59]

If it was *wrought*; fragments of blooms, scales, heavy hammers (of metal or stone), tongs and files and anvils might be found.[60]

Other work might be done nearby or in neighbouring rooms. This might include *sheet-working*, cutting, riveting and soldering, and characteristic tools (shears, tracers and hammers). Debris (rivets, strip and solder-splashes) might be recognisable.

Specialist manufactories (e.g. for coins, buckets, pins) should be recognisable from the objects found.[61] The whole process of manufacture should be worked out.

## BONE, IVORY AND ANTLER

If these were worked there is some chance of identifying the area from the industrial debris.

At its simplest this manufacturing area may be part of a hunter-gatherers' camping site where the debris (antlers with tines and strips removed, cut or sawn bones and tusks) is concentrated.[62] A study of this may show the objects produced (e.g. prickers or needles); the techniques (e.g. grooving and splintering) and the tools (saws, gravers, grinding stones) used. If the tools were of stone their sharpening spalls may lie around. Similar remains may be found in the huts or compounds of farmers.

In larger communities, manufactories for specialised objects, for example carriage fittings or belt fittings, are more likely. These should be recognisable from the tools and from the industrial debris.[63]

## TEXTILES

Weaving and tailoring workshops may also vary from the corner of a room to a large factory.

*Weaving* should leave the most evidence, since looms will usually be necessary and, depending on the type in use, pits, post-holes and rows of loom weights as well as bobbins or spindles, spools, swords and shears may be found.[64]

*Tailoring* may leave evidence in the form of shears, pins and needles, but unless actual cloth-fragments survive, they will be inconclusive.

## WOOD[65]

Although this was probably the first and is still the commonest material used by man, little evidence of specialist workshops will be likely from simple societies. Hunter-gatherers' tools, like hollow scrapers and arrow-straighteners, may suggest wood-working areas if found in concentrations, but this cannot be proved unless concentrations of actual debris survive. Specialised craftwork-shops (e.g. wheelwrights or coopers) might be identifiable from their tools.[66]

## GLASS AND FAIENCE

These may be considered together since the industrial processes are similar[67] (Fig. 70).

Sites are likely to be recognised by the industrial debris, especially slag and clinker, crucibles or glasspots, broken and distorted fragments and moulds. The heaps of raw *former* (probably quartz sand or crushed flint), or of *modifier* (oxides of sodium, potassium, calcium and lead) might be located. So might the *ovens* or the debris from them, and some of the *blowing, moulding, cutting* and *grinding* equipment[68] (Plate xx).

The finished products (beads, bottles, etc.) should be recognisable from wasters and rejects in the same way as potteries (page 278). Faience manufactories will be similar in general organisation.[69]

## SELECTED READING

*Artifacts*\*\*, Hodges, H. 1965. Part I (with good bibliography).
*Notes and Queries on Anthropology*\*, BAAS 1962. 257–96.
*Industrial Archaeology; an introduction*, Hudson, K. 1963 (for the last few centuries only unfortunately).
*Handbook for Industrial Archaeologists*, Hudson, K. 1967.
*Techniques of Industrial Archaeology*, Pannell, J. 1966; see especially gazetteer p. 172 (from AD 1500 only unfortunately).
*Theory and Practice of Industrial Archaeology*, Buchanan, R. (ed) 1968.
*Industrial Archaeology of the East Midlands*, Smith, D. 1965.
*Mines, Mills and Furnaces*, Rees, D. 1969.
Mines and Quarries of the Indians of California *JMGC* 40 1940. 292.
*A Diderot Pictorial Encyclopaedia of Trades and Industries*, Diderot, D. 1959.
British Industries of the Middle Ages, Salzman, L. 1923.
*Crafts, Trades and Industries*, Jewell, A. 1968.
Stone: No reports are wholly satisfactory but see Harrow Hill: *SAC* 66 (1926) and 78 (1937): 230 and Mynydd Rhuw: *PPS* XXVII 1961. 108.
Salt: *Salt*\*, Nenquin, J. 1961. For a regional study in Lincolnshire: *LAAS* VIII 1960. 26.
Metal: *Metallurgy in Archaeology*\*, Tylecote, R. 1962. *De re metallica*, Agricola, G. 1950. African Smiths, *Kuml* 1962.
Clay: *Ceramics for the Archaeologist*\*, part II. Shepard, A. 1961. *Roman Potters' kilns of Colchester*. Hull, M. 1963. Potterton, *AntJ* XLVI 1966. 225.
Textiles: Pits, looms and loomweights *Kuml* 1963. 104. Studies in Primitive Looms *JRAI* XLVI-VIII 1918. Grimstone End *PSIA* 1954.
Leather: Leather and Parchment . . . of the Dead Sea Scrolls Community *TC* 31 1962 with good bibliography.
Glass: Glastenburg *JGS* V 1963.

## NOTES

1. See a whole series of books in recent years. e.g. Hudson, K. 1967 and Pannell, J. 1966. For the kinds of evidence from less sophisticated sources see *JMGC* 40, 1940. 292.
2. e.g. For Roman mining techniques see Davies, O. 1935.
3. A good general idea is given by the Fallowfield Mine, *IndArch* 4 1967. 311.
4. Beresford, M. and St. Joseph, K. 1958. 229.
5. For stone for tools see Mynydd Rhuw: *PPS* XXVII 1961. 108.
6. Rosenfeld, A. 1965. Slags especially, must be well known. For examples see Tylecote, R. 1962. 252.
7. For ochre in South Australia see Elkin, A. 1954. 145.
8. Grimes Graves, Pit 12: *PPS* (*PPSEA*) 7, 1934. 382.
9. Pike of Stickle; *PPS* XV, 1949, 1. Umm es Sawan (gypsum): Caton-Thompson, G. and Gardiner, E. 1934. 104. For chalk mining (deneholes) *AntJ* XXXVIII 1881 and 2.
10. Turra, Ma'sara and Gebelein: Lucas, A. 1962. 12. Sinai: Forbes, R. 1950. 333.
11. e.g. Umm es Sawan (loc. cit.).
12. Muhlbach Bischshofen (copper): *MZUO* VI, 1952. For a plan see Fallowfield (lead) *IndArch* 4 1967.
13. Harrow Hill (flint): *SAC* 66 1926, and 78 1937. 230; Easton Down: *WAM* XIV 1931. 61.
14. e.g. Hallein-Durrnberg (salt) where much organic matter was preserved. Nenquin, J. 1961. 49; also Singer, C., Holmyard, E. and Hall, A. 1957.

15. Harrow Hill (loc. cit.); Grimes Graves (loc. cit.).

16. Mynnydd Rhuw (op. cit.) 108. Kimmeridge (shale): *ArchJ* XCIII 1936. 200.

17. Nenquin, J. 1961. For a local study: *LAAS* VIII 1960. 26.

18. e.g. Redmore and near St. Michael Mount: Hencken, H. 1932.

19. Gold: Forbes, R. 1950. 145, especially his translation of Diodorus III; Example: Dolancothi *BBCS* XIV 1950. Tin: Agricola, G. 1950.

20. Tylecote, R. 1962 and Forbes, R. 1950.

21. e.g. Muhlbach-Bischshofen (loc. cit.). Summarised in Clark, J. G. D. 1954. 190.

22. As in the Sussex iron industry: Straker, E. 1931 and *TNS* I. 1920–1.

23. Beresford, M. and St. Joseph, K. 1958. 230.

24. e.g. Mining and Metal in Negro Africa: *AmAnth* 5 1937. For details of West African smelting: *JISI* 56 1904. 91. For excavating problems: The Iron Industry of Roman Britain, Cleere, H. 1966 *LRS* (duplicated).

25. e.g. Ashwicken: *NorArch* XXXII 1966. 142.

26. For an example of charcoal burning see *IndArch* I 1964/5. 27.

27. Prehistoric Iron-smelting in Denmark: *Kuml* 1962. For sites see High Bishopley: *JISI* 192 1959. 26: 1967. 187. Byrkeknott: *JISI* 194 1960. 451.

28. West Runton: *NorArch* XXXIV 1967. 187. Ashwicken: *NorArch* XXXII 1960. 142.

29. A good summary of copper processing: Forbes, R. 1950. 234. Bronze: Heron-bridge: *JCNW* 41 1954. 1. Tin: Hamilton-Jenkins, A. 1927 Chapters 1–3. Chun Castle: *Arch* LXXVI 1927. 238—this to be read with Tylecote R. 1962. 49.

30. Gold: *Antiq* 1942. 193, and Mennell, F. et al. 1955. Lead: Clough, R. 1962. *PFHS* XIII 1953. 5. Silver: *Arch* 57 1900. 113 and Wacher, J. 1966. 81.

31. *RTIC* 45.2 1953. For a good regional study in Israel see *TC* 3.1 1962.

32. No attribution should be made unless supported by analysis.

33. e.g. Diderot, D. 1959.

34. For the kind of evidence to be expected see Grant, I. 1961.

35. Fulling stocks: *IndArch* I, 1964/5. 9. See also Rudenko, S. 1953.

36. Clark, J. G. D. 1954. 232. Retting pits should be recognisable.

37. For silk-reeling machines see Hoffmann, M. 1964.

38. Rose, W. 1937 Chapters 4 and 5. Note the evidence for sawpits. See also Singer, C. et al. Vol. I 1954. 388.

39. Excellent specialist accounts exist (e.g. Rose, W. 1937 for carpentry).

40. As Pike of Stickle was found (loc. cit.).

41. Slow-moving cars were used with great success in the Nubian surveys 1964–7.

42. *PPS* XXX, 1964. 400.

43. For a recent technique see McBurney, C. 1968.

44. As for example in the Congo. *AT* VIII, 1962. 61.

45. e.g. in Great Britain at Brandon for gunflints and Kirkcaldy for flintdust. *IndArch* 31, 1966. 171.

46. e.g. Turra, Ma'sara and Gebelein: Lucas, A. 1928. 12. Mokattam: Petrie, F. 1936. 69.

47. As in the finds from Dead Sea region: *TC* 31, 1962.

48. Semenov, S. 1967. 190.

49. Deventer: *BROB* 10–11 1961. 253. Valkenburg: Groenman von Waateringe, W. 1967.

50. Hodges, H. 1965 Chapter I. Linne, S. in Matson, F. (ed) 1966. 20.

51. In Britain for example see Eilean an Tighe—*PSAS* LXXVI. 130; Upper Heaton—*ArchJ* CXXI, 1964, Hull, M. 1963; and Potterton—*AntJ* XCVI 2.

52. At the most elaborate level, see Kirkcaldy: *IndArch* 3.1 1966. 171.

53. For a good example of a tile-kiln see Boston: *JBAA* 28–29 1966. 86 (Mediaeval).

54. Hodges, H. 1965. 35.

55. e.g. Clay Pipe Works. *BMQN* XXVI. 1944. For a general account *JBAA* XXIII, 1960. 40.
56. Brickworks at Childerley (to be published in *PCAS*).
57. e.g. Holt: *y Cymrodor* XII 1930.
58. For ethnographic evidence of black-smiths: *Kuml* 1962. For bronze: Vindblaes—*Kuml* 1956; Jarlshof—*PSAS* LXVII, 91; Heronbridge—*JCNW* 41 1954.
59. Tzŭ Hsing Shan: Watson, W. 1961. 79.
60. Cornwall, I. in Brothwell, D. and Higgs, E. (ed) 1964. 120.
61. For coins see Bagendon—Clifford, E. 1961. 97.
62. General: Ancient Europe. Clark, J. G. D. 1954. 222. Example: Meiendorf: Rust, A. 1937. 92.
63. Hsin T'ien: Chang, K.-C. 1963.
64. General: *Kuml* 1963. 104. Examples: Grimstone End: (Saxon weaving shed) *PSIA* 1954. Goldberg: Vogt, E. 1937, 112. For recent weaving cottages in England see *IndArch* 3.4 1966. 25.
65. Singer, C. et. al. 1954 Vol. I. 142.
66. For the kind of evidence from a carpenter's shop: Rose, W. 1937, Chapters III and IV.
67. Hodges, H. 1965. 54.
68. Glastenbury: *JGS* V, 1963. Tell el Amarna: Petrie, F. 1923. 123. For the kind of evidence from a glass furnace: *The Connoisseur*, 92, 1933. For Roman Britain see Wacher, J. 1966, 78. Varva, J. (undated).
69. Tell el Amarna: Petrie, F. 1923. 117.

# BIBLIOGRAPHY, other than Journals

(Select bibliographies are given at the end of each chapter).

Adcock, F.: *The Greek and Macedonian Art of War*, Cambridge 1968.
Ager, D.: *Principles of Palaeo-ecology*, New York 1963.
Agricola, G.: *De re metallica* (Hover translation), New York 1950.
Aitken, M.: *Physics and Archaeology*, New York 1961.
Albright, W.: *The Archaeology of Palestine*, London 1960.
Allan, W.: *The African Husbandman*, London 1965.
Allchin, F.: *Neolithic cattle keepers of S. India*: A study of the Deccan Ash mounds, Cambridge 1963.
Ashbee, P.: *The Bronze Age Round Barrow in Britain*, London 1960.
Atkinson, R.: *Field Archaeology*, London 1953.
Atkinson, R.: *Stonehenge*, London 1960.
Atkinson, R., et al.: *Dorchester*, Oxford 1951.

(BAAS). British Association for the Advancement of Science. *Notes and Queries on Anthropology*. London 1962.
Barley, M.: *The English Farmhouse and Cottage*, London 1961.
Benać, A.: *Glasinac I and II*, Sarajevo 1956 and 1964.
Beresford, M.: *The Lost Villages of England*, London 1963.
Beresford, M.: *History on the Ground*, London 1957.
Beresford, M. and St. Joseph, K.: *Mediaeval England: an aerial survey*, Cambridge 1958.
Best, E.: *Fishing methods and devices of the Maori*, London 1929.
Beveridge, W.: *The Art of Scientific Investigation*, London 1961.
Binford, S.: *New Perspectives in Archaeology*, Chicago 1968.
Blegen, C. (et al.): *Troy* (I–VII), Princeton 1950–8.
Boon, G.: *Isca*, Cardiff 1960.
Bowen, H.: *Ancient Fields*, London 1963.
Bradford, J.: *Ancient Landscapes*, London 1957.
Braidwood, R. and Willey, G. (ed): *Courses towards Urban Life*, Edinburgh 1962.
Brønsted, J.: *Danmarks Oldtid* III, Copenhagen 1960.
Brothwell, D. and Higgs, E. (ed): *Science in Archaeology*, London 1964 and (new edition) 1970.
Brothwell, D.: *Digging up Bones*, London 1965.
Bruce-Mitford, R. (ed): *Recent Archaeological Excavations in Britain*, London 1956.
Brunton, G. and Caton-Thompson, G.: *The Badarian Civilisation*, London 1924.
Buchanan, R. (ed): *The Theory and Practice of Industrial Archaeology*, Bath 1968.
Bulleid, A. and Gray, H.: *The Meare Lake Village*, Taunton 1948–66.
Bushe Foxe, J. *Richborough* I–IV, Oxford 1926–49. Published as Soc. of Ant. research reports 1, 2, 10, 16. (V edited by B. Cunliffe 1969).
Buttler, W. and Haberey, K.: *Das bandkeramische Ansiedlungbec Köln-Lindenthal*. (Rom-Germ. Forschungen 11), Berlin 1936.
Butzer, K.: *Environment and Archaeology*, London 1964.

CBA (Council for British Archaeology): *A Handbook of Scientific Aids and Evidence for Archaeologists*, London 1970.
CBA: *Notes for the Guidance of Archaeologists in the Use of Codes*, London 1964 (duplicated).
CBA: *The Investigation of Smaller Domestic Buildings*, London 1964.
CBA: *Rural Settlement in Roman Britain* (Research Report), London 1966.
CUP: (Cambridge University Press) *The Preparation of Manuscripts and Correction of Proofs*, Cambridge 1964.

Carr, R. and Hazard, J.: *Map of the Ruins of Tikal*, Tikal Report II, Philadelphia 1961.
Carter, H.: *The Tomb of Tut-Ankh-Amen*, London 1927.
Caton-Thompson, G. and Gardiner, E.: *The Desert Fayum*, London 1934.
Caton-Thompson, G. and Bates, D.: *The Stone Age on Mount Carmel*, Cambridge 1934.
Chang, K.-C.: *The Archaeology of Ancient China*, Yale 1963.
Cheng, Te-K'un: *Archaeology in China*, 1 Cambridge 1960 and 2 1964.
Childe, V.: *Skara Brae*, London 1931.
Clark, C. and Haswell, M.: *The Economics of Subsistence Agriculture*, London 1966.
Clark, J. D.: *Kalambo Falls*, Cambridge 1969.
Clark, J. D.: *Prehistory of Southern Africa*, London 1959.
Clark, J. G. D.: *Star Carr*, Cambridge 1954.
Clark, J. G. D.: *Prehistoric Europe: the Economic foundation*, Cambridge 1954.
Clarke, D.: *Analytical Archaeology*, London 1968.
Clarke, D.: *Beaker Pottery of Great Britain and Ireland*, Cambridge 1970.
Clarke, S. and Englebach, R.: *Ancient Egyptian Masonry*, London 1930.
Cleland, C.: *Ethno-zoology of the Upper Great Lakes Region* (MAUM 29), Ann Arbor 1966.
Clifford, E.: *Bagendon*, Cambridge 1961.
Clough, R.: *The Lead Smelting Mills of the Yorkshire Dales*, Leeds 1962.
Coe, M. *The Maya*, London 1966.
Collingwood-Bruce, J.: *Handbook to the Roman Wall*, Newcastle-on-Tyne 1957.
Colvin, H. (ed): *The History of the King's Works*, Vol. I, London 1963.
Combier, J.: *Solutré 1907-25*, Macon 1956.
Cook, J. and Plommer, W.: *The Sanctuary of Hemitrea at Kastabos*, Cambridge 1966.
Cook, S. and Heizer, R.: *Studies on the Chemical Analysis of Archaeological Sites* (UCPA 2) 1965.
Cookson, M.: *Photography for Archaeologists*, London 1954.
Corder, P.: *Great Casterton* (3rd report), Nottingham 1961.
Cornwall, I.: *Bones for the Archaeologist*, London 1956.
Cornwall, I.: *Soils for the Archaeologist*, London 1958.
Cornwall, I.: *The World of Ancient Man*, London 1964.
Crawford, O.: *Archaeology in the Field*, London 1953.
Crawford, O.: *Topography of Roman Scotland*, Cambridge 1949.
Cunnington, M.: *Woodhenge*, Devizes 1929.


Davey, N.: *A History of Building Materials*, London 1961.
Davies, O.: *Roman Mines in Europe*, Oxford 1935.
Davies, O.: *West Africa before the Europeans*, London 1967.
Delougaz, P.: *The Temple Oval at Khafajah*, Chicago 1940
Desborough, V.: *The Last Mycenaeans and their Successors*, Oxford 1964.
Devore, I. and Lee, R. (ed): *Man the Hunter*, Chicago 1968.
Diderot, D. (ed. Gillespie): *A Diderot Pictorial Encyclopaedia of Trades and Industries*, New York 1959.
Dimbleby, G.: *Environmental Studies and Archaeology*, London 1963.
Dimbleby, G.: *Plants and Archaeology*, London 1967.
Dittert, A. and Wendorf, F. (ed): *Procedural Manual for Archaeological Field Research Projects*, Santa Fe 1963.
Drake, R. (ed): *Molluscs in Archaeology and the Recent*, Vancouver 1962.
Dunham, D. (ed): *Naga-ed-Dêr*, Berkeley 1965.

Elkin, A.: *The Australian Aborigines*, London 1954.
Emery, W.: *Buhen*, NYP.
Emmison, F.: *Archives and Local History*, London 1966.
Evans, Sir Arthur John: *The Palace of Minos*, Oxford 1921–36.
Evans, Joan: *Monastic Architecture in France*, Cambridge 1964.
Evans, J.: *Malta*, London 1959.
Eyre, S.: *Vegetation and Soils*, London 1963.


Fagan, B.: *Southern Africa during the Iron Age*, London 1966.
Falk, R.: *The Business of Management*, London 1963.
Fay, G.: *Archaeological Field Equipment* (Museum of Anthropology, Wisconsin
    University. 4), Oshkosh 1965.
Feininger, A.: *Manual of Advanced Photography*, London 1970.
Finegan, J.: *The Archaeology of World Religions*, Princeton 1952.
Firth, R.: *Primitive Economies of the New Zealand Maori*, London 1929.
Fletcher, B.: *A History of Architecture*, London 1943.
Forbes, R.: *Notes on the History of Ancient Roads and their Construction* (Arch. Hist.
    Bijdragen III), Amsterdam 1934.
Forbes, R.: *Metallurgy in Antiquity*, Leiden 1950.
Forbes, R.: *Studies in Ancient Technology* (I–VI), Leiden 1955, 1956, 1957, 1958.
Forde, C.: *Habitat, Economy and Society*, London 1964.
Fouché, L.: *Mapungubwe*, Cambridge 1937.
Fox, C.: *A Find of the Early Iron Age from Llyn Cerrig Bach*, Cardiff 1946.
Fox, C.: *Offa's Dyke*, Oxford 1955.
Fox, C.: *Pattern and Purpose*, London 1958.
Fox, C.: *Life and Death in the Bronze Age*, London 1959.
Frankfort, H.: *Art and Architecture of the Ancient Orient*, London 1958.
Freese, S.: *Windmills and Millwrighting*, Cambridge 1967.
Frere, S.: *Britannia*, London 1967.
Frere, S. (ed): *Problems of the Iron Age in Southern Britain*, London 1958.
Fryer, D.: *Surveying for Archaeologists*, Durham 1960.


Garlake, P.: *The Early Islamic Architecture of the East African Coast*, Oxford 1966.
Garrod, D. and Bate, D.: *The Stone Age of Mount Carmel*, Oxford 1937.
Gibb, H.: *Ibn Battuta*, London 1929.
Giddings, J.: *The Archaeology of Cape Denbigh*, Providence 1964.
Gilyard-Beer, R.: *Abbeys*, London 1958.
Gjerstad, E.: *Early Rome*, III, Lund 1960.
Glasbergen, W.: *Barrow Excavations in the Eight Beatitudes* (Palaeohistoria II and III),
    Groningen 1954.
Glob, P: *The Bog People*, London 1969.
Goodman, W.: *The History of Woodworking Tools*, London 1964.
Goody, J.: *Death, Property and the Ancestors*, London 1962.
Grakov, B.: *Kamenskoe*, Moscow 1954.
Grant, I.: *Highland Folk Ways*, London 1961.
Gray, H. and Bulleid, A.: *The Glastonbury Lake Village*, Glastonbury 1911, 1948 and
    1953.
Green, C.: *Sutton Hoo*, London 1963.
Griffin, J. (ed): *Essays on Archaeological Method* (Michigan Museum of Anthropology
    8), Ann Arbor 1957.
Grimes, W.: *Excavations on Defence Sites 1939–45*, London 1960.
Grimes, W.: *The Excavation of Roman and Medieval London*, London 1968.

T

Grinsell, L., Rahtz, P. and Warhurst, A.: *The Preparation of Archaeological Reports*, London 1965.
Grinsell, L.: *Ancient Burial Mounds*, London 1953.
Groenman van Waateringe, W.: *Romeins Lederwerk uits Valkenburg*, Groningen 1967.

Haekel, J. (ed): *Theorie und Praxis der Zusammenarbeit zwischen der Anthrop. Disziplinen*, Horn 1961.
Hamilton, J.: *Excavations at Jarlshof*, London 1956.
Hamilton-Jenkins, A.: *The Cornish Miner*, London 1927.
Hammond, P.: *Archaeological Techniques for Amateurs*, Princeton 1963.
Hartley, B.: *Notes on the Roman Pottery Industry in the Nene Valley*, Peterborough 1960.
Hatt, G.: *Oldtidsagre*, Copenhagen 1951.
Hawkes, C.: *St. Catherine's Hill, Winchester* (HFCAS XI), Southampton 1930.
Heizer, R. and Cook, S. (ed): *The Application of Quantitative Methods to Archaeology*. Viking Fund Publications in Anthropology 28, Chicago 1960.
Heizer, R. and Graham, J.: *A Guide to Field Methods in Archaeology*, Palo Alto 1967.
Heizer, R. (ed): *The Archaeologist at Work*, New York 1959.
Hencken, H.: *The Archaeology of Cornwall*, London 1932.
Hencken, H.: *Tarquinia* (Peabody Museum Bulletin 23), Cambridge (USA) 1968.
Herrnbrodt, A.: *Der Husterknupp*, Koln-Graz 1958.
Hester, J. and Shoenwetter, J. (ed): *The Reconstruction of Past Environments*, Fort-Burgwin 1964.
Hodges, H.: *Artifacts*, London 1965.
Hodson, F.: *The La Tène Cemetery at Münsingen-Rain*, Berne 1968.
Hoffmann, M.: *The Warp weighted Loom*, Studia Norvegica 14, Oslo 1964.
Howard, H.: *The Avifauna of the Emeryville Shellmound* (University of California Publications in Zoology 32), Berkeley 1939.
Howell, F. (ed): *Early Man*, Netherlands 1968.
Hudson, K.: *Industrial Archaeology*, London 1963.
Hudson, K.: *Handbook for Industrial Archaeologists*, London 1967.
Hull, M. R.: *The Roman Potters' Kilns of Colchester* (Soc. of Ant. 21), Oxford 1963.
Hull, M. R.: *Roman Colchester* (Soc. of Ant. 20) Oxford 1958.
Hutchinson, J. (ed): *Essays on Crop Plant Evolution*, Cambridge 1965.

ICE (Institution of Civil Engineers) *Manual for Civil Engineering*, London 1966.

Jessup, R.: *Archaeology of Kent*, London 1930.
Jewell, A.: *Crafts, Trades and Industries*, London 1968.
Jewell, P. (ed): *The Experimental Earthwork on Overton Down*, London 1963.
Jope, E. (ed): *Studies in Building History*, London 1961.

Kargen, M.: *Drevnii Kiev*, Moscow 1958.
Keiler, A. (ed I. Smith): *Windmill Hill and Avebury*, London 1965.
Kenyon, K.: *Beginning in Archaeology*, London 1952.
Kenyon, K.: *The Jewry Wall, Leicester*. (Soc. of Ant. 15), Oxford 1948.
Kenyon, K.: *Digging up Jericho*, London 1957.
Kenyon, K.: *Archaeology of the Holy Land*, London 1960.
Kerr, R.: *The Gentleman's House*, London 1864.
Klima, B.: *Dolní Věstoniée*, Prague 1963.
Knowles, M. and St. Joseph, K.: *Monastic Sites from the Air*, Cambridge 1952.
Kostrewski, J.: *Osada Vagrenna w Biskupinie*, Poznan 1936. English summary *Antiq* XII 1938. 311.
Kramer K.: *Hallstatt*, Vienna 1960.

La Porte, L.: *Ancient Environments*, New Jersey 1968.
Leakey, L.: *Olduvai Gorge I*, Cambridge 1965.
Lerici, C.: *Prospezioni archeologiche a Tarquinia*, Milan 1959.
Lerici, C.: *Alla Scoperata della Civilta sepolte*, Milan 1960.
Lewis, M.: *Temples in Roman Britain*, Cambridge 1966.
Libby, W.: *Radio Carbon Dating* (2nd ed), Chicago 1955.
Linton, D. (ed.): *Sheffield and its region*, Sheffield 1956.
Liversidge, J.: *Furniture in Roman Britain*, London 1955.
Lucas, A.: *Ancient Egyptian Materials and Industries* (4th ed), London 1962.

MOL (Ministry of Labour): *Safety Precautions in Civil Engineering Works*, London 1967.
McBurney, C.: *The Haua Fteah*, Cambridge 1968.
McCown, D. (et al.): *Nippur I*, Chicago 1967.
Mackay, E.: *Further Excavations at Mohenjo Daro*, London 1938.
MacPherron, A. *The Juntunen Site* (Museum of Anthropology, University of Michigan 30), Ann Arbor 1967.
Margary, I.: *Roman Roads in Britain* (2nd ed), London 1967.
Marshall, J. (et al.): *Mohenjo Daro . . .*, London 1931.
Martin, L.: *Houses and House Life of the American Aborigines* (reprint from 1881), Chicago 1965.
Mathiassen, T. (et al.): *Dyrholmen*, Copenhagen 1942.
Matson, F. (ed): *Ceramics and Man*, London 1966.
Matthews, S.: *Photography in Archaeology and Art*, London 1968.
Mennell, F. and Summers, R.: *The 'Ancient Workings' of Southern Rhodesia* (Nat. Mus. of S. Rhodesia 20), Salisbury (Rhodesia) 1955.
Merrifield, R.: *The Roman City of London*, London 1965.
Michalowski, K.: *Faras*, Warsaw 1966.
Monkhouse, F. and Wilkinson, H.: *Maps and Diagrams*, London 1964.
Munby, L. (ed): *East Anglian Studies*, Cambridge 1968.
Mylonas, G.: *Mycenae and the Mycenaean Age*, Princeton 1966.

Nash-Williams, V.: *The Roman Frontier in Wales*, Cardiff 1954.
Neitzel, R.: *Archaeology of the Fatherland site: The Grand Village of the Natchez* (Am. Museum of Natural History 51), New York 1965.
Nenquin, J.: *Salt: a study in economic prehistory* (Stud. Arch. Gandenses VI), Brugge 1961.
Norman, E. and St. Joseph, K.: *The Early Development of Irish Society*, Cambridge 1970.

OS (Ordnance Survey): *Field Archaeology* (Professional Paper 13), London 1963.
Oakeshot, R.: *The Archaeology of Weapons*, London 1960.
Oakley, K.: *Frameworks for Dating Fossil Man*, London 1964.
Oman, C.: *The Art of Warfare in the Middle Ages*, London 1924.
Orwin, C. and C.: *The Open Fields*, London 1938.

Pannell, J.: *Techniques of Industrial Archaeology*, Bath 1966.
Petrie, F.: *Methods and Aims in Archaeology*, London 1904.
Petrie, F.: *Arts and Crafts of Ancient Egypt*, London 1923.
Piggott, S.: *West Kennet Long Barrow*, London 1962.
Piggott, S.: *Prehistoric India*, London 1961.
Plenderleith, H.: *The Conservation of Antiquities and Works of Art*, Oxford 1956.
Polach, H. and Golson, J.: *Collection of specimens for Radio Carbon Dating . . . .* Canberra 1966.
Powell, T. and Daniel, G.: *Barclodiad y Gawres*, Liverpool 1956.
Pyddoke, E.: *Stratification for the Archaeologist*, London 1961.

RCHM (Royal Commission on Historical Monuments): *Eboracum: Roman York*, London 1962.
Raikes, R.: *Water, Weather and Prehistory* (Part I), London 1967.
Rajewski, Z.: *Biskupin . . .*, Warsaw 1959.
Rees, D.: *Mines, Mills and Furnaces*, Cardiff 1969.
Reinerth, H.: *Das Federseemoor*, Leipzig 1929 and 1936.
Reisner, G.: *Naga ed Der* III, *A Provincial Cemetery*, Oxford 1932 (plan redrawn in Heizer, R. 1959.
Renn, D.: *Norman Castles in Britain*, London 1968.
Richmond, I. (ed Brailsford): *Hod Hill*, London 1968.
Richmond, I.: *The City Wall of Imperial Rome*, London 1930.
Rivet, A.: *Town and Country in Roman Britain*, . . . . 1965.
Robertson, A.: *The Antonine Wall*, Glasgow 1960.
Robinson, K.: *Khami Ruins*, Cambridge 1959.
Robinson, K., Summers, R. and Whitty, A.: *Zimbabwe Excavations*. Bulawayo 1961 (NMSPOP 3. 23a).
Rose, W.: *The Village Carpenter*, Cambridge 1937.
Rosenfeld, A.: *The Inorganic Raw Materials of Antiquity*, London 1965.
Roth, H.: *Great Benin*, London 1903.
Rudenko, S.: *Pazirik*, Moscow 1953. English trans. by M. Thompson, London 1970.
Rust, A.: *Das Altsteinzeitliche Rentierjägerlager Meiendorf*, Neumunster 1937.
Ryder, M.: *Animal Bones in Archaeology*, Oxford 1969.

SPF (Société préhistorique française): *Manuel des Recherches Préhistoriques*, Paris 1929.
St. Joseph, K.: (et al.): *The Roman Occupation of South Western Scotland*, London 1952.
St. Joseph, K. (ed): *Uses of Aerial Photography*, London 1967.
Salisbury, E.: *Weeds and Aliens*, London 1964.
Salzman, L.: *British Industries of the Middle Ages*, London 1923.
Schmidt, R.: *Die Burg Vucedol*, Zagreb 1945.
Schwartz, G.: *Archaeologische Feldmethode*, Munich 1967.
Scranton, R.: *Greek Walls*, Cambridge (USA) 1941.
Semenov, S.: *Prehistoric Technology*, New York 1967.
Sharma, Y.: *Archaeological Remains in Monuments and Museums* I (Arch. Survey of India), Delhi 1964.
Shepard, A.: *Ceramics for the Archaeologist*, 1961.
Simmonds, N.: *The Evolution of the Bananas*, London 1962.
Simmons, H.: *Archaeological Photography*, London 1969.
Singer, C., Holmyard, E. and Hall, A. (ed): *History of Technology* (I–III), Oxford 1954, 1956, 1957.
Smith, D.: *The Industrial Archaeology of the East Midlands*, London 1965.
Smith, N.: *Victorian Technology*, London 1970.
Sollas, W.: *Ancient Hunters*, London 1924.
Soudsky, B.: *Libenice*, Prague 1962.
Soudsky, B.: *Principles of Automatic Data Treatment applied on Neolithic Pottery*, Prague 1967.
Stafaniszym, B.: *Material Culture of the Ambo* (Rhodes-Livingstone Museum 16), Lusaka 1964.
Stead, I.: *The La Tène Cultures of Eastern Yorkshire*, York 1965.
Steensberg, A.: *Ancient Harvesting Implements*, Copenhagen 1943.
Stone, J.: *Wessex*, London 1958.
Summers, R.: *Inyanga*, Cambridge 1958.
Straker, E.: *Wealdon Iron*, London 1931.
Syson, L.: *British Watermills*, London 1965.

Talbot-Rice, T.: *The Scythians*, London 1958.

Taylor, W. (ed): *The Teaching of Anthropology* (American Anthropological Association 94), New York 1963.

Taylor, W. (ed): *The identification of non-artifactual archaeological Material* (American National Academy of Sciences, 565), Washington 1957.

The Times: *Atlas of the World*, London 1964.

Towle, M.: *Ethno-Botany of Pre-Colombian Peru* (Viking Fund Publications in Anthropology 30), New York 1961.

Townsend, D.: *Underwater Photography*, London 1964.

Trorey, L.: *Handbook of Aerial Mapping and Photogrammetry*, Cambridge 1950.

Trump, D.: *Skorba* (Soc. of Ant. 22), Oxford 1966.

Tylecote, R.: *Metallurgy in Archaeology*, London 1962.

Ucko, P. and Dimbleby, G. (ed): *The Domestication and Exploitation of Plants and Animals*, London 1969.

Ucko, P. and Rosenfeld, A.: *Palaeolithic Cave Art*, London 1967.

Varva, J.: *5000 Years of Glassmaking*, Prague (n.d.).

Viatores: *Roman Roads in the S.E. Midlands*, London 1964.

Vogt, E.: *Geflechte und Gewebe der Steinzeit*, Basel 1937.

Wacher, J. (ed): *The Civitas Capitals of Roman Britain*, Leicester 1966.

Wailes, R.: *The English Windmill*, London 1954.

Wainwright, F.: *Archaeology, Place-names and History*, London 1962.

Watson, W.: *China before the Han Dynasty*, London 1961.

Webster, G.: *Practical Archaeology*, London 1966.

Webster, G.: *The Roman Imperial Army . . .*, London 1969.

Wells, C.: *Bones, Bodies and Disease*, London 1965.

Wenham, L.: *The Romano-British Cemetery at Trentholme Drive, York*, London 1969.

West, J.: *Village Records*, London 1962.

Wheeler, R.: *Lydney Park* (Soc. of Ant. 9), London 1932.

Wheeler, R.: *Verulamium* (Soc. of Ant. 2), Oxford 1936.

Wheeler, R.: *Maiden Castle* (Soc. of Ant. 12), Oxford 1943.

Wheeler, R.: *Archaeology from the Earth*, London 1954.

Wheeler, R.: *Stanwick* (Soc. of Ant. 17), Oxford 1954.

Wheeler, R. and Richardson, K.: *Hillforts of Northern France*, London 1957.

White, K.: *Agricultural Implements of the Roman World*, Cambridge 1968.

Willey, G. *An Introduction to American Archaeology*, New York 1966.

Williams, J.: *A Petrological Study of the Prehistoric Pottery of the Aeolian Islands* (typescript doctoral thesis), University Library, London 1967.

Williams, J. C.: *Simple Photogrammetry*, London 1970.

Winbolt, S.: *With a Spade on Stane Street*, London 1936.

Wood, E.: *Field Guide to Archaeology*, London 1963.

Wood, M.: *The English Mediaeval House*, London 1965.

Woolley, C.: *The Ur Excavations II (The Royal Cemeteries)*, London 1934.

Woolley, C.: *The Ur Excavations V (The Ziggurat and its surroundings)*, London 1939.

Woolley, C.: *Dead Towns and living Men*, London 1942.

Yadin, Y.: *Masada* London 1967.

Yadin, Y.: *Art of Warfare in Biblical Lands*, London 1963.

Zeuner, F.: *Dating the Past*, London 1952.

# ABBREVIATIONS USED IN NOTES AND BIBLIOGRAPHY
(unless otherwise stated these are British publications)

| | |
|---|---|
| AAM | American Anthropological Memoirs (USA) |
| AHR | Agricultural History Review |
| AJA | American Journal of Archaeology (USA) |
| AJS | American Journal of Science (USA) |
| AmAnt | American Antiquity (USA) |
| AmAnth | American Anthropologist (USA) |
| AMN | American Museum Novitates. Am. Mus. Nat. History (USA) |
| ANA(AP) | American National Academy of Sciences (Anthropology and Psychology Division) (USA) |
| AnInd | Ancient India (India) |
| Antiq | Antiquity |
| AntJ | Antiquaries Journal |
| APAMNH | Anthropological Papers of the American Museum of Natural History (USA) |
| APAO | Archaeology and Physical Anthropology in Oceania (New Zealand) |
| Arc | Archaeology (USA) |
| Arch | Archaeologia |
| Archeom | Archaeometry |
| ArchAel | Archaeologia Aeliana |
| ArchCam | Archaeologia Cambrensis |
| ArchCant | Archaeologia Cantiana |
| ArchJ | Archaeological Journal |
| ArcJ | Archaeologia Jugoslavica (Jugoslavia) |
| AS | Antiquity and Survival (Netherlands) |
| AT | Africa Tervuren (Belgium) |
| | |
| BAEB | Bureau of American Ethnology Bulletin (USA) |
| BBCS | Bulletin of the Board of Celtic Studies |
| BIA | Bulletin of the Institute of Archaeology, London University |
| BMQN | Belfast Museum Quarterly Notes |
| BNSS | Bulletin of the National Speleological Society |
| BSPF | Bulletin de la Société Préhistorique Française (France) |
| BROB | Berichten van der Rijksdienst von het Oudheidkundig Bodemonderzoek (Netherlands) |
| | |
| CA | Current Anthropology (USA) |
| CBA | Council for British Archaeology |
| CornArch | Journal of the Cornwall Archaeological Society |
| CUP | Cambridge University Press |
| | |
| Ex | Expedition (Bulletin of the University Museum of Pennsylvania) |
| | |
| Germ | Germania (Germany) |
| | |
| HSNJ | Journal of the Historical Society of Nigeria (Nigeria) |
| | |
| IMM | Journal of the Institute of Mining and Metallurgy |
| IndArch | Journal of the Society for Industrial Archaeology |

| | |
|---|---|
| JAH | Journal of African History |
| JBAA | Journal of the British Archaeological Association |
| JBAAS | Journal of the British Association for the Advancement of Science |
| JCNW | Journal of the Chester and North Wales Architectural Society |
| JGS | Journal of Glass Studies |
| JISI | Journal of the Iron and Steel Institute |
| JMGC | Journal of Mineralogy and Geology of California (USA) |
| JPMA | Journal of the Society for Post-Mediaeval Archaeology |
| JRAI | Journal of the Royal Anthropological Institute |
| JRIC | Journal of the Royal Institute of Chemistry |
| JRS | Journal of Roman Studies |
| JRSAI | Journal of the Royal Society of Antiquaries of Ireland |
| | |
| Kuml | Arborg for Jysk Arkaeologisk Selskab (Denmark) |
| Kush | Journal of Archaeology in the Sudan (Sudan) |
| | |
| LAAS | Lincolnshire Archaeological and Architectural Society |
| LRS | London Research Seminar in Archaeology and Related Subjects (Institute of Archaeology) |
| MAGZ | Mitteilungen der Antiq. Gesellschaft, Zurich (Switzerland) |
| MAUM | Museum of Archaeology, University of Michigan (USA) |
| MedArch | Journal of the Society for Mediaeval Archaeology |
| MZUO | Material zur Urgeschicht Österreich (Austria) |
| | |
| NDS | Notizia degli Scavi (Italy) |
| NGM | National Geographical Magazine (USA) |
| NMSROP | National Museums of S. Rhodesia. Occasional Papers |
| NorArch | Norfolk Archaeology |
| | |
| Ocean | Oceania (New Zealand) |
| Oxon | Oxoniensia |
| | |
| PA | Prospecioni Archeologiche (Italy) |
| PBA | Proceedings of the British Academy |
| PCAS | Proceedings of the Cambridge Antiquarian Society |
| PDNH | Proceedings of the Dorset Natural History and Archaeological Society |
| PFHS | Proceedings of the Flintshire Historical Society |
| PhotJ | The Photographic Journal |
| PIM | Prace i Materialy (Poland) |
| PMB | Peabody Museum Bulletin (American Society for Prehistoric Research) (USA) |
| PPACP | Proceedings 1st Pan African Congress on Prehistory, Oxford 1952 |
| PPH | Proceedings of the Congresses of Pre- and Proto-History (VI Italy) VII (Czechoslovakia) |
| PPS | Proceedings of the Prehistoric Society (incorporating the Prehistoric Society of East Anglia) |
| PSAS | Proceedings of the Society of Antiquaries of Scotland |
| PSIA | Proceedings of the Suffolk Institute of Archaeology |
| | |
| RCHM | Royal Commission on Historical Monuments |
| RevArch | Revue Archaeologique (Czechoslovakia) |
| RSL | Revista di Studi Liguri (Italy) |
| RTIC | Revue Technologique de l'Institut de Cuir (France) |

| | |
|---|---|
| SA | Scientific American (USA) |
| SAC | Sussex Archaeological Collections |
| SAMA | South African Museums Association Bulletin (South Africa) |
| SARP | Society of Antiquaries of London Research Reports |
| SASRP | Surrey Archaeological Society Research Papers |
| SDAS | Sunderland and Durham Archaeological Society |
| SIMC | The Smithsonian Institute (Miscellaneous Collections) (USA) |
| SR | The Smithsonian Report (USA) |
| SS | Studies in Spelaeology |
| Sumer | Sumer: a journal of Archaeology in Iraq (Iraq) |
| TAPS | Transactions of the American Philosophical Society (USA) |
| TC | Technology and Culture (USA) |
| TNS | Transactions of the Newcomen Society |
| UCPA | University of California Publications in Anthropology (USA) |
| UCPZ | University of California Publications in Zoology (USA) |
| VFPA | Viking Fund Publications in Anthropology (USA) |
| WA | World Archaeology |
| WAM | Wiltshire Archaeological Magazine |
| WCFC | Journal of the West Cornwall Field Club |
| YCY | y Cymrodor |
| YUPA | Yale University Publications in Anthropology (USA) |
| ZTZ | Zeitschrift vor Tierzuchtung und Zuchtungs biologue (Germany) |

## ACKNOWLEDGEMENTS

I should like to thank Professor W. F. Grimes, Mr. and Mrs. P. Woudhuysen, Mrs. G. Wilson, Dr. P. Ucko, Messrs. R. A. H. Farrar, G. Rye, C. Sparrow and J. Brownfield for reading and commenting on various parts of the script; Miss B. Powell for undertaking the indexing, and Mr. J. Scott for taking the photographs for the plates not otherwise acknowledged.

I am also grateful for the permission given by their authors to publish the following figures and plates: Figures—13, R. Riley; 14, N. Simmonds; 16a, K. P. Oakley; 16b, C. E. M. McBurney; 17, J. G. D. Clark; 21, J. D. Evans; 22, I. Stead; 26, J. Desmond Clark; 29, W. Allan; 32, J. R. C. Hamilton; 37, W. F. Grimes; 38, P. Jewell and the British Association for the Advancement of Science; 40, C. W. Phillips; 43, P. Ashbee; 44a, R. Hodson; 44b, J. Close-Brook; 48, S. Greenfield; 49, R. Goodchild; 50, 55, 56, 57b, 60 and 67, Sir Mortimer Wheeler; 51, Penguin Books Ltd.; 52, M. Biddle; 54, A. L. F. Rivet; 57a, C. F. C. Hawkes; 65, B. Hope-Taylor; 64, A. Redmayne; Plates I, XI, XII, XIII, XV and XVII (taken by M. Cookson for Sir Mortimer Wheeler); X, O. G. S. Crawford; IX, J. Coles; XVIII, G. Sieveking; III, K. St. Joseph; Frontispiece, J. N. Hampton for Royal Commission on Historical Monuments (crown copyright reserved).

I am also grateful to W. Heffer and Sons Ltd. for the loan of the blocks for Figure 34 and Plate III and to the Society of Antiquaries of London for prints of Mr. Cookson's photographs.

# SOURCES OF ILLUSTRATIONS

Illustrations not included in this list are previously unpublished originals by the author

13. Essays: *Crop Plant Evolution*, J. Hutchinson (ed), Cambridge 1965. 122.
14. *The Evolution of the Bananas*, N. Simmonds, London 1962. 137.
15. *Dolní Věstoniée*, B. Klima, CAMA XI Prague 1963. 90.
16a *Frameworks for Dating Fossil Man*, K. Oakley, London 1964. 165.
16b *The Haua Fteah*. C. McBurney, Cambridge 1968. 6.
17. *Star Carr*. J. G. D. Clark, Cambridge 1954.
19. *The Gentleman's House*. J. Kerr, London 1864.
21. J. D. Evans (unpublished drawing).
22. I. Stead, *AntJ* XLVI pt. i 1966. 75–6.
23. I. Richmond, *PBA* XLI 1955 plate V.
26. *The Prehistory of Southern Africa*. J. D. Clark, London 1959. 291.
28. C. Fox, *Antiq.* XII 1937. 430.
29. *The African Husbandman*, W. Allan, London 1965. 80.
30. *Houses and House Life of the American Aborigines*, Washington 1881 Fig. 15.
32. *Recent Archaeological Excavations in Britain*, R. Bruce-Mitford (ed), London 1956. 209.
34. *East Anglian Studies*, L. Munby (ed), Cambridge 1968. 49.
37. *Recent Archaeological Excavation in Britain*. R. Bruce-Mitford (ed), London 1956. 121.
38. *The Experimental Earthwork on Overton Down*. P. Jewel (ed), London 1963. 87.
40. C. W. Phillips.
41. J. Alexander, *PPS* XXVI 1960. 265 and 272.
42. J. Alexander, *ArchCant* LXXVI 1961. 4 and 7.
43. P. Ashbee, *PPS* XXIII 1957. 147 and 151.
44a R. Hodson, *Proceedings VI Congress Pre- and Proto-History* Pt. III Rome 1966 plate XXV.
44b J. Close-Brooks, *Notizia degli Scavi* 1965. 63.
47. *Wessex*, J. Stone, London 1958. 89.
48. E. Greenfield, *AntJ* XLIII 1963. 230.
49. R. Goodchild and J. Kirk, *Oxoniensia* XIX 1954. 36.
50. R. Wheeler, Society of Antiquaries Research Report IX, London 1932 plate LI.
51. *The Archaeology of Palestine*, W. Albright, London 1960. 164.
52. M. Biddle, *AntJ* XLVIII 2 1968. 269 and part of plate LXVII.
54. *The Problems of the Iron Age in Southern Britain*. S. Frere (ed), London 1968.
55. R. Wheeler, *AntJ* XXXII 1952. 4.
56. R. Wheeler, *AntJ* XV 3 1935 plate XXX.
57a C. Hawkes, *Antiq.* V 1931. 75.
57b R. Wheeler, Society of Antiquaries Research Paper, London 1932.
58. I. Richmond, *PSAS* LXXIII 1939. 154.
59. I. Richmond. *PBA* XLI 1955 plate 2.
60. R. Wheeler, in S. Piggott, 1950.
61. I. Richmond, *PBA* XLI 1955. 312.
64. A. Redmayne JAH.
65. B. Hope-Taylor, *ArchJ* CVII 1950. 24 and 27.
67. R. Wheeler, Society of Antiquaries Research Report IX, London 1932 plate VIII.
70. D. Atkinson, *Caistor Excavations*, London 1931 plate XII.

Plate xx D. Diderot, plate 70.
Plate xxi *Antiq.* XVI 1942. 193.

# INDEX

Accidents *see* Insurance *and* Safety
Precautions
Aerial Photographs *see* Photographs
Agriculture: evidence from excavation,
142, 144–5; shifting, evidence for,
163; *see also* Botanical Evidence *and*
Ethnographic Evidence
Animal Husbandry, information from
excavation, 145–6; *see also* Zoological
Evidence
Antler, industrial working, evidence
for, 282
Archaeomagnetic Dating, sampling for,
92, 132, 272
Architects: training for field
archaeology, 17–18; when specially
necessary, 38
Archives and Libraries: ethnographic
information, 26, 97, 196, 198;
geological information, 26; historical
information, 25, 168, 182; industrial
information, 262
Assistants, Archaeological and
Environmental, 18, 38–9; *see also*
Camp Commandant, Photographer
*and* Surveyor
Augers, use of, 28; *see also* Probe,
Auger and Drill Surveys
Aural Information, collection before
excavation, 22–4

Backfilling *see* Excavation
Banks: boundary, of settlements and
fields, 142; counterscarp, 227, 232;
defensive, 189–90; identification and
excavation, 233–8; religious sites, 201;
*see also* Mounds, Fortified Sites *and*
Ramparts
Barbicans *see* Entrances
Barracks, 256
Barrows, Long and Round,
excavation of, 213–15
Bastions *see* Fortified Sites
Battue, recognition of sites, 106
Bone: artifacts, manufacture of, 282;
conservation, of, 90; excavation of,
199–201; processing of, 65; *see also*
Burials, Human Remains *and*
Zoological Evidence
Botanical Evidence: excavation and
identification, 89, 145, 185, 202, 208,

210–11, 232, 237; from settlements,
137, 139, 140, 141; place in
archaeological studies, 88–9; seasonal
occupation, indicated by, 98
Bricks: excavation, 124–7; manufacture,
280–1; *see also* Archaeomagnetic
Dating
Bridges, 148, 255
Building Material, processing, 64; *see
also* Clay, Stone, *and* Wood
Buildings: baths, public and private,
133, 175; commercial, 171, 173;
excavation techniques, 117; industrial,
175, 265, 282; judicial and prison,
160–1, 174, 175–6; military, 256–7;
religious, 176, 190, 193–6; storage,
159, 173, 280; theatres and stadia,
174–5; *see also* Byres, Dwellings *and*
Rooms
Burials: coffins, 208; cremations,
excavation of, 200–1; grave-goods and
offerings, 200, 210–11, 215; grave-pits
or platforms, excavation of, 199–200;
inhumations, excavation of, 199–200;
location of, 197–8; mortuary
chambers, 203–7; mounds, 213–15;
rituals, of burial, 207–11; rituals, of
preparation, 119–207; rituals, of
remembrance, 211–15; subsidiary,
215; *see also* Cemeteries

Camp-Commandant, need for, 53
Campaign Camp *see* Fortified Sites
Caves: excavation of, 110–12, 187, 267;
location of, 107–8; religious use of,
187; *see also* Hunter-Gatherer
Settlements
Cemeteries: burial patterns, 218;
chronological and sociological
importance, 216–18; ethnographic
evidence, use of, 196, 218; excavation
problems, 198, 215–16, 218–20;
location of, 196, 216–18; recording of
220; town, 176; village, 161; *see also*
Burials *and* Human Remains
Ceremonial Centres, excavation of,
195–6
Charcoal: analysis of, 68; -burning,
evidence of, 271; funeral pyres,
samples from, 200; kilns and firing
areas, samples from, 280–1; *see also*

Fires, Hearths *and* Radio-Active
Isotopes
Chimneys, identification of, 122
Church *see* Sanctuaries *and* Worship,
places of
Clay Quarries, identification and
excavation, 264; *see also* Bricks,
Geological Evidence, Pottery *and* Tiles
Climate, interpretation from
environmental finds, 88–91
Coffins *see* Burials
Collecting Sites, industrial, 268–9
Conchology *see* Molluscs
Conservation of finds, 40, 62–3
Cooking Areas: kitchens, 137, 196;
ovens, 132–3; pits, 103, 132; *see also*
Hearths
Coroner, 32
Costing Excavations, 27–8, 226
Cotton, 273
Cremation *see* Burial
Cultivation: implements, 145; locating
sites, 134; lynchets, 142; recognition
of ancient, 144–5; *see also* Farms and
Farmbuildings
Cursus, excavation of, 195

Dating Methods: in the education of a
director, 14–15; relative stratigraphy,
71–2; sampling methods, 92–3; *see also*
Archaeomagnetic Dating, Radio-
Active Isotopes, Thermoluminescence,
Tree-Ring Analysis *and* Varve Analysis
Dedication and Foundation Deposits,
185
Defences *see* Fortified Sites
Dendrochronology *see* Tree-Ring
Analysis
Digging-Stick Cultivation, 145
Director, Field: organisational
problems, 49–50; public relations,
need for, 33–6, 50; qualities, necessary
for success, 12–16; relations with
environmentalists, 87; responsibilities,
11; writing report, 70–2
Ditches: boundary, 142; burials,
surrounding, 201–2; cursus, 195;
defensive, 227–8, 230; henge, 189–90;
infilling, deliberate, 230, 232;
intersection and re-entrants, 228–31;
problems in excavating, 232–3; recut,
232; relative chronology of, 137,
228–30; silting, natural, 230

Docks and Harbours, excavation of,
176–7
Doors, location of, 130
Drains, excavation of, 133
Drip-Trench, excavation of, 128
Dwellings: alterations and additions,
124–7; clay, peat and turf
constructions, 124; heating, 131;
location of, 116–17, 156; mansions and
palaces, 158–9, 171, 257; military,
256; reconstruction of, 122, 124;
religious, 195, 196; single family, 156,
158, 170–1; stone, dry, 122–4; stone,
mortared, 124–8; temporary, 104;
terraced, 156; timber, 117, 120–2; *see
also* Buildings, Chimneys, Doors,
Drains, Floors, Roofs, Rooms,
Settlements, Shelters, Tents *and*
Windows

Earth Ovens *see* Pits, Cooking
Echo-Sounding Surveys, 30, 109
Education: assistant, 17–18; director,
12–16; helpers, 18
Entomological Evidence: possibilities,
91; sampling, 139–41
Entrances: bridges, 251; causeways, 251;
excavation of, 142, 228; gates, 251–2;
outworks, 250; location of, 248, 250;
revetting of, 251–2
Environmental Studies: archaeological
possibilities of, 85–7; assistants, 18,
38–9, 60; director, importance to, 14,
87; material, treatment of, 65; *see also*
Botanical Evidence, Entomological
Evidence, Geological Evidence,
Molluscs, Pedology, Pollen Evidence
*and* Zoological Evidence
Equipment: assessing needs, 42–4;
caves, special needs, 112; ditches,
special needs, 232–3; mines, special
needs, 267; towns, special needs, 164–5
Ethnographic Studies; agricultural
economics, aid in interpretating,
144–7; director, importance to 12–13;
local, use in pre-excavation studies,
26; farming, use in excavations, 134,
144; hunter-gatherer-fisher, use in
excavations, 97; religious, use in
excavations, 196, 198; urban, use in
excavations, 164
Excavating Machinery: economic use of,
41; varieties and handling of, 52–3, 216

Excavation: backfilling, 66; costing, 37; domestic arrangements during, 53–5; equipment, 42–4, 164–5, 232–5, 267; financing, 8; insuring, 32–3; legal problems of, 30; licensing, 30–1; open, 102; organising, director's problems, 15–16; previous, checking results of, 25; recording during, 55–7; safety during, 32, 165, 232–3, 238, 267; siting, 65–6; surveys, primary and secondary, 23–30; tropical lands, special problems in, 45; *see also* Finds, Grid, Report *and* Personnel

Faience *see* Glass-Making
Farms and Farmbuildings: animal shelters, 140–1; crop-drying kilns and racks, 137; defences, 226, 257; excavation, 134–42; haystacks and platforms, 137; presses, 138–9, 160; stores, 139–40, 160; threshing floors, 137; yards, 136–7, 141–2; *see also* Cultivation, Dwellings, Field Systems, Mills *and* Roads
Fibre-Processing, evidence for, 273
Field Systems: location and excavation, 142, 144, 161–3; temperate zones, interpretation of, 144–5; tropical zones, interpretation of, 146–7; *see also* Cultivation *and* Roads
Field Walking, 100, 116
Finance of Excavations, 37
Finds, Cultural: analysis by material, 63–5, 76–7; burials, associated with, 200, 210–11, 215; conservation of, 40, 61–2; fortified sites, associated with, 233; drawing of, 79; industrial sites: mining, 267, 268; processing, 270–1; finishing, 274–83; ownership of, 31–2; photographs for publication, 79; processing, 39, 45, 60–2; registering special, 56; urban sites, associated with, 164; *see also* Building Material, Bone, Burials, Glass, Metal, Pottery, Stone *and* Wood
Finds, Non-Cultural, sampling and processing, 88–91; *see also* Environmental Studies
Fires: camp, 102; kitchen, 132; religious, 187, 200–2, 211; vitrified walls, 246; *see also* Chimneys, Hearths, Ovens, Pyres *and* Stoves
Fish: excavation and examination, 89–90

Flax: retting, cleaning and spinning, 273
Flint: processing, 275–6; quarries and mines, 264
Flotation, use of, 89
Floors: construction and materials, 129–30; drains under, 133; excavation of, 125–7, 129; hypocaust systems under, 131; renewal of, 129–30
Forecourts, 207
Fortified Sites: bastions and towers, 252; civilian, special problems, 176, 226; excavation problems, general, 227; interiors, 255–8; keep or citadel, 255; location, general problems of, 226; military strategy, need for knowledge of, 224; religious, 196; *see also* Barracks, Banks, Ditches, Entrances, Ramparts *and* Walls
Funeral Pyre, excavation of, 200–1
Furnace *see* Iron

Gateway *see* Entrances
Geo-Electrical Surveys *see* Resistivity Surveys
Geological Evidence: excavation problems, 51–2; field archaeology, importance of, 87–8, 101; mining, identification by, 263; pre-excavation information, source of, 26; specialist visits, need for, 101
Glass-Making; evidence for, 283
Government, Control of Excavations, 30–1
Graves *see* Burials
Gravel: pits, 264; problems of working in, 52
Grid, Setting Out, 65–6; *see also* Caves, Cemeteries, Dwellings, Entrances, Farms, Forecourts, Industrial Areas *and* Settlements
Grinding or Pounding Areas, 133
Ground Surface, Old, importance of, 101, 144, 207, 237–8

Hair-Processing, evidence of, 273
Hamlets *see* Villages
Harbours *see* Docks
Hearths: dwellings, 132; excavation of, 102–3, 131–2; sanctuaries, 187; *see also* Cooking Areas *and* Fires
Helpers and Volunteers: director's relations with, 50–1; recruitment of, 40–1; training of, 18

Hemp *see* Flax
Hoe-Cultivation, 145
Horizontal Stratigraphy *see* Stratigraphy
Houses *see* Building *and* Dwellings
Human Remains, legal and religious procedures during excavation, 32; *see also* Bone, Burials *and* Cemeteries
Hunter-Gatherer settlements: approach to excavation, 97–8; caves and rockshelters, 107–8; dwellings, 104–6; excavation, 101–2; identification of, 99–100; industrial areas of, 104, 274–7; open-air, 99–100; *see also* Battue, Cooking Areas, Fires, Kill Sites, Middens *and* Sleeping Hollows
Hypocaust Systems, 131

Industrial Areas and Sites: dwellings, in, 159; farms, in 137, 277; finishing, 273–83; hunter-gatherers, of, 104, 275; processing, 269–73; towns, in 173, 277; villages, in, 161, 277; *see also* individual materials
Inns, evidence for, 161
Insects *see* Entomological Evidence
Insurance: accident, 32; national, 33
Iron-working: finishing sites, 281–2; processing sites, 271–2
Ivory-Working, evidence for, 282

Kill-Sites, 107
Kitchens *see* Cooking Areas
Kilns *see* Bricks, Farms and Farming, Pottery *and* Tiles

Labelling, excavation, in, 57; site hut, in, 61
Labour *see* Helpers and Volunteers *and* Personnel
Landowner: permission to excavate, 31; relations with, 35
Latrines, evidence of, 131; provision of, 54
Leather-Working: finishing, evidence of, 276–7; processing evidence for, 272; shops, 283
Libraries *see* Archives
Licences to Excavate, 30–1
Lynchets *see* Cultivation

Machines *see* Excavating Machines
Magnetic Surveys, 29, 117, 154, 226, 248, 255, 273
Market Places, evidence for, 160
Megalithic Chambers *see* Burials

Metallurgical Industries: collecting sites, 268–9; finishing sites, 281–2; location, 269–70; processing sites, 271–2; selling produce of, 173; *see also* Mining
Middens, Identification and Excavation, 103–4
Military Sites, categories of, 224–6; *see also* Fortified Sites
Mills: animal, water and wind, 139; communal, 160
Mines: deep, excavation of, 267; galleries, 267; location of, 263; open-cast, excavation of, 264–5; shafts, 268; tunnels, 267–8; *see also* Gravel, Flint *and* Iron
Molluscs: identification, 185, 202, 232, 237; importance in archaeology, 90; sampling, 90–1
Mortuary Chamber *see* Burials
Motte *see* Mounds, Defensive
Mounds: burial, 196, 204–5, 207–8, 212–15; defensive, 212–15; excavation problems, 164, 213; haystack and press foundations, 138–40; refuse, of, 268; revetting of, 214; sanctuaries, 187; settlements, as indication of, 153–4; *see also* Banks, Middens *and* Ramparts
Museums: curators, courtesy to, 35; information from, 168

National Insurance, obligations of a director, 33
Negligence, Law of, 33

Ore-Roasting Sites *see* Industrial Areas
Ovens, excavation of, 132
Overburden, problems of, 101

Palisades, excavation of, 239–40
Panning *see* Collecting Sites
Pedology: director's education, importance in a, 14, 91; sampling for, 91
Personnel of Excavation: control and economic use of, 41, 49–51; payment of, 37; recruitment of, 38–41; shelter, feeding and transport of, 53–5; training of, 17–18; *see also* Assistants *and* Helpers and Volunteers
Petrology *see* Stone
Photographer: duties of, 58; training of, 18, 38